IMAGES
of America

IONE AND THE JACKSON VALLEY

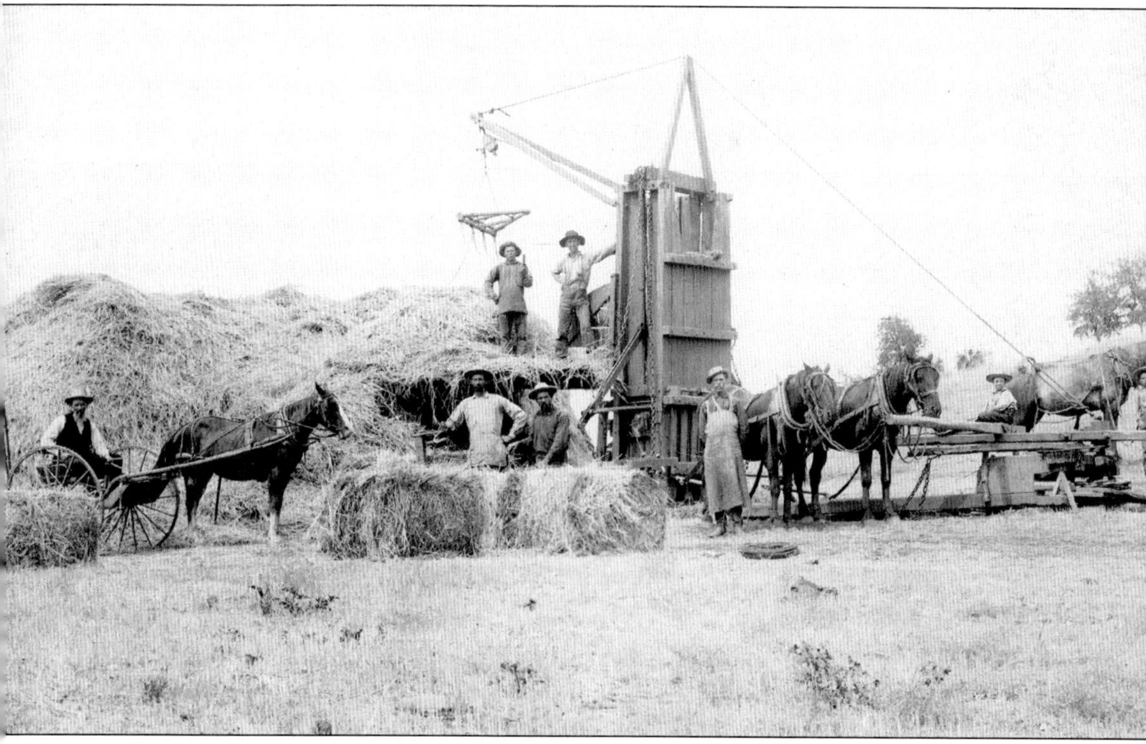

This 1897 image of Fred Grover's hay-bailing crew, by Ione photographer Clem Sutterley, depicts a familiar scene in the Ione Valley. Long known for its rich, fertile soil, the valley has produced bumper harvests of grains and crops for over 100 years. See page 77 for more information about this photograph.

IMAGES
of America

Ione and the Jackson Valley

Deborah Coleen Cook

ARCADIA
PUBLISHING

ISBN 978-0-7385-5602-4

Published by Arcadia Publishing
Charleston SC, Chicago IL, Portsmouth NH, San Francisco CA

Printed in the United States of America

Library of Congress Catalog Card Number: 2007934171

For all general information contact Arcadia Publishing at:
Telephone 843-853-2070
Fax 843-853-0044
E-mail sales@arcadiapublishing.com
For customer service and orders:
Toll-Free 1-888-313-2665

Visit us on the Internet at www.arcadiapublishing.com

To Uncle Dick, who always laughed, and to Mike, who brought music and art to life. A clarinet solo of "Stranger on the Shore" will never sound as sweet as it did on D Street.

Contents

ACKNOWLEDGMENTS

The compilation of this book became an adventure in learning for the author. It would not have been possible without the information provided by many local historians and residents, who have told stories of various people, events, and institutions comprising the history of the Ione and Jackson Valleys. Although they are too many to name here, I would like to thank several specific people. First of all, my hat goes off to Judy Allen, the true authority on Ione history, for the work she has done and deposited at the Amador County Archives. Secondly, I would like to thank John Strohm, a lifelong resident of the Jackson Valley, for the information he provided on growing up at Buena Vista. Next, I am grateful to Jim Scully, who is a tireless champion at keeping the physical evidence of Ione Valley history protected from destruction. In addition, I would like to thank the County of Amador for the generous use of the historic photograph collection held at its archives. Unless otherwise noted, the images used in this book are from that collection.

Introduction

In 1857, when a local newspaper reporter known as "the Traveler" wrote about Ione in his weekly column, he described it as "a place that has probably received more encomiums than any other section of the State. Well, it is deserving of all it receives, and more. Its fine brick stores, well filled with goods; rich and tasteful gardens in which the strawberries are now ripe, (large delicious ones they are too) its excellent schools, order-loving citizens and refined society are surely worthy of commendation." From that early day unto the present, this little community and surrounding valley have pleasantly surprised all who pass through.

Geographically, Amador County is a study in variety, with the Ione and Jackson Valleys forming most of the lowland region on the western margin of the county. Botanically it appears sparse, hosting grasses and scrubs, with occasional stands of oak trees and bull pine. This appears stark in contrast to the more densely populated slopes of the higher hills on the Gold Belt and Sierra Nevada to the east. The area is also geologically different than the famous Mother Lode, which cuts through Amador County. Here a unique geologic formation known as the Ione Formation stretches from Carbondale on the north to the Mokelumne River on the south. Mining of the deposit, rich in clays and limited deposits of lignite coal, has contributed a great deal to the economic stability of these valleys, much as have the agrarian endeavors of those who pursued a livelihood cultivating the land and raising livestock.

In those first years of the Gold Rush, settlement here by European American immigrants was limited to those few who took up large tracts of land to raise livestock; however, it was discovered that both valleys contained prime agricultural land, and grain crops were soon added to the equation. Those first into the area discovered it occupied by several thousand Miwok, the Native Americans who had lived here for centuries. In addition to the ranchers and farmers, there were those small scattered mining camps. Many came and went as quickly as the meager deposits of gold that were mined along the streambeds flowing through the valleys. Those deposits could not compete with the heart of the Mother Lode, situated to the east. The majority of gold-mining success in this area was found to the south of the Jackson Valley along the Mokelumne River at places such as Lancha Plana. Here a thriving town grew around rich strikes but did not survive once the cliffs and bars were mined out. Other small bergs and camps that came and went included Muletown, Quincy, and Boston Store. On the southern margin of the Jackson Valley, another Boston Store, located at the crossroads of Jackson and Lancha Plana, was likewise short-lived. Still, by the start of the 20th century, both valleys were settled with farmers and ranchers, and Ione City was considered an important economic center and transportation crossroads.

In 1894, with construction of the Preston School of Industry, a new type of resident was added to the community: the youth offender. Previously, boys who had committed crimes were remanded to the custody of the state prison system, but the school provided an alternative. It also brought an economic boost to the town, employing many local residents. In 1987, when Mule Creek State Prison was built west of Preston, residents took employment there, while others moved into Ione from towns and cities outside Amador County to work there.

Today Ione continues to thrive as a small California town. Many residents are descendants of the first settlers who came into the Ione and Jackson Valleys. The buildings that line Main Street stand the same as they did 100 years ago, with only cosmetic changes. The rural background is much as it was over a century ago, with many old farmhouses still occupied, with a few newer homes are tucked in here and there. Several new housing developments, including the Castle Oaks golf course community, are now situated around Ione. The Jackson Valley to the south, with its rolling hillocks and meandering seasonal streams, now boasts three recreational lakes within five miles of one another but still exudes a comforting rural ambiance. It is guaranteed that anyone who passes through these valleys will not soon forget them.

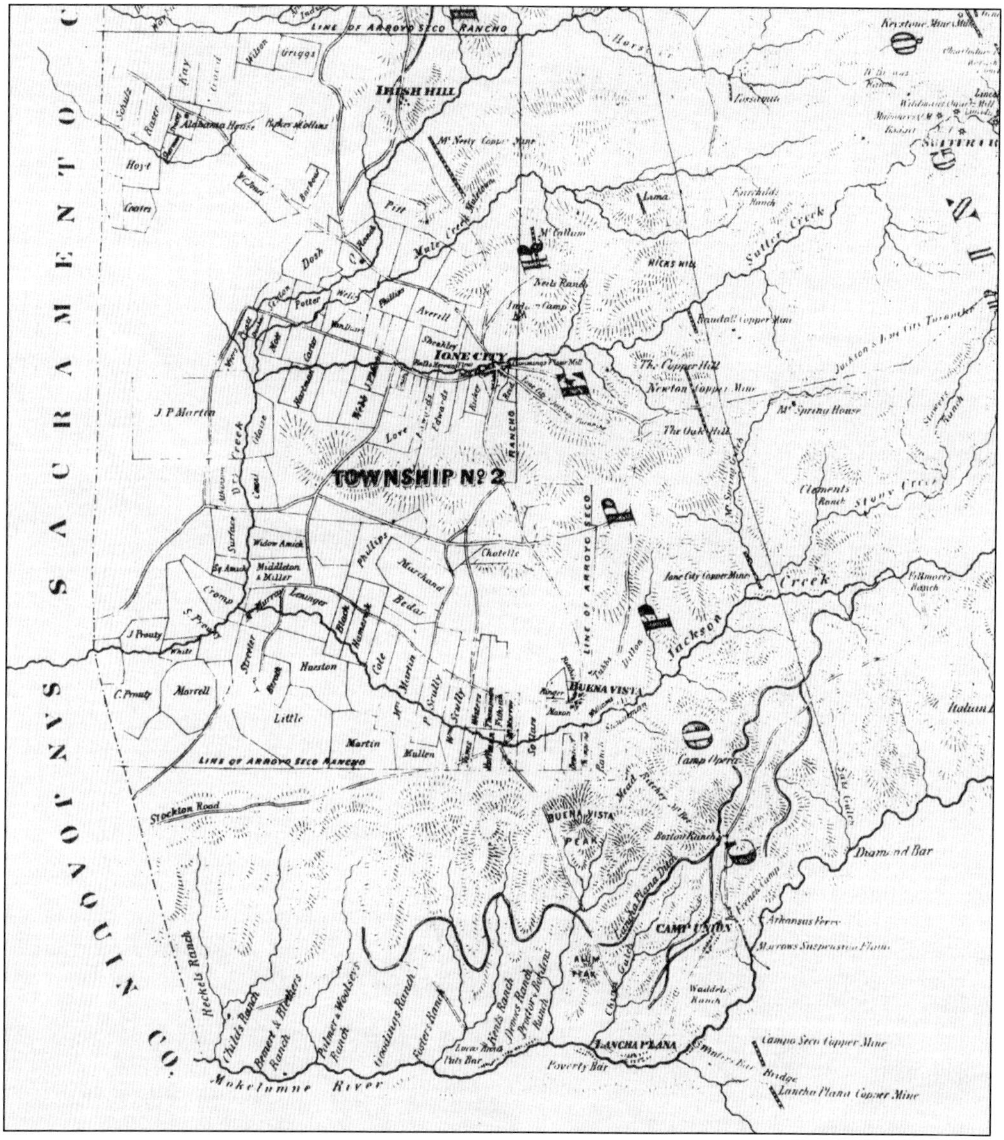

The Ione and Jackson Valleys, situated at the western margin of Amador County, butt against the Sacramento and San Joaquin County lines. The 1866 Amador County map shows just how well settled this fertile agricultural region had become within just two decades of the arrival of the first Argonauts.

One

The Native Land and the Newcomers

In 1848, when William Hicks and Moses Childers arrived in the Ione Valley, the only settlers they found were the Patterson family, living in an adobe house, and a man named Edward Robinson. Shortly after their arrival, John Sutter passed through the valley with workers on their way to the mountains to cut timber along Sutter Creek. Andres Pico, the brother of Mexican governor of California Pio Pico, also passed through the valley that same year. He would later lay claim to a bogus Mexican land grant that took in both the Ione and Jackson Valleys. In 1849, a man named Diggs claimed a large tract of land to the south, which took in the entire expanse of the Jackson Valley. Awaiting him were fertile lands ideal for livestock and farming. After the discovery of gold at Coloma, these people were followed by miners, who set up camps from the Mokelumne River, south of the Jackson Valley, to Dry Creek, north of Ione. Settlers and merchants followed them, hoping to cash in on both the land and profits from selling goods.

When the newcomers arrived, they discovered large numbers of the native Mi-wuk (or Miwok) people, who had occupied the land for more than 500 years. One early account states that there were at least 5,000 Miwoks living in the Ione and Jackson Valleys; however, with the influx of more pioneers, many natives were forced off their land and died from disease brought in by the European Americans. The Jackson Valley Miwoks have occupied their rancheria since at least 1817. Likewise the Ione band has lived in the region for over a century, although many were displaced from their village sites near the Consumes River and the town of Plymouth. Despite the devastation suffered by these people, descendants remain in the area, maintaining their cultural identity and passing along their heritage to younger generations.

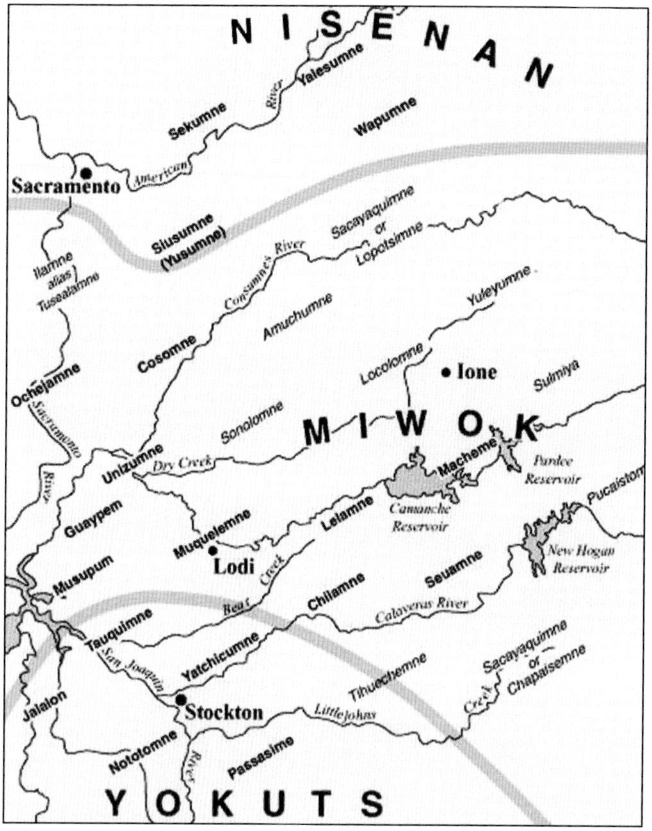

This map shows the geographic area around Ione occupied by the Miwok people at the time of European American contact and notes some of their village sites. The wide gray lines mark the approximate territorial boundaries between them and the neighboring native groups, the Nisenans and the Yokuts. Ione is shown in the center. (Author's collection.)

In 1903, naturalist and ethnographer C. Hart Merriman photographed the Miwok village site near Buena Vista in the Jackson Valley. An overview of the area appears much the same today, with little change in the landscape. The Buena Vista Buttes, seen in the background, are considered a sacred place by the Miwok tribe. (Courtesy Bancroft Library.)

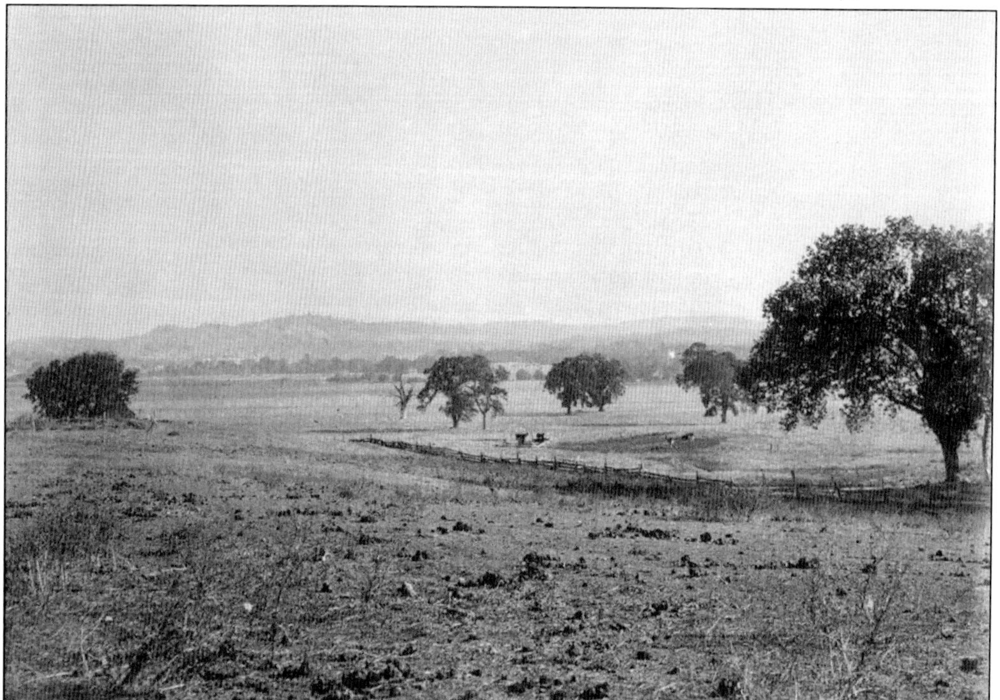

The Miwok people utilized a number of plants and seeds to supplement their diet of wild game. Of these, the staple plant food was the acorn, which was ground into meal by the use of a handheld stone pestle that was pressed into a stone cup, or mortar. The bedrock mortar station pictured here is known as *Chaw'se*, the Miwok word for grinding rock. It is located near the town of Volcano at Indian Grinding Rock State Historic Park.

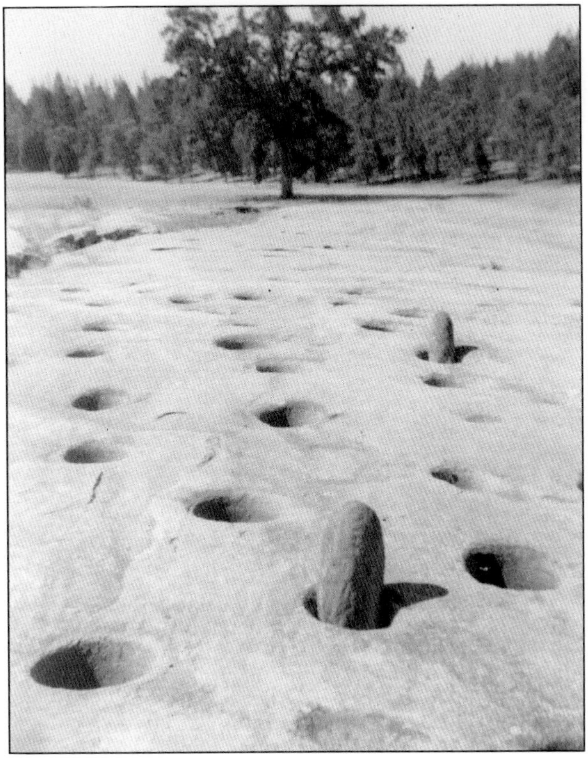

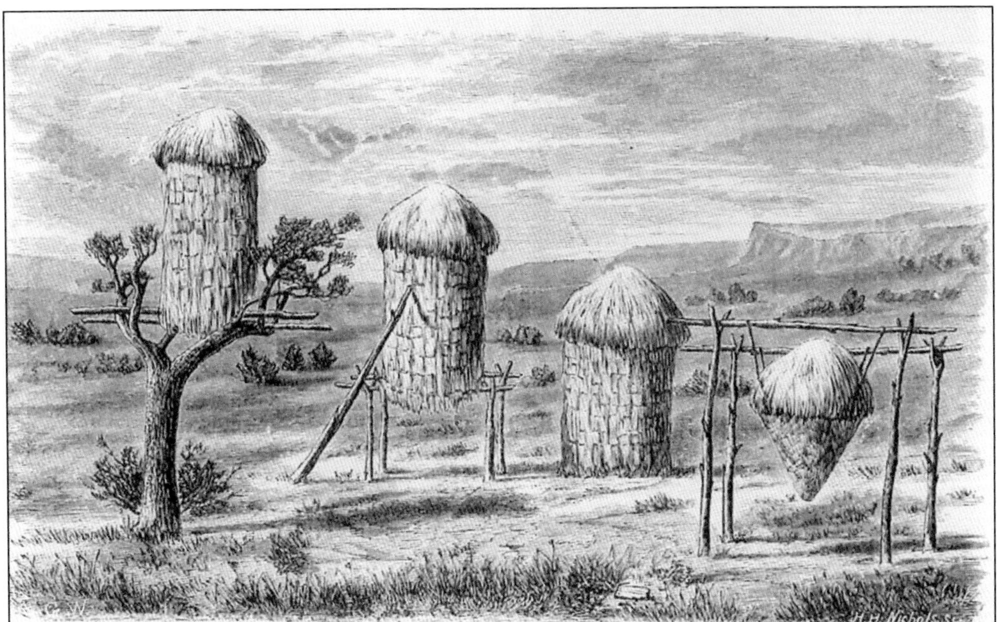

Just as we store flour in quantity, the Miwoks stored acorns. Once gathered, the acorns were cached in a granary, generally built with tree branches hewn into posts, over which the sides were constructed of sticks and brush. The granary was lined with grass, and a thatched roof was added. This 1877 lithograph shows four different types of granaries used by the Miwok. (Author's collection.)

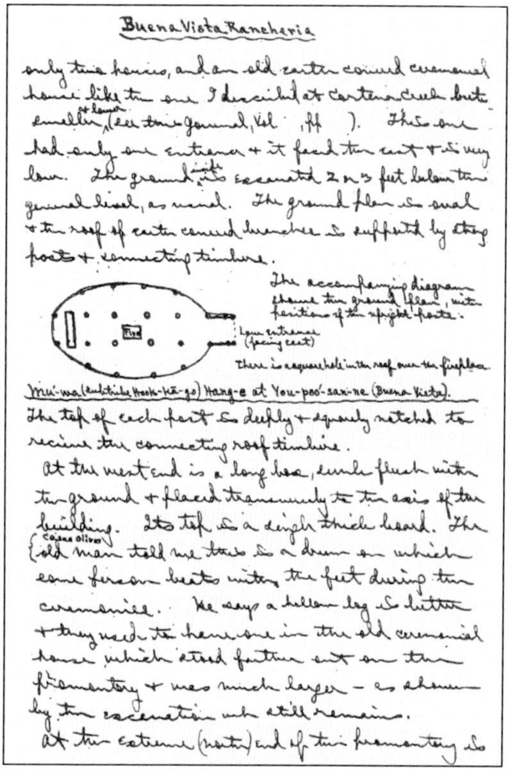

Buena Vista Rancheria

only two houses, and an old earth covered ceremonial house like the one I described at Cosumnes Creek but smaller (& lower) (see this journal, Vol. , pp). This one had only one entrance & it faced the east & is very low. The ground inside is excavated 2 or 3 feet below the general level, as usual. The ground plan is oval & the roof of earth covered branches is supported by strong posts & connecting timbers.

The accompanying diagram shows the ground plan, with positions of the upright posts.

There is a square hole in the roof over the fireplace.

Mu'-wa (substitute Hook-kā-go) Hang-e at You-poo'-san-ne (Buena Vista).

The top of each post is deeply & squarely notched to receive the connecting roof timbers.

At the west end is a long box, sunk flush with the ground & placed transversely to the axis of the building. Its top is a single thick board. The (Cajeme Oliver) old man told me this is a drum on which some person beats with the feet during the ceremonies. He says a hollow log is better & they used to have one in the old ceremonial house which stood farther out on the promontory & was much larger — as shown by the excavation wh still remains.

At the extreme (north) end of this promontory is

Each Miwok village included a dance house, a place for ceremonial assembly. These buildings were constructed over a large pit 40 to 50 feet in diameter and about 3 to 4 feet in depth. Posts set into the ground around the perimeter and heavy beams supported the roof, which was built in the form of a low cone and covered with thatch and earth. At the center of the floor was a fire pit attended by a *wükü'ppe* (fire tender) and a *t'mma* (foot drum). The drum, usually 5 to 10 feet long, was made from a hollowed-out log and set into the ground. During ceremonies, a dancer stamped upon the drum. The photograph below shows the entrance to the dance house at the Buena Vista Rancheria in the Jackson Valley. At left is a page from the journal of ethnographer C. Hart Merriam telling of the rancheria with a drawing of the dance house. Merriam visited the village site in 1903 and recorded what he experienced. (Courtesy Bancroft Library.)

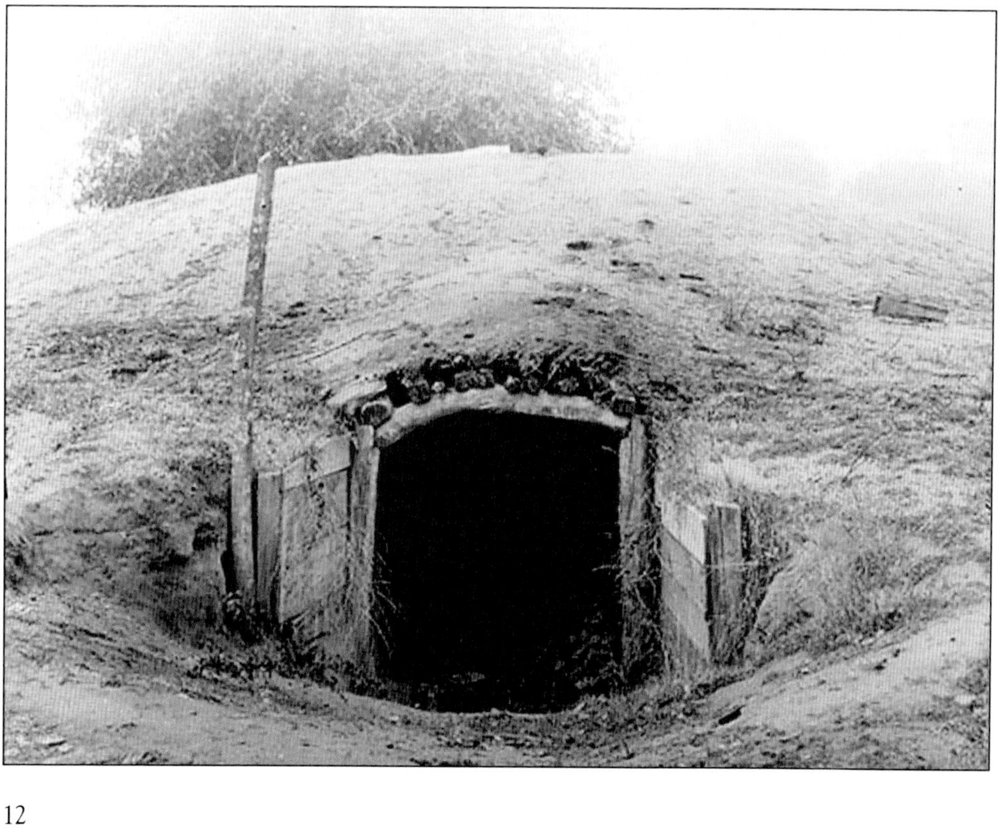

This photograph of Casus Oliver and his wife, Amanda, was taken at the Buena Vista Rancheria by C. Hart Merriam in 1903. Oliver was baptized as Jesus Alvarez, but later anglicized his name. He was known as a Miwok captain of great hospitality. Amanda, a Nisenan woman from the village near Gold Hill in Eldorado County, was the daughter of Capt. John Oitey. (Courtesy Bancroft Library.)

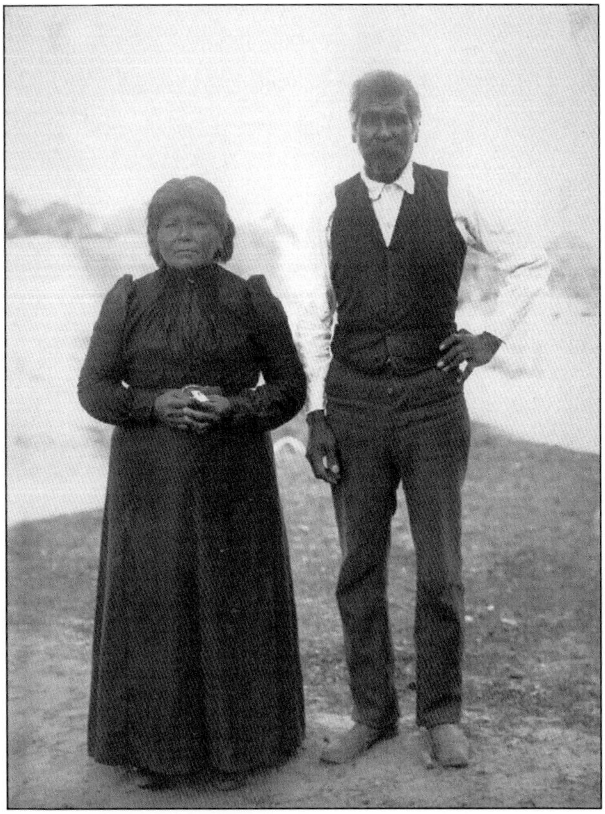

Casus Oliver and his family stand in front of their homestead at the Buena Vista Rancheria. The roundhouse mound can be seen at the right edge. This photograph was also taken by Merriam during his 1903 visit to the village. (Courtesy Bancroft Library.)

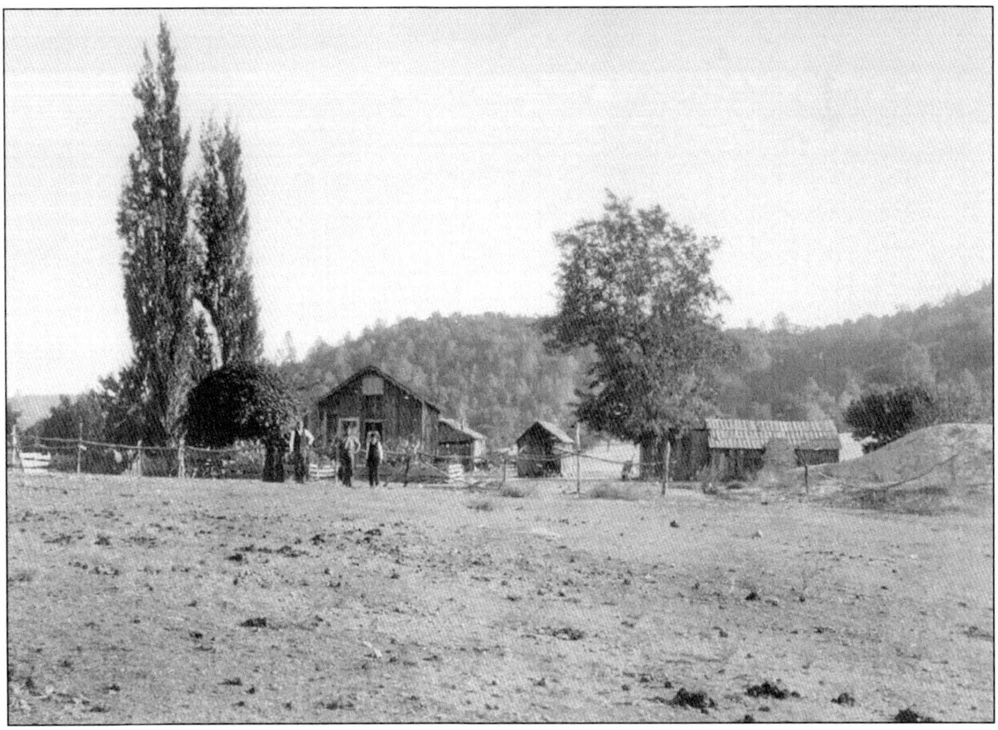

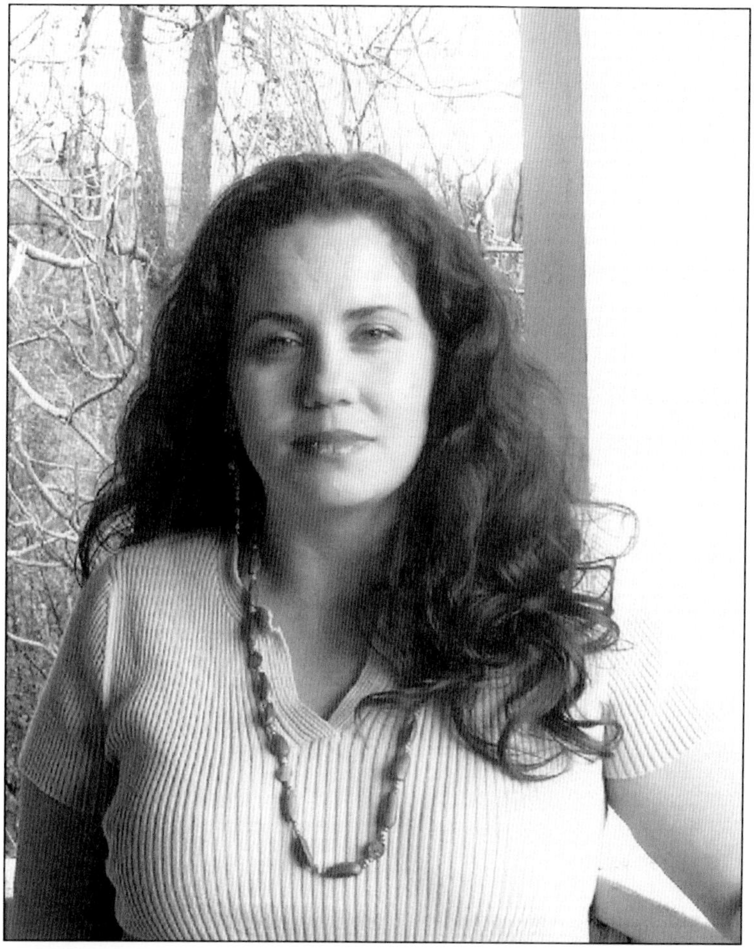

Rhonda Morningstar Pope is the current tribal chairperson for the Buena Vista band of Miwok Indians. She is the great-granddaughter of Louis and Annie Oliver, who were federally recognized as leaders of the band in 1927. Pope is working toward the construction of the Flying Cloud Casino on the rancheria property in the Jackson Valley. Below is an artist's rendition of the proposed facility.

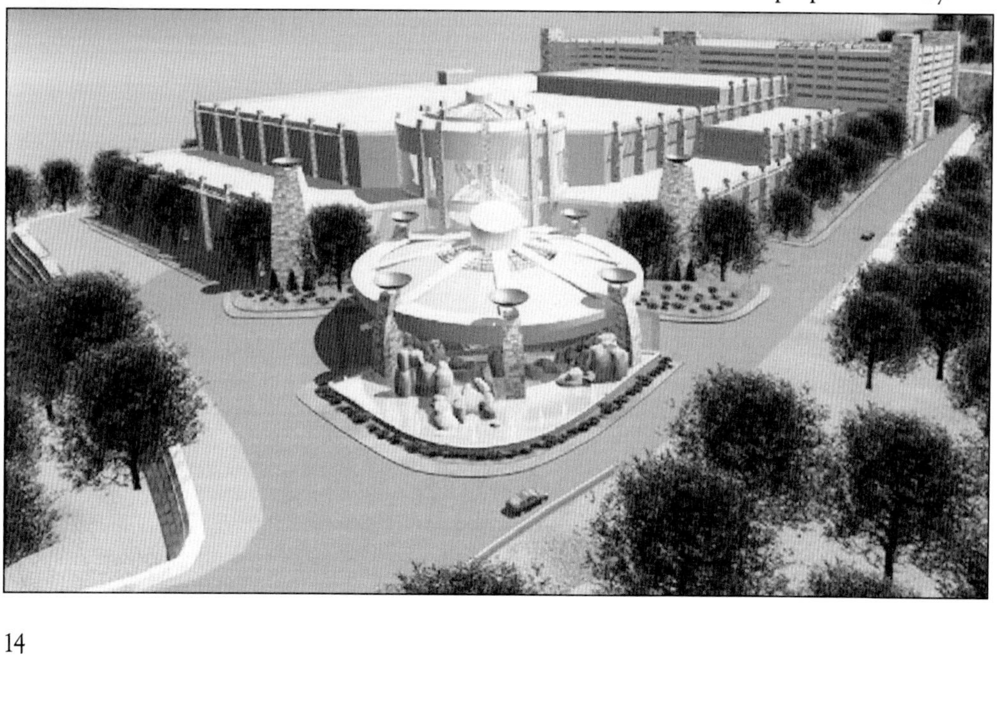

In 1915, John Terrell took a census of Native Americans in the Ione area and identified 101 homeless native people. Due to both poverty and disease, many children were orphaned. In 1922, an orphanage for homeless Native American children was opened in Ione and operated by the Free Methodist Church Home Missionary Board. This pamphlet solicited donations to pay off the property and perform repairs to the facility.

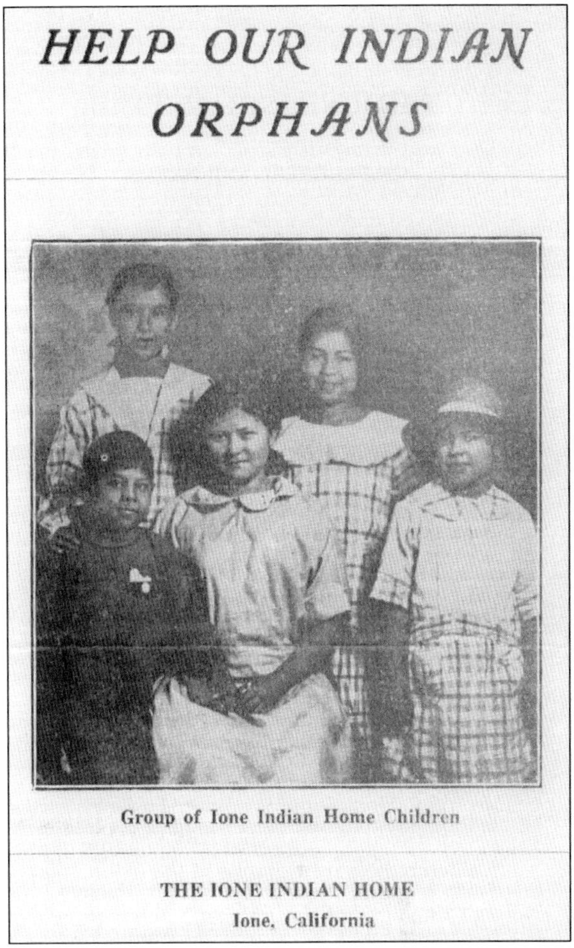
HELP OUR INDIAN ORPHANS

Group of Ione Indian Home Children

THE IONE INDIAN HOME
Ione, California

Despite the misery, suffering, and death that the Miwok Indians experienced during the Mission Period in California history, by the time the Gold Rush was well under way, they had begun to assimilate into European American culture. This c. 1888 image shows members of an all-Miwok baseball team organized and coached by Clarence W. Swain (left).

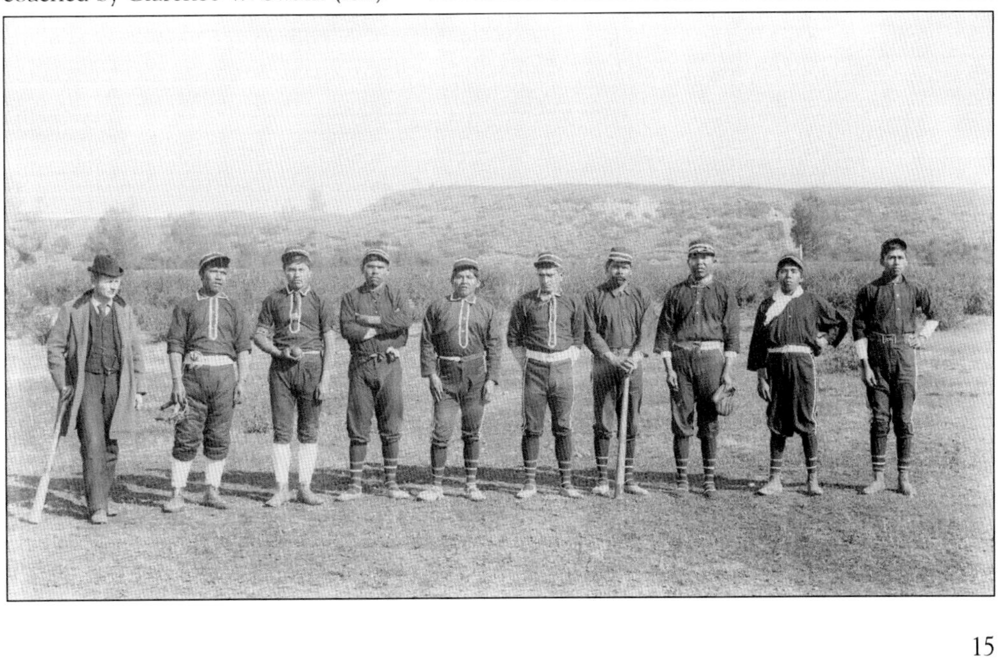

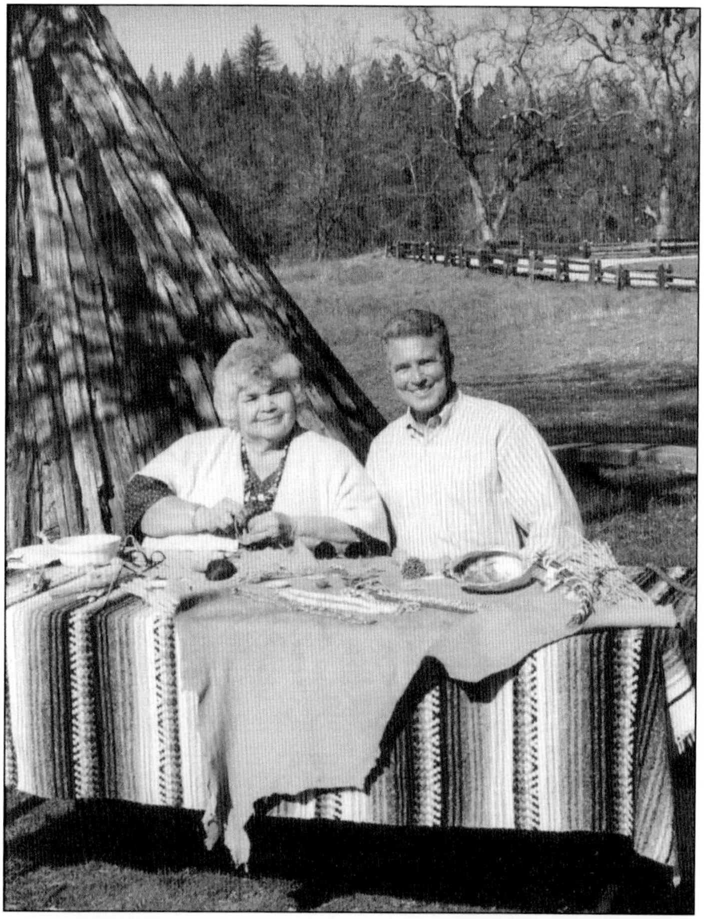

The Ione Miwok keep their heritage alive by practicing traditional material culture and passing it along to younger generations. Basketry and beadwork are two of the traditional crafts that tribal women continue today. Many such items are displayed each year at the Amador County Fair, as seen in the photograph below. Ramona Dutschke, a noted basket maker from Ione, is seen at left with television host Huell Howser at a *Chaw'se* celebration. Dutschke, who passed away in 2006, was a distinguished and much-loved elder of the Ione band of Miwok and a member of the Sierra Native American Council, the California Indian Basket Weavers Association, and the Chaw'se Association.

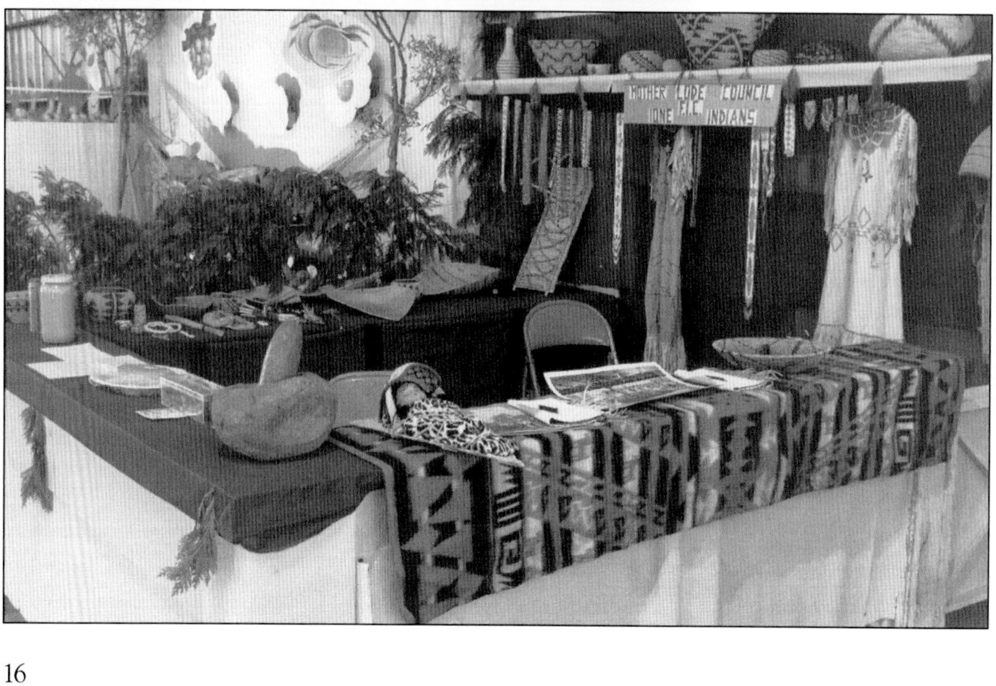

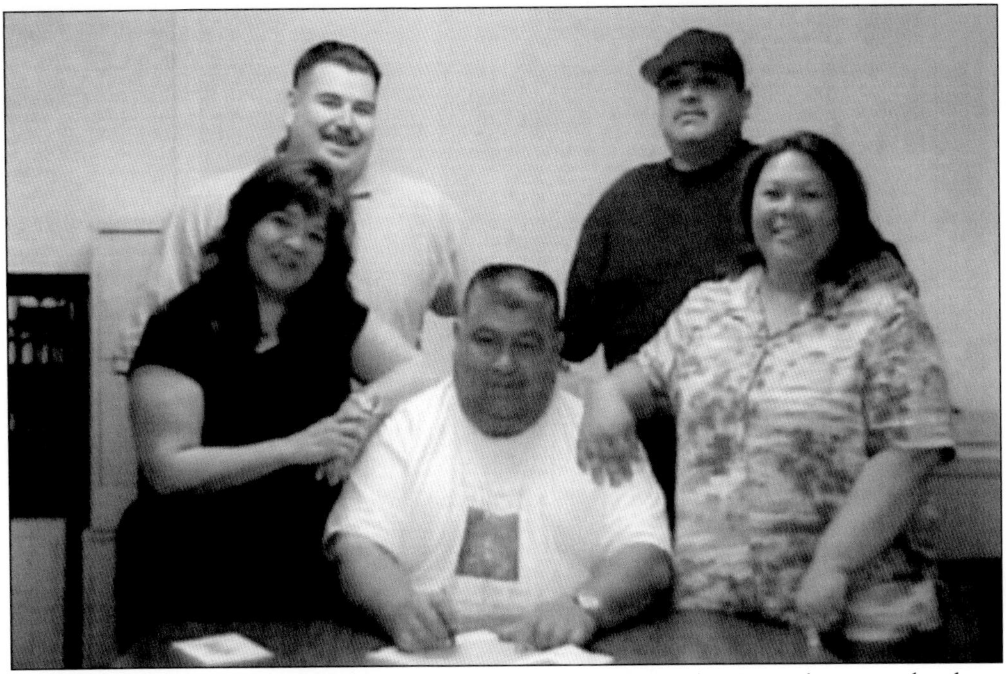

In 1994, the Ione Miwoks obtained federal recognition for their tribe. Since that time, they have experienced many controversies within the group over rightful leadership but nonetheless have operated as a sovereign nation with a democratically elected tribal government. The members pictured here were elected to the tribal council in April 2006 and will serve for three years. From left to right are secretary Tracy Tripp, chairman Matthew Franklin, vice chairman John "Gil" Jamerson, member-at-large Ralph "Troy" Hatch, and treasurer Barbara "Barbie" Sanchez. The office out of which the council conducts business is located on Main Street in Ione.

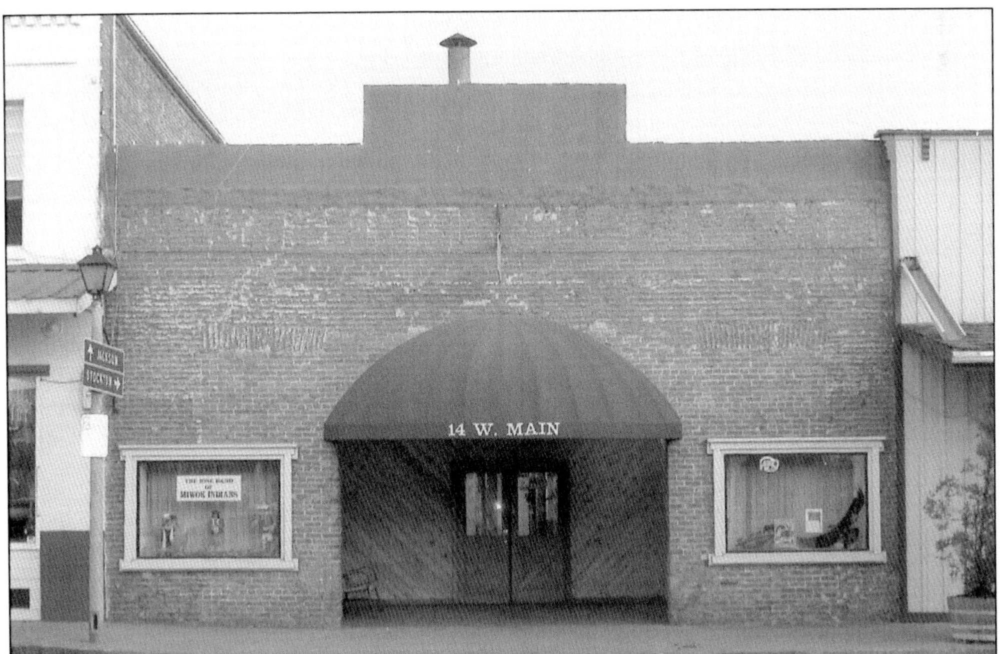

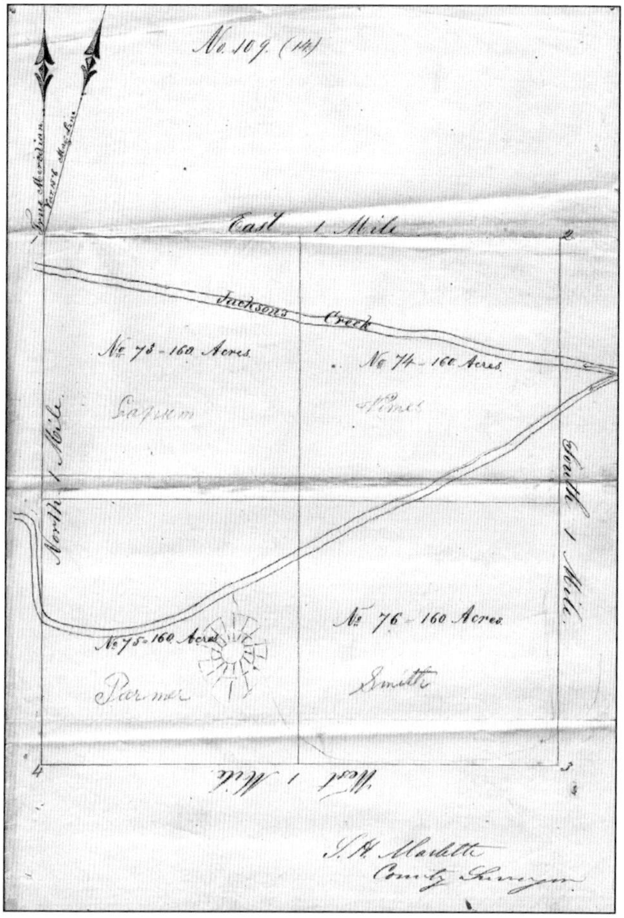

The first settler to the Jackson Valley was a man named Diggs, who arrived in 1849 and sold his land to Charles Stone, Warren Nimms, and Fletcher Baker in 1850. Within two years, the partnership had dissolved, with Stone and Nimms remaining. These two divided the land by half. In 1852, Nimms commissioned Seneca H. Marlette to survey his portion. This map was drawn from that survey.

These stone-building remains stand in a pasture next to Jackson Valley Road. According to the Scully family, this house was the structure sold to William Scully when he took up residence here in 1855. It is probable that it was built by either Diggs or Stone, Nimms, and Baker. (Author's collection.)

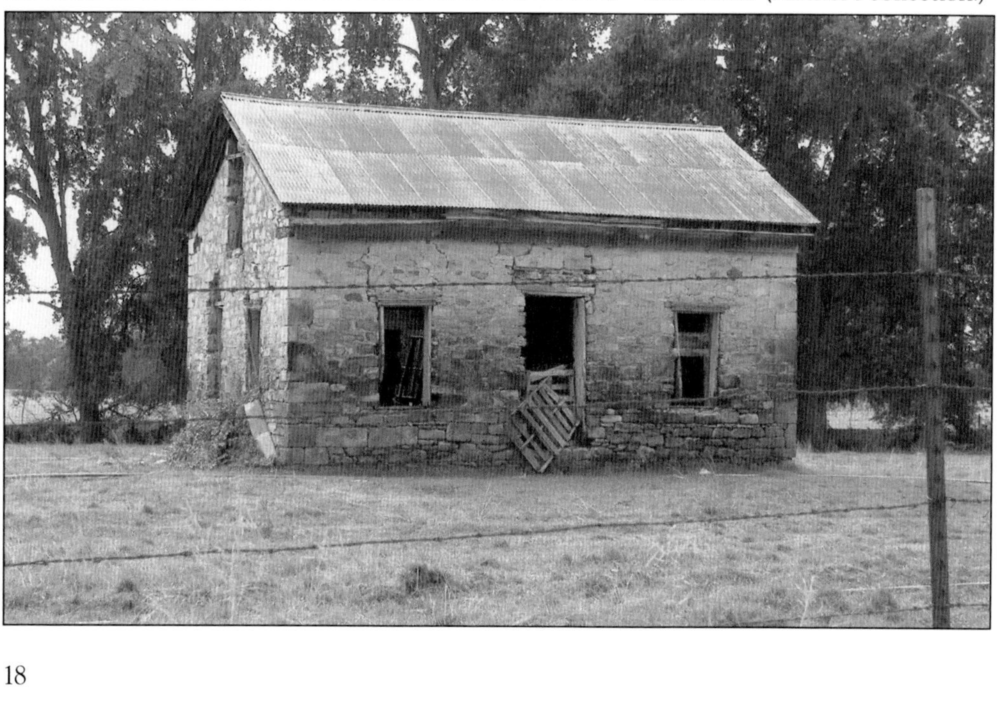

William Hicks is credited as the first white businessman in the Ione Valley. He came to California in 1843 and, after working as a rancher for John Sutter, arrived in the valley in 1848. Hicks became a wealthy man, first operating a trading post and then entering into the livestock business.

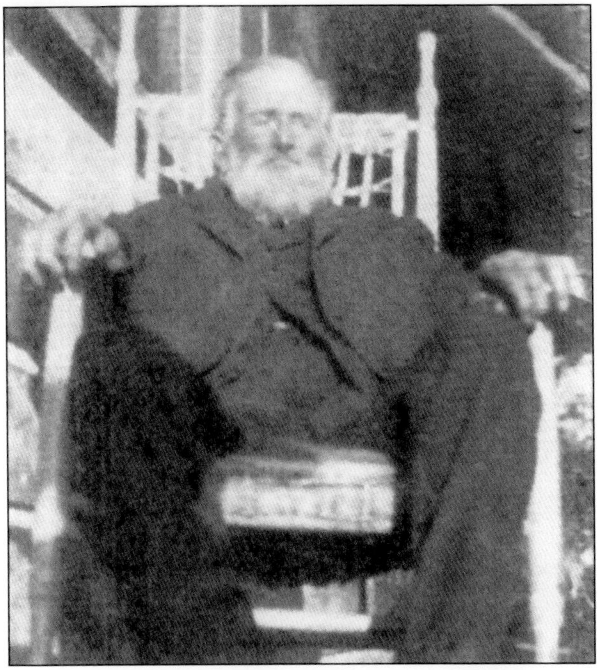

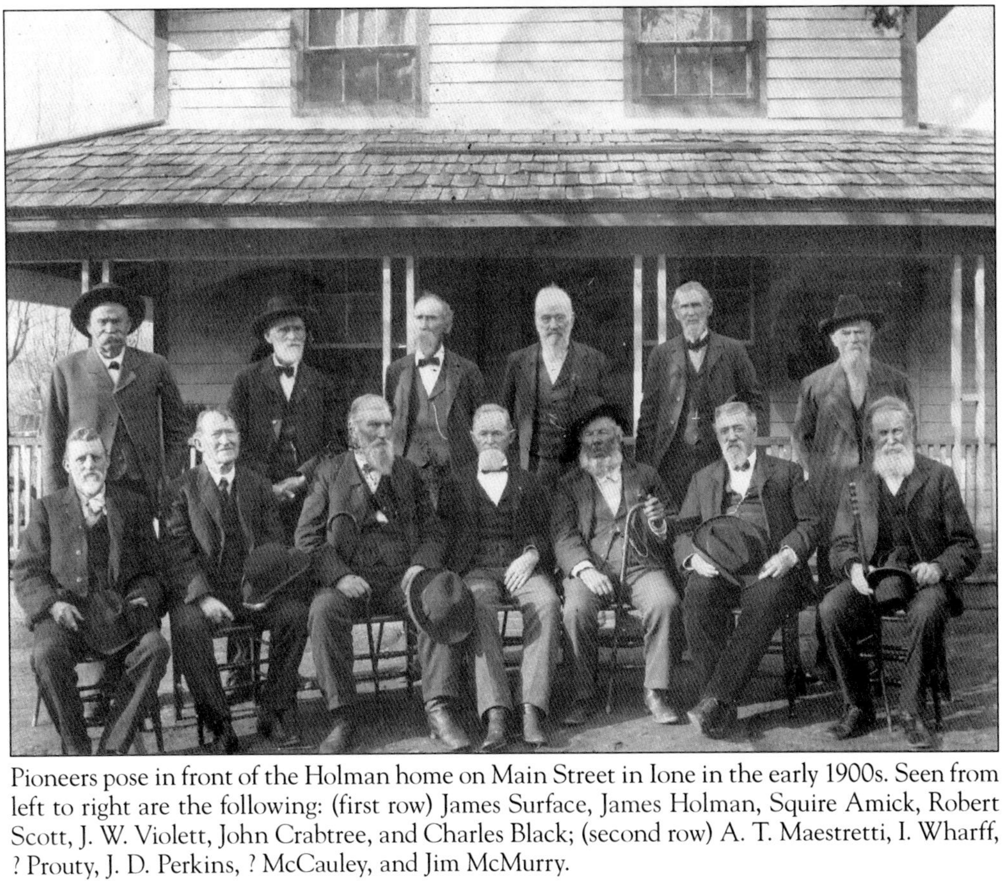

Pioneers pose in front of the Holman home on Main Street in Ione in the early 1900s. Seen from left to right are the following: (first row) James Surface, James Holman, Squire Amick, Robert Scott, J. W. Violett, John Crabtree, and Charles Black; (second row) A. T. Maestretti, I. Wharff, ? Prouty, J. D. Perkins, ? McCauley, and Jim McMurry.

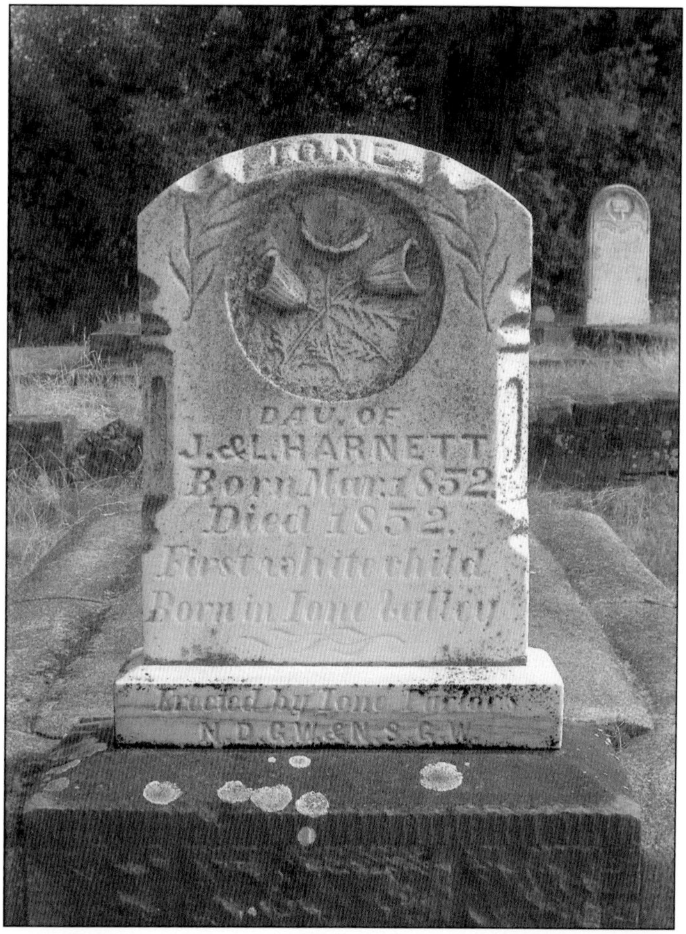

Not just single men came to the fertile land of western Amador County. In the early 1850s, many families also set down roots. Pictured here is the headstone of Ione Harnett, the first white child born in the Ione Valley. There are varying accounts of how the valley was named. Could it be that it was named in her memory? (Author's collection.)

The Tom Cook family settled in the Ione Valley at the onset of the Gold Rush. Cook is seated at center, with his wife to his left.

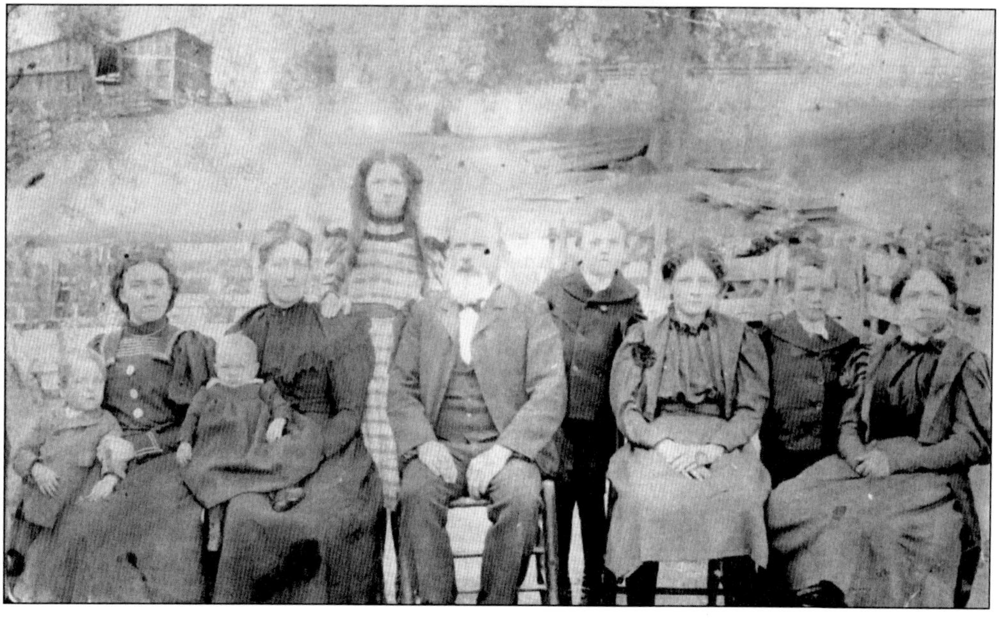

Two

The Arroyo Seco Grant

Straddling the boundary lines between Amador, Sacramento, and San Joaquin Counties is a large, open tract of land covered by low rolling hills that give way to flatlands to the west. This sparsely inhabited expanse is all that remains of what is known as Rancho Arroyo Seco, which began as a bogus Spanish land grant.

By 1853, the region that was to become Amador County was well populated, and many citizens were determined to form a new county. During a trip to the state legislature at Benicia in 1853, Dr. E. B. Harris and H. A. Carter, both of Ione, discovered that the Arroyo Seco claim had been filed in the General Land Office. It took in 11 square leagues of land, including their town. The document, filed by Andres Pico, a Mexican Californian, stated that Gov. Juan B. Alvarado had granted the tract to Teodocio Yerba on May 8, 1840, who in turn sold it to Pico on October 4, 1852.

This was not the first spurious grant that had surfaced at the end of the war with Mexico. Many settlers in the region that was to become Amador County were aware of the fact that they could lose their land. A few of them living within the boundaries of the claim actually paid Pico for the land they had lived on for years. Others, determined to stay their ground, ignored Pico's claim and continued to battle him through the courts. By 1861, Pico had tired of the battle and sold the grant to J. Mora Moss, H. W. Carpentier, E. F. Beale, Herman Wohler, and others. Soon thereafter, these partners employed the military to eject settlers from their homesteads and businesses, which did not prove to be too successful. It was not until 1865 that the battle for the land finally subsided.

Between those early years and today, some sections of the grant have been sold, with a large portion in Sacramento County placed into a nature reserve. The open grant land that remains in Amador County has been used for both livestock ranching and mining operations and has been associated with several people of world renown. In this chapter, the reader will meet some of those whose lives and livelihood have been linked to the controversial piece of land.

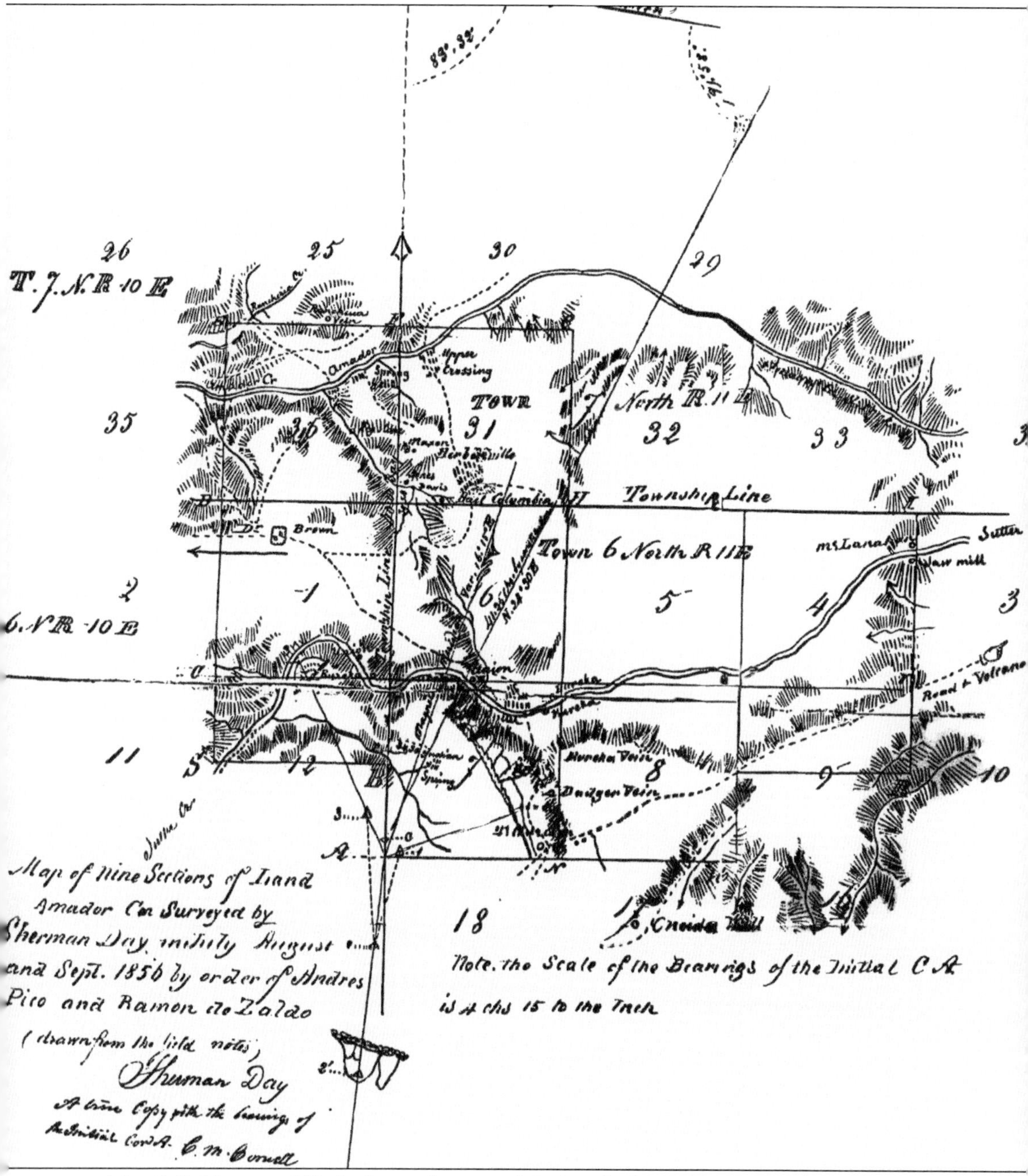

After E. B. Harris and H. A. Carter discovered the Pico's claim, they returned to Ione and helped form a committee to fight Pico. In February 1855, Pico's claim was rejected by commissioners of the federal government; however, their decision was reversed by the U.S. District Court. Pico employed engineer Sherman Day to survey the tract, and this 1865 map resulted. Note that the boundaries of the claim extend well beyond the Ione and Jackson Valley area to include land to the east and north. Over time, the boundaries moved to include valuable mining claims along the Mother Lode and north of Ione along Dry Creek. Also included were the town sites of Amador City, Sutter Creek, and Jackson.

Andre Pico was the villain behind the claim to the Arroyo Seco Grant. During the Mexican-American War, he commanded Mexican soldiers in California and, like his brother Pio Pico, served for a time as governor of Alta California. In 1846, he led a successful attack on U.S. general Stephen Kearny at San Pascual. It was Pico who signed the Treaty of Cahuenga with John C. Fremont on January 13, 1847, ending the war in California.

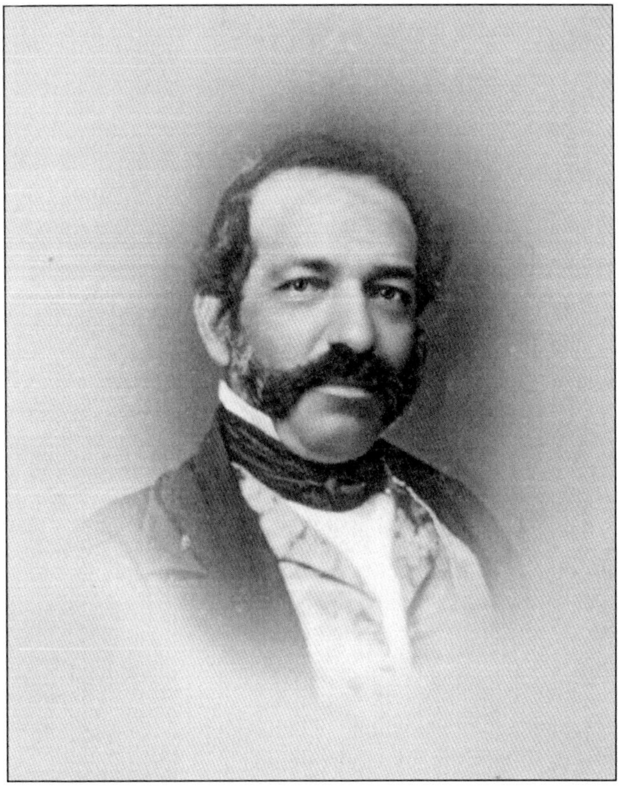

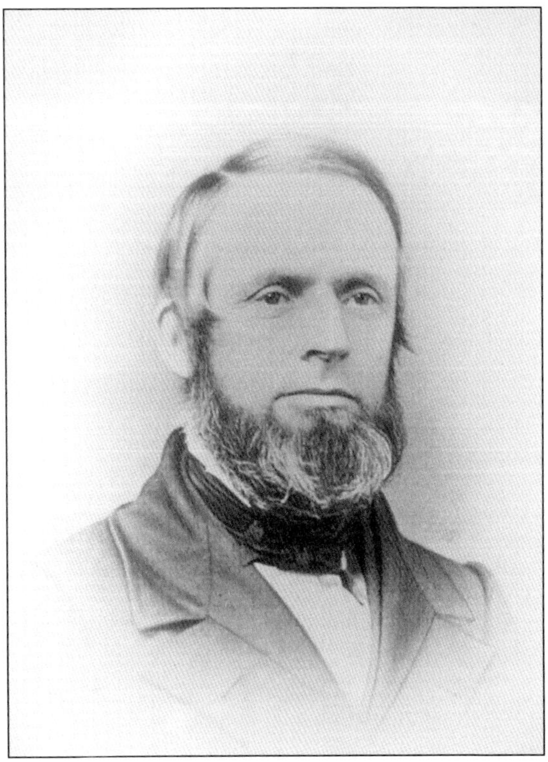

Sherman Day, a well-known author and civil engineer, first arrived in California in 1849 and set up business in both civil and mine engineering. In 1855, he surveyed wagon routes across the Sierra Nevada. His survey for Pico was completed in August and September 1856. Day also served in the California State Senate during the 1855–1856 session and as U.S. surveyor general for California from 1868 to 1871. As an original trustee of the University of California, he taught as a professor of mine construction and surveying.

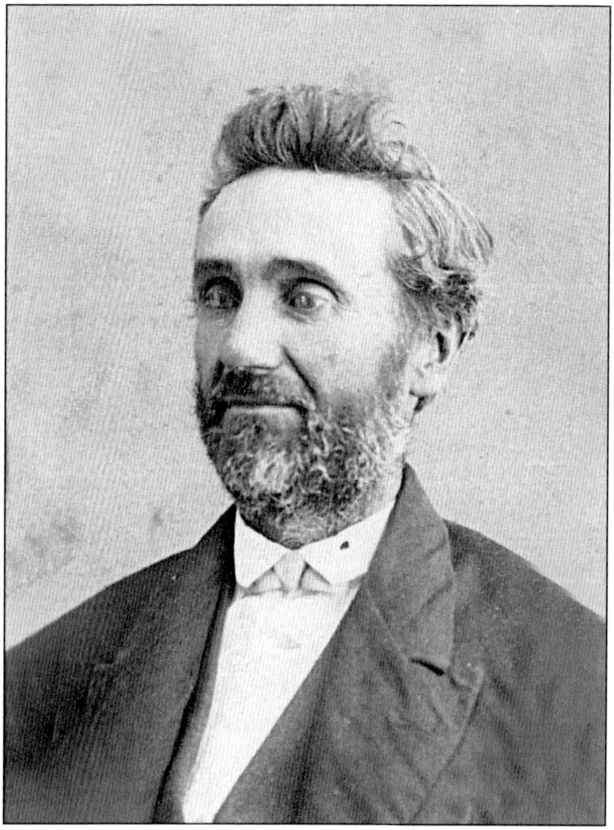

Joseph Fithian, an Ohio native, arrived in California in 1849. After a stint in mining and brick making, he returned to Ohio, married Leanora Fowler, and in 1856 returned to Amador County. Fithian became a victim of the grant dispute when soldiers under the direction of Herman Wohler marched into the Jackson Valley and ejected settlers from their homes.

This 1860s view of Ione and the surrounding valley gives one a sense of just how settled the region had become amid the controversy of Pico's claim to the Arroyo Seco Grant. This photograph was taken from atop a hill to the east of town. The boulevard at the center is Main Street. (Courtesy Library of Congress.)

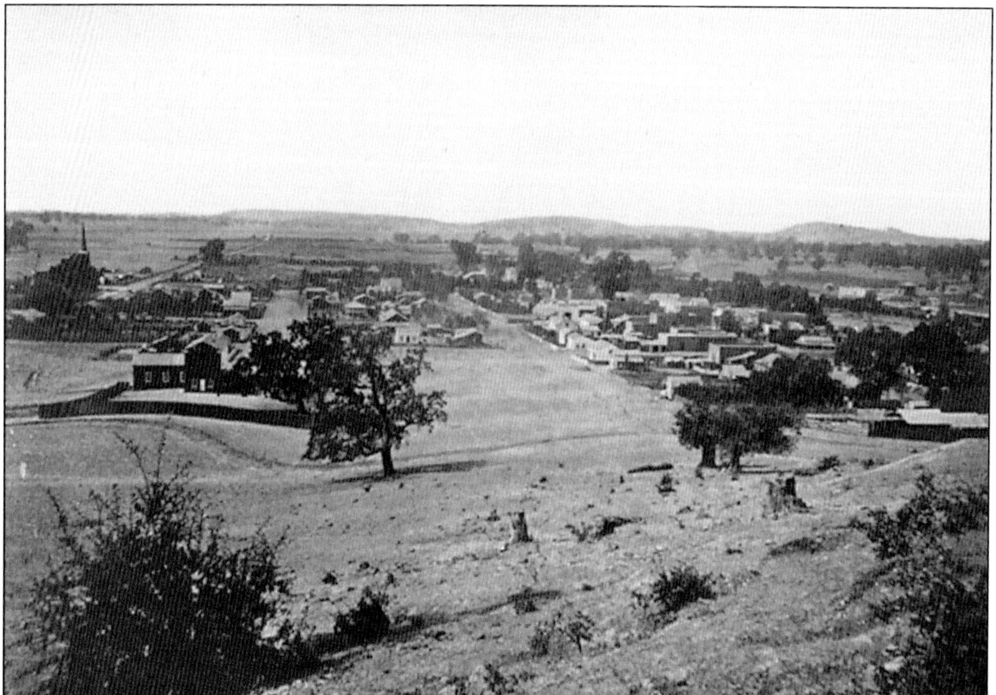

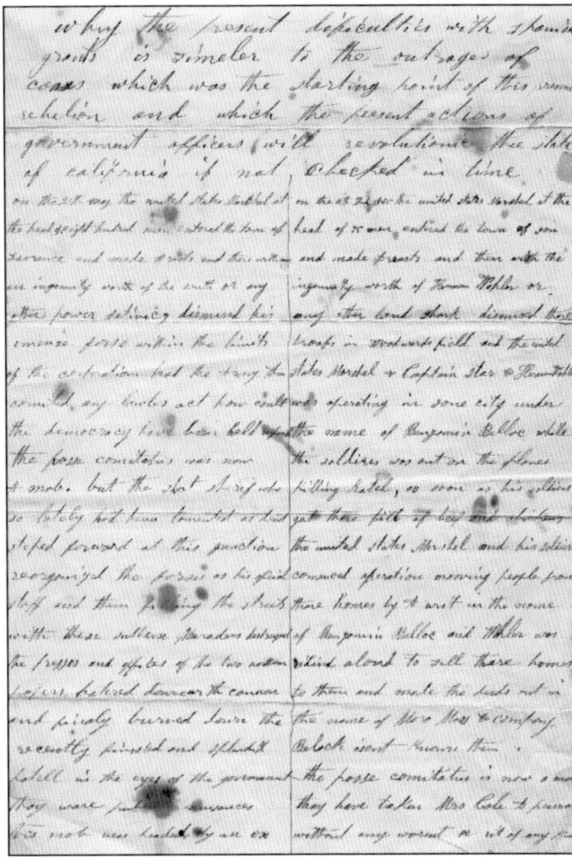

why the present difficulties with spanish grants is simeler to the outrages of [illegible] which was the starting point of this [illegible] rebelion and which the present actions of government officers will revolutionise the state of california if not checked in time

on the 2th may the united states Marshal at the head of eight hundred men entered the town of [illegible] and made [illegible] and then with an ingenuity worth of the [illegible] or any other power [illegible] dismissed his imense force within the limits of the [illegible] that the [illegible] comitted any [illegible] act how could the democracy have been held up the posse comitatus was now a mob. but the [illegible] sheriff who so lately had been [illegible] as [illegible] steped forward at this junction reorganized the posse as his special staff and then [illegible] the streets with these [illegible] [illegible] destroyed the presses and offices of the two [illegible] papers battered down with the cannon and finaly burned down the recently finished and splendid hotell in the eyes of the government they were [illegible] [illegible] this mob was headed by an ex

on the [illegible] the united states Marshal at the head of 75 men entered the town of Ione and made [illegible] and then with the ingenuity worth of Herman Wohler or any other land shark dismissed those troops in Woodwards field and the united states Marshal & Captain Star & Herman Wohler was operating in Ione city under the name of Benjamin Belloc while the soldiers was out on the plains killing [illegible], as soon as his soldiers got there fill of beef and chickens the united states Marshal and his soldiers commenced operations moving people from there homes by a writ in the name of Benjamin Belloc and Wohler was [illegible] alond to sell there homes to them and make the deeds out in the name of [illegible] [illegible] & company Belock [illegible] knows them. the posse comitatus is now a mob they have taken Mrs Cole to prison without any warrent or writ of any kind

This letter was penned shortly after the settlers were thrown off their property in the Ione and Jackson Valleys. It is apparent from the introduction that not only was the Arroyo Seco claim causing problems, but difficulties were also arising across the state over other Spanish grants. The author of the letter is not known.

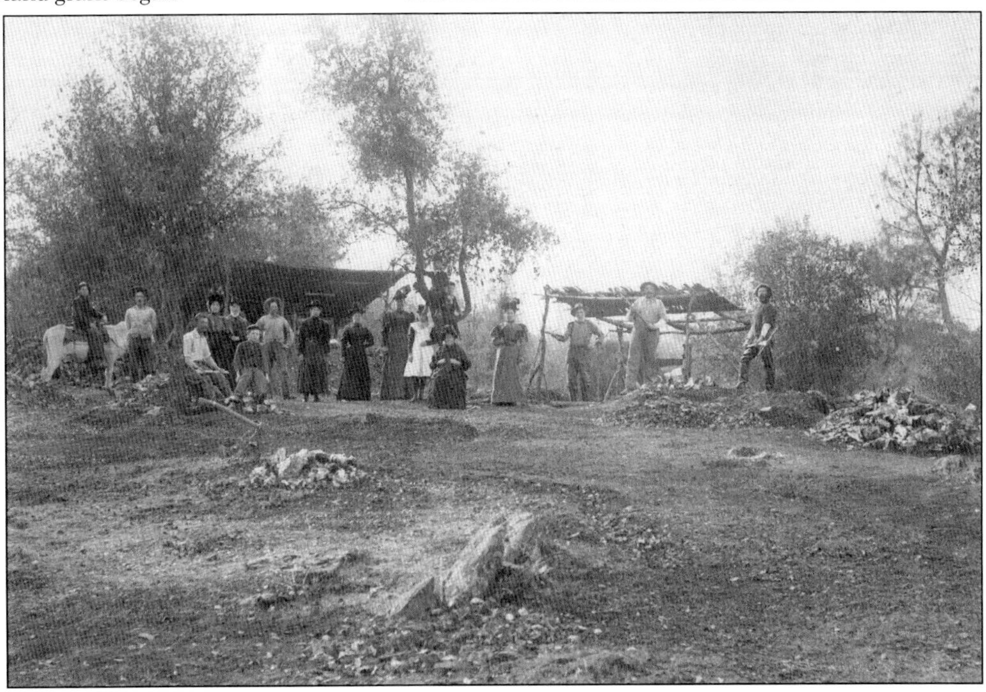

Many early pioneers of the region lived and worked in large extended families. Here a family gathers at an Ione Valley mining claim that may have been considered a "squatter's claim" when controversy over the land grant began.

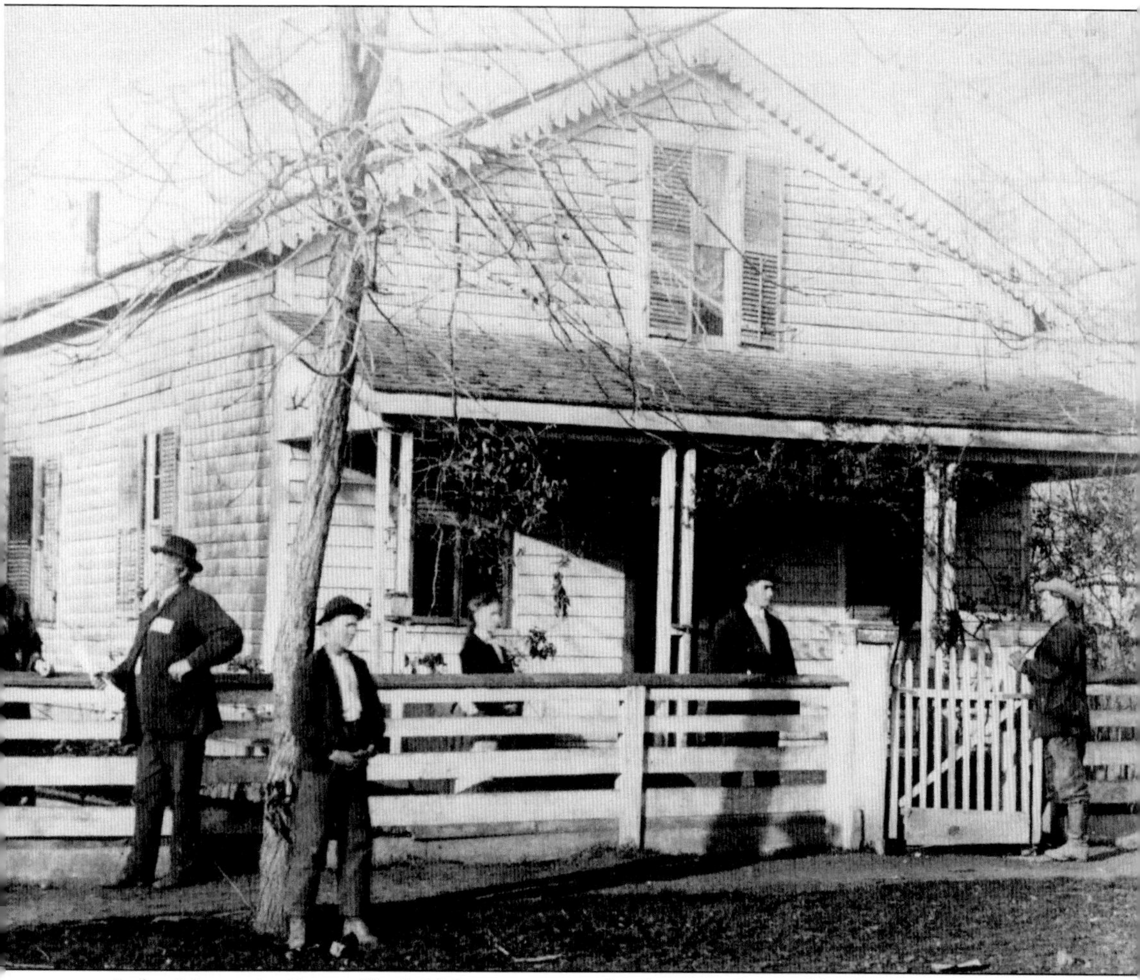

Judge Henry A. Carter (far left) leans against the fence in front of his home in Ione. Carter's frame house was the first built in the county, being brought round the horn from the east and erected in 1850. In an 1852 letter, he described the lawlessness here: "The code of morals highest in authority is Colt backed by Bowie. Occasionally, Lucy Lynch reaches a villain and there at the hands of an infuriated and uncontrollable mob the crime is expiated upon the first limb. Religion is not of course in a very flourishing condition here." Carter, in company with Dr. E. B. Harris, first discovered Pico's claim to Arroyo Seco during a visit to Benicia in 1853 while organizing the new county of Amador. In addition to serving many years as a judge, he became the first district attorney for Amador County and served in the state assembly in 1875.

Another settler ejected from his land, John W. Surface first settled along Dry Creek, near Ione, in 1852. Surface engaged in raising grain and livestock with his brothers and established a livery stable in partnership with Robert Ludgate in 1863. In 1895, he opened the Ione Valley Bank with his son. He also served as county assessor from 1869 to 1874.

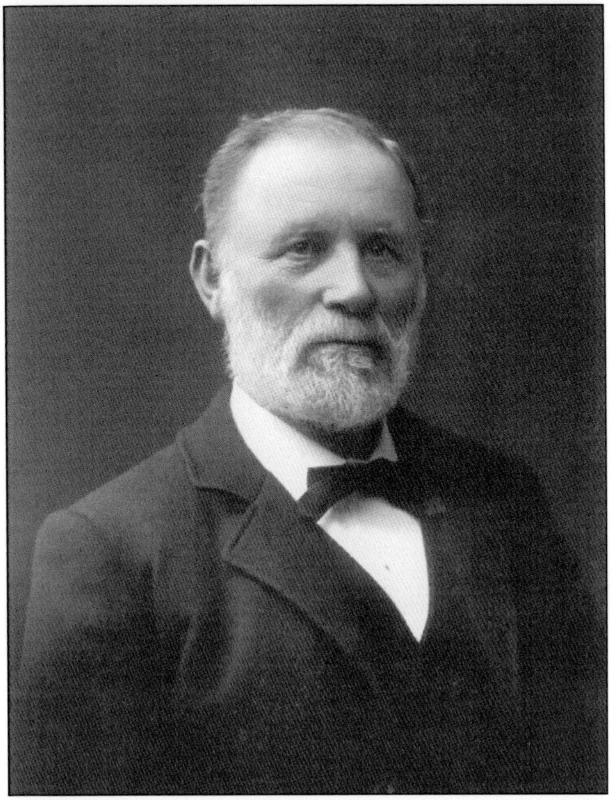

Gerald Cullen (seated at center, surrounded by his children) arrived in the Ione Valley in April 1851. Like many early settlers, he suffered displacement over the land dispute. Apparently, the episode was something that stuck with those who endured it. He recounted in a 1932 newspaper article how he was instrumental in keeping Pico from claiming all the land in Jackson.

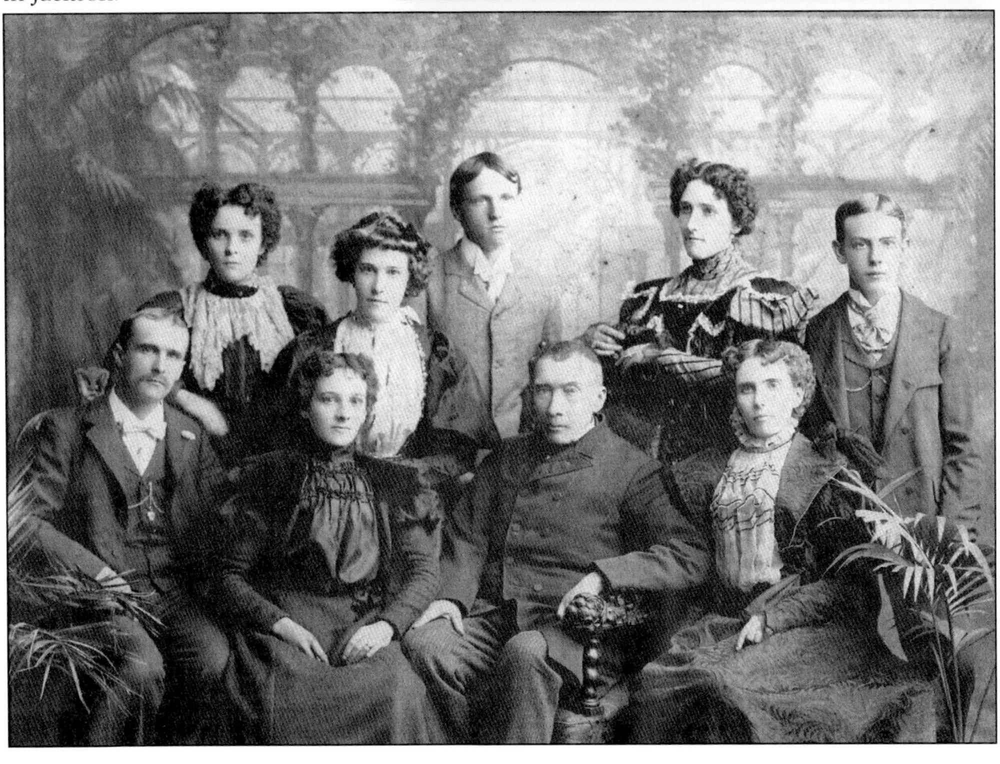

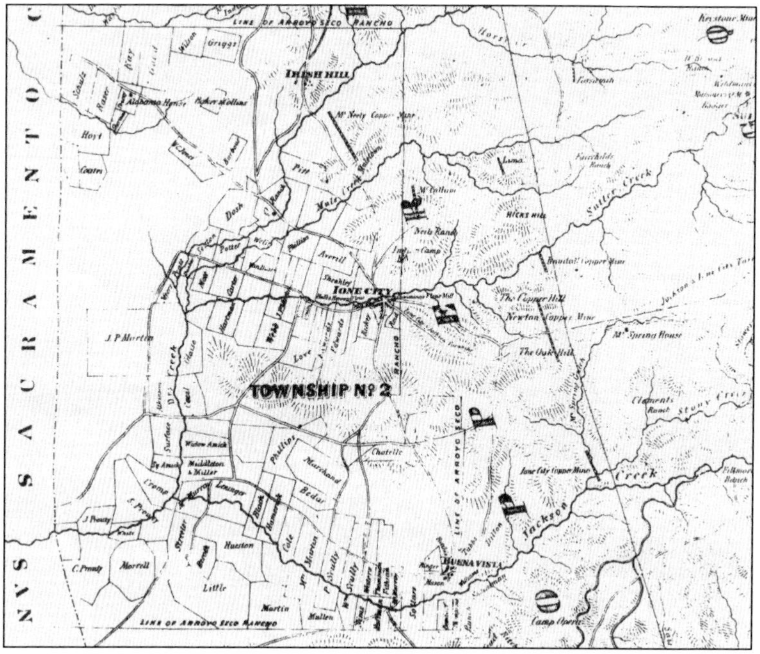

This section of the 1866 Official Map of Amador County shows the finalized boundary lines of the Arroyo Seco Rancho. It is apparent from the property owner names and the locations of both Ione and Buena Vista that a great number of people in this area were affected by Pico's claim. (Author's collection.)

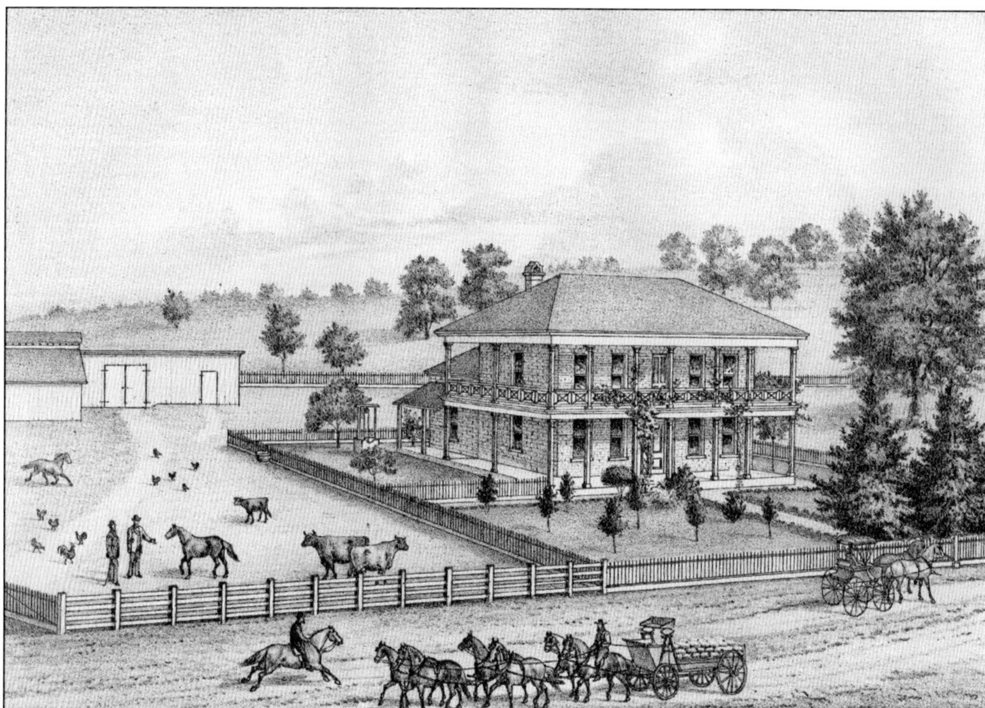

The home of Frank Frates was known as the Grant House. A native of the Azores, Frates came to the Ione Valley in 1876. By 1881, when the *History of Amador County* was written, he was serving as manager of both the Ione grant ranching operation and the Ione Coal and Iron Company. That company leased and mined portions of the grant property. (Author's collection.)

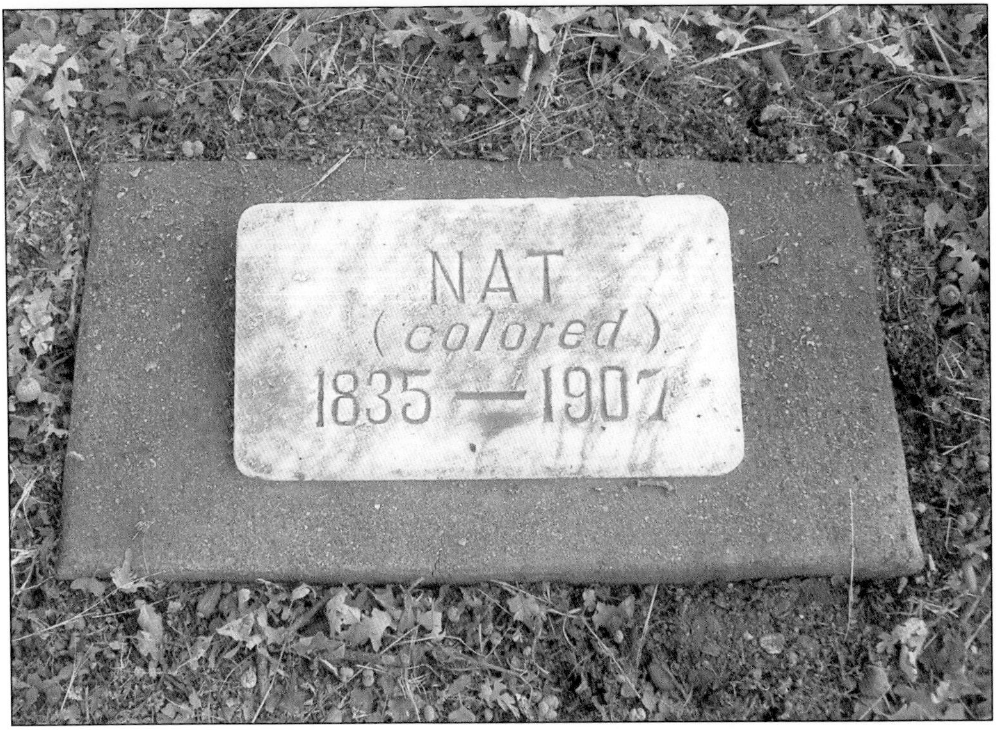

A well-known cowboy associated with the grant, Nat Cecil was the only African American resident of the Ione Valley for many years. Born a slave in Henry County, Missouri, in 1838, he traveled west to Ione with his owners, the Cecil family, in 1857. After purchasing his freedom, he became a wrangler on the Arroyo Seco, where he worked until his death in 1907. (Author's collection.)

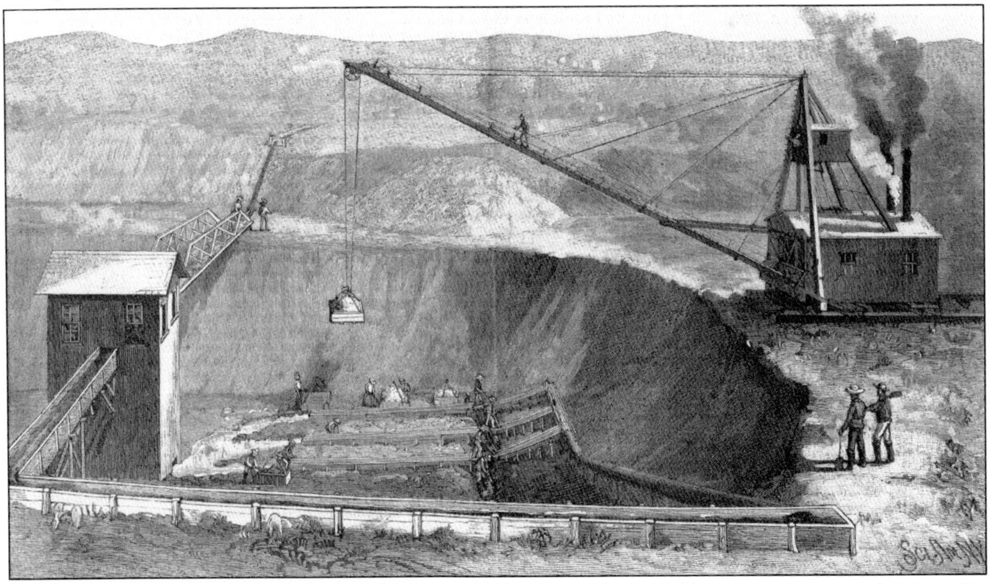

The soils of the Arroyo Seco are rich in minerals. As early as 1849, miners were exploiting the gravels along drainages, and by the 1880s large-scale mining operations were in place. Pictured here is an orange-peel dredge at the Arroyo Seco Mine in 1886. In the summer of 1887, the mine produced between $8,000 to $12,000 per month. (Courtesy *Scientific American*.)

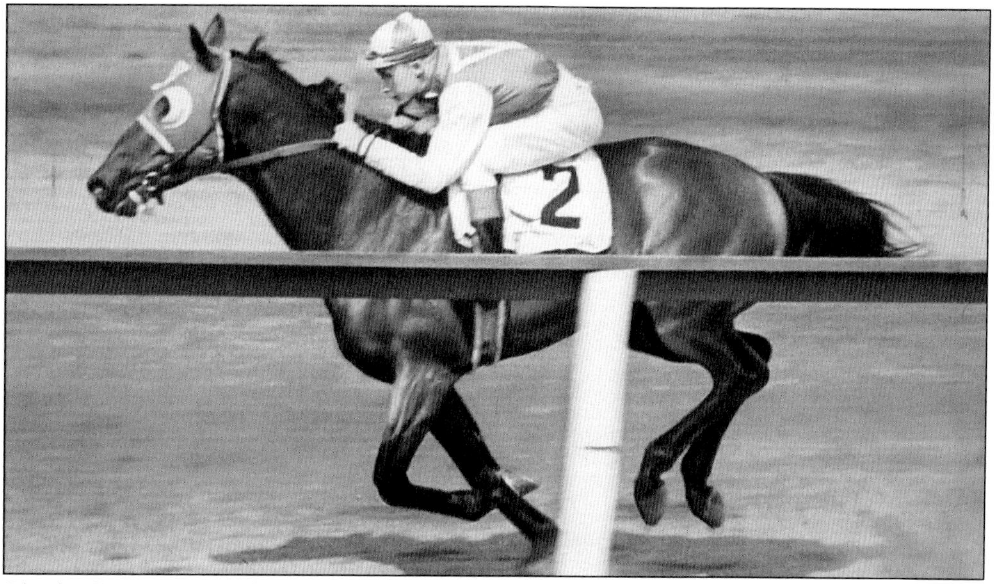

Charles Stewart Howard, owner of the famed racehorse Seabiscuit (pictured above), purchased 32,000 acres of the Rancho Arroyo Seco in 1942 from his friend W. H. Moffat. Included in the sale were the Ione Racetrack and an adjacent 89-acre parcel, now known as Howard Park. The park was leased to the City of Ione for $1 per year until Howard's heirs sold it to the city in 1995. A 12,362-acre section of the grant in Sacramento County also was sold by the heirs to the Nature Conservancy. Then, in November 2006, they sold 16,000 acres of grant property in Amador County to a partnership of private developers. The sign pictured below, one of many that hang on perimeter fences of the grant, bears the Howard Ranch brand.

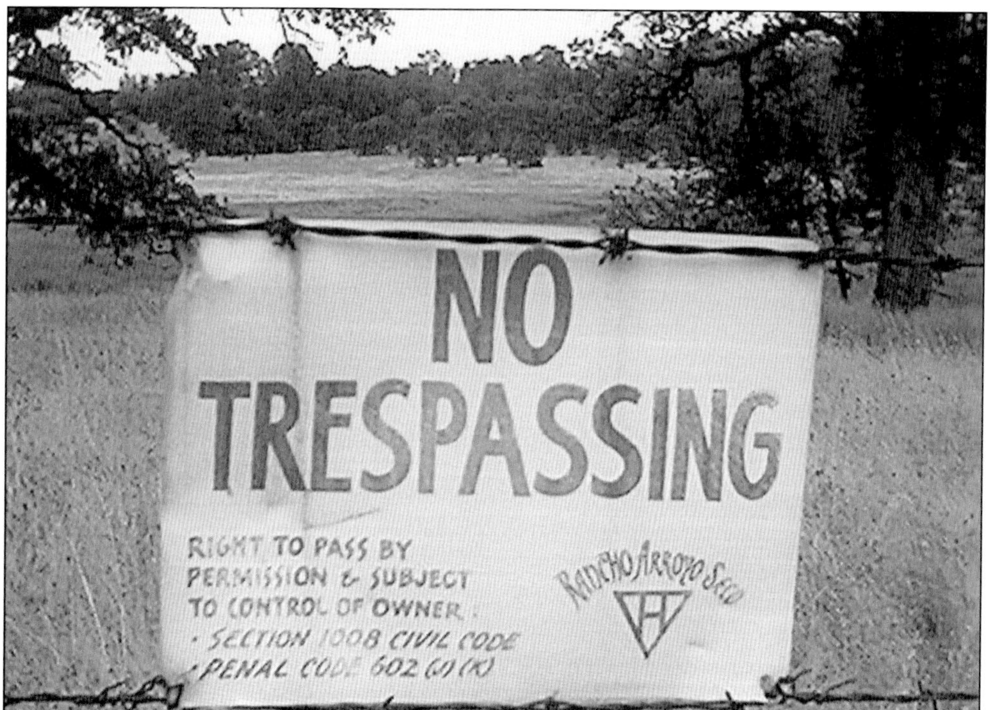

Another famous person associated with the Arroyo Seco Grant is jazz legend Dave Brubeck. When he was 12 years old, his family moved from Concord, California, to the grant, where his father managed the 45,000-acre spread. Brubeck was drawn to ranching like his father but also developed an interest in music like his mother.

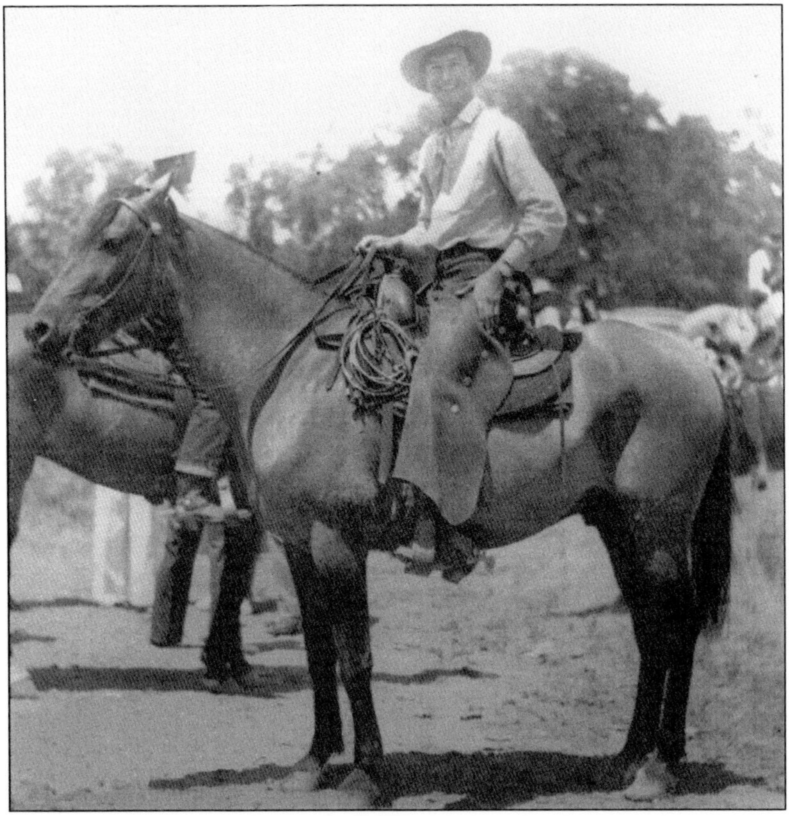

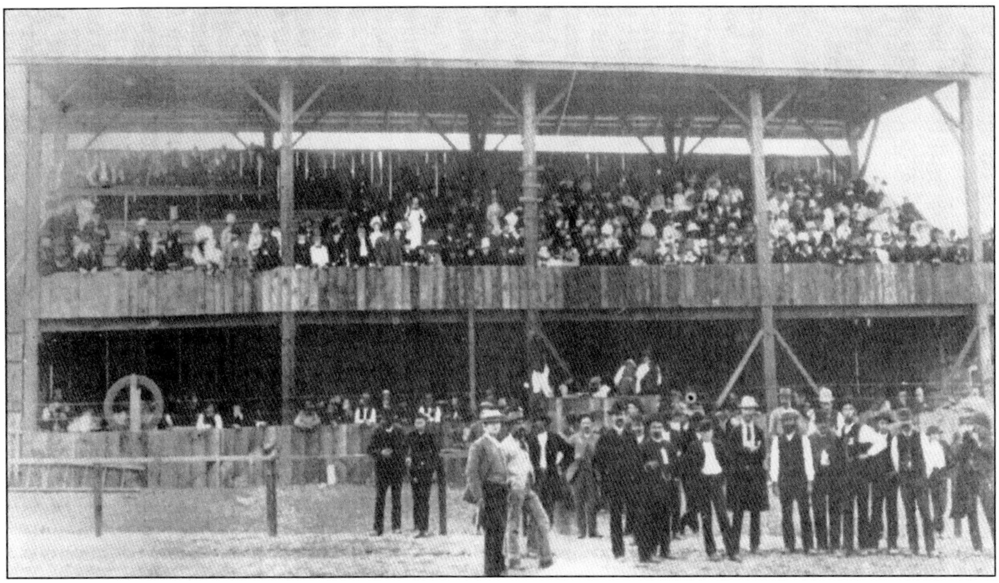

Racehorses have long been a favorite of Ionians. Here a crowd gathers in the grandstand at the old Ione Racetrack, built for the first fair, held in 1877. Horses from around the world, including some from England, ran its course. The grandstand stood where the horse arena is now located at Howard Park. The racetrack also boasted stable room for 100 horses.

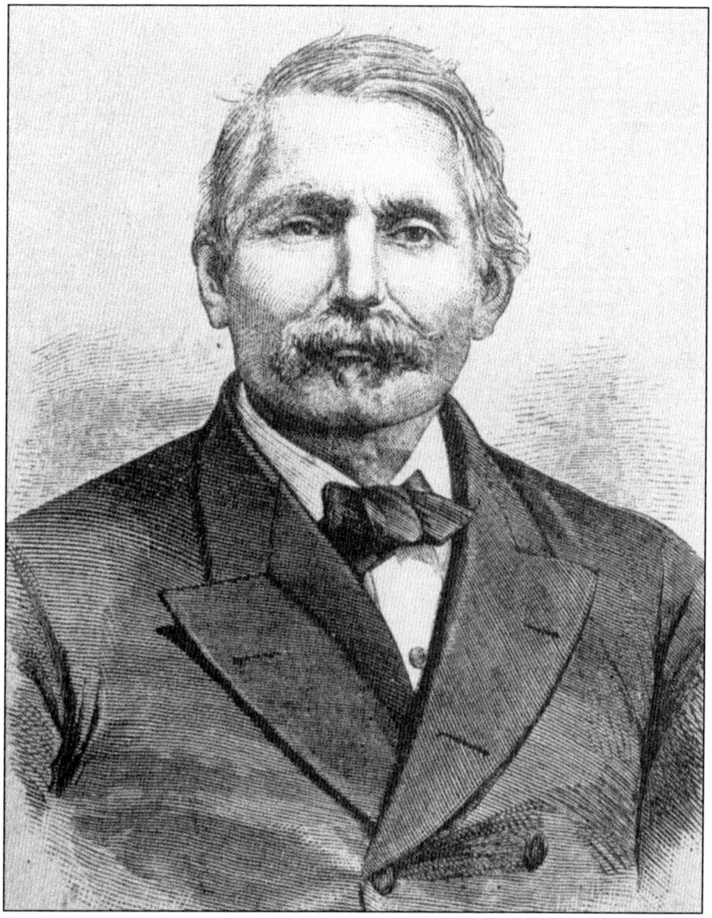

In partnership with J. Mora Moss and others, Brig. Gen. Edward Fitzgerald Beale purchased the Arroyo Seco Grant from Andres Pico. Beale Air Force Base is named for him. (Courtesy U.S. Naval Historical Center.)

These artifacts, which include both domestic and military items, were discovered on the Arroyo Seco Grant property. Could it be that the military items were left behind by soldiers associated with the grant dispute? Further study could reveal the actual site of the soldiers' camp. (Author's collection.)

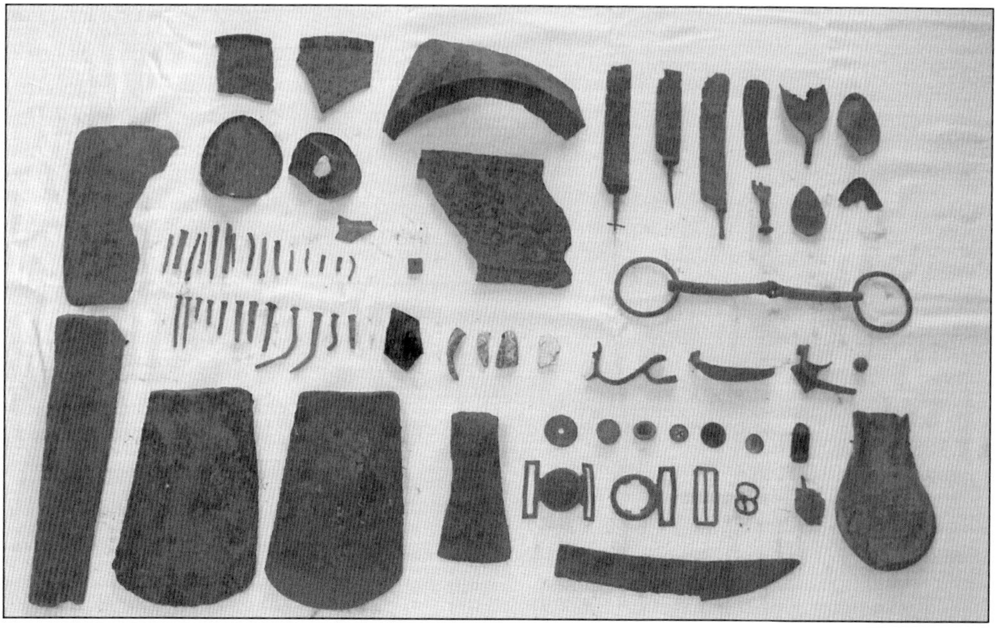

Three

Down to Business in Ione City

In 1849, when California saw a rising tide of immigrants to the goldfields, the land surrounding the Mother Lode was a sparse, uninhabited expanse. With the exception of a few quickly erected trading posts, the availability of goods and services was meager compared to what the Argonauts were accustomed to; however, it was not long before entrepreneurs took advantage of the growing number of both miners and settlers, and discovered that a central district for trading and living was a very profitable enterprise.

Ione City proper, also known in its infancy as "Bedbug" and "Freezeout," had its beginnings in early 1850s, when Thomas Brinley Rickey had the idea of establishing a town. He arrived in the Ione Valley, where he purchased a tract of land that would become Ione City. In 1853, he hired S. H. Marlette to survey the property and lay out town lots, which he soon sold off to settlers and merchants. As discussed in the previous chapter, many of these settlers suffered the distress of being ejected from their property when the land was claimed by Andres Pico. The town also endured several floods and a fire that destroyed a number of buildings on Main Street. Despite these hardships, the settlers persevered and the town continued to thrive. In those early years, a steam flouring mill was built by Rickey; several livery, harness, and saddlers provided services to the agricultural community of Ione Valley; and dry goods merchants, such as Daniel Stewart, provided the necessities of everyday life.

When one enters Ione today, what they see along Main Street, and the avenues and alleys that transect that artery, are vestiges of the evolution of a Gold Rush settlement. All manner and form of architecture and domestic landscaping takes the visitor on a visual journey from the earliest days of the town to the present.

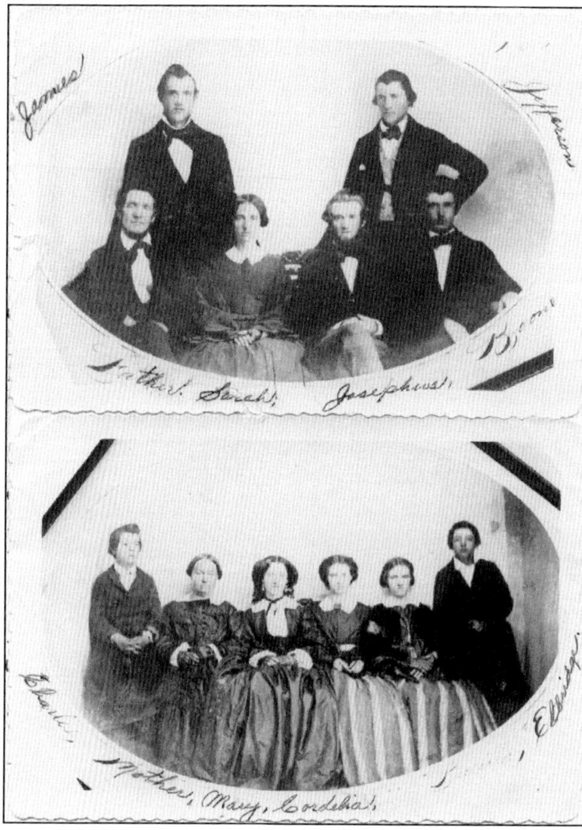

Thomas Brinley Rickey is often called "the Father of Ione." In this interesting compilation of two photographs, Thomas and his wife, Mary Harper Robbins Rickey, pose with their 10 children. Pictured above from left to right are Thomas, James, Sarah, Josephus, Jefferson, and Daniel Rickey. Seated below from left to right are Charles, Mary (the mother), Mary (the daughter), Cordelia, Priscilla, and Eldbridge.

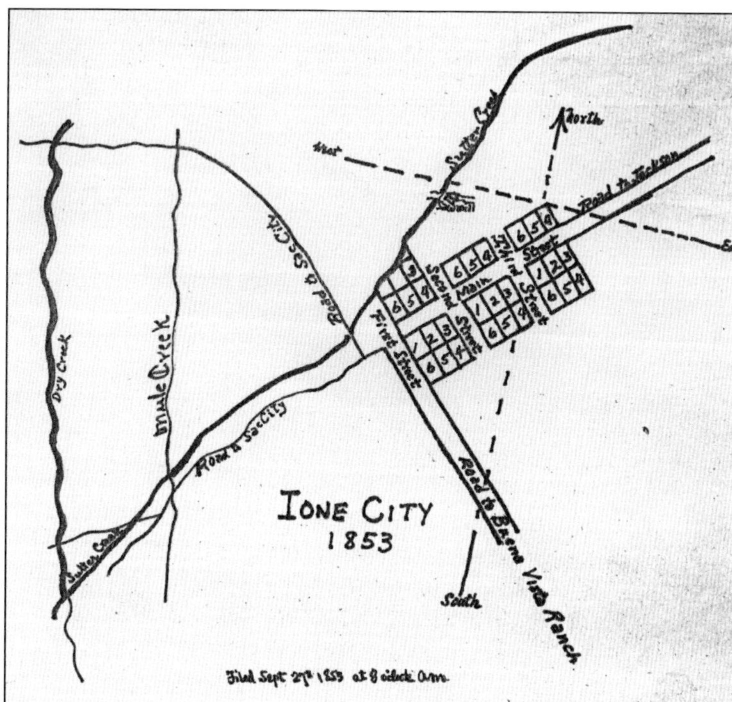

In 1853, Thomas Rickey employed S. H. Marlette to survey his land and lay out town lots for Ione City, as pictured on this map. At that time, Marlette was serving as county surveyor and would go on to become California's surveyor general. Note that the entire settlement at that time was south of Sutter Creek.

Robert Ludgate, a native of Ireland, came to America as a young boy, settling with his parents in New Orleans. In the early 1850s, he arrived in the Ione Valley, where he took up stock raising and farming. He then partnered with J. W. Surface in a livery business in 1863. Ludgate also served in the state assembly from 1877 until his death in February 1878.

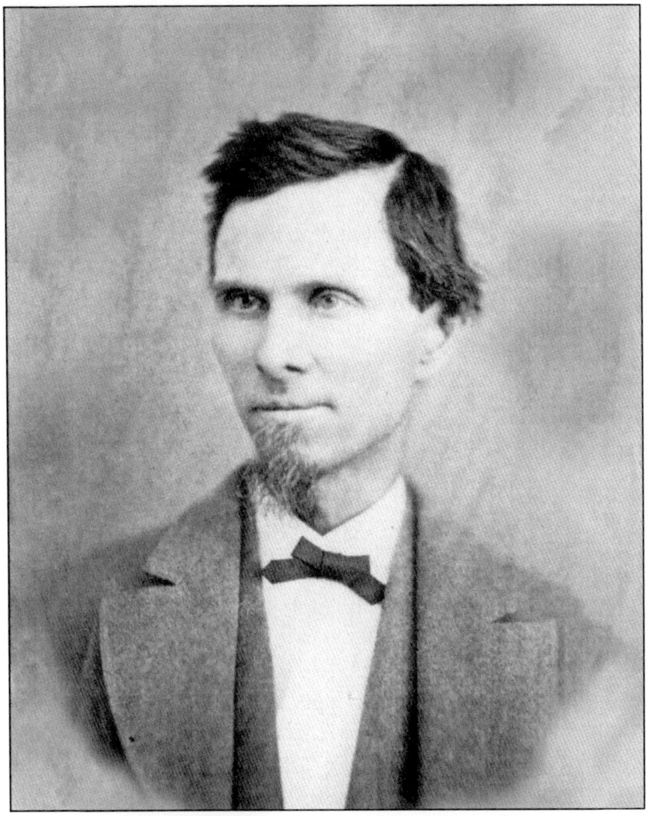

Men take a break from their work to pose in front of the Ludgate and Surface livery stable. The business was established in 1863 in a wood-frame building that stood at this site. That structure burnt in a fire two years later and was replaced by this brick building. When Robert Ludgate died in 1878, J. W. Surface's brother James became his partner.

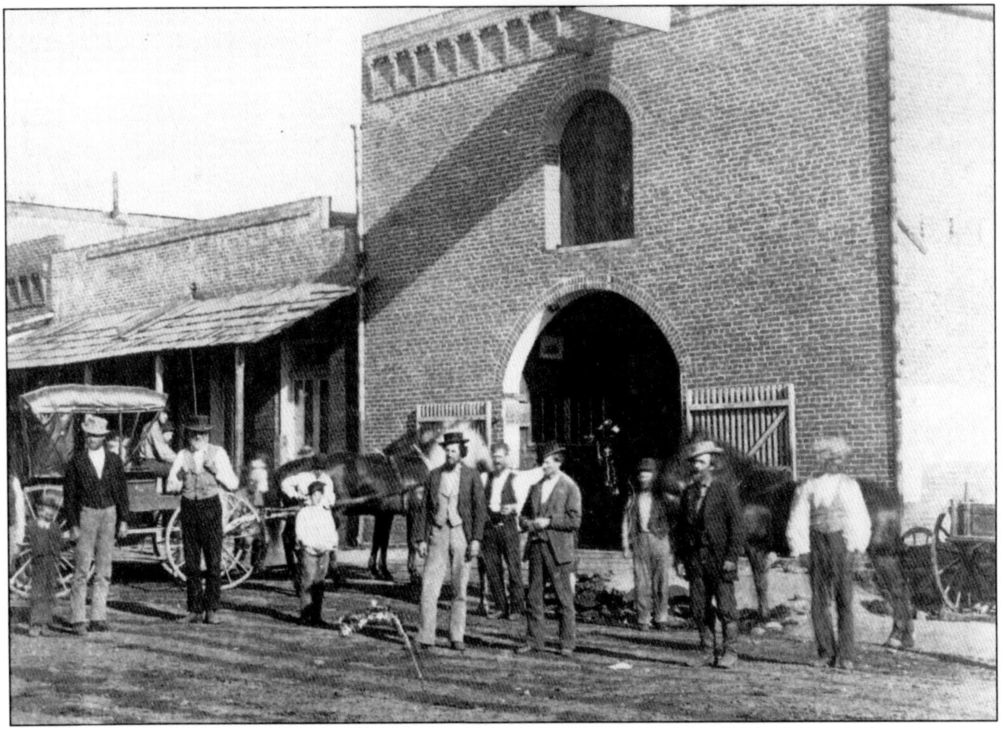

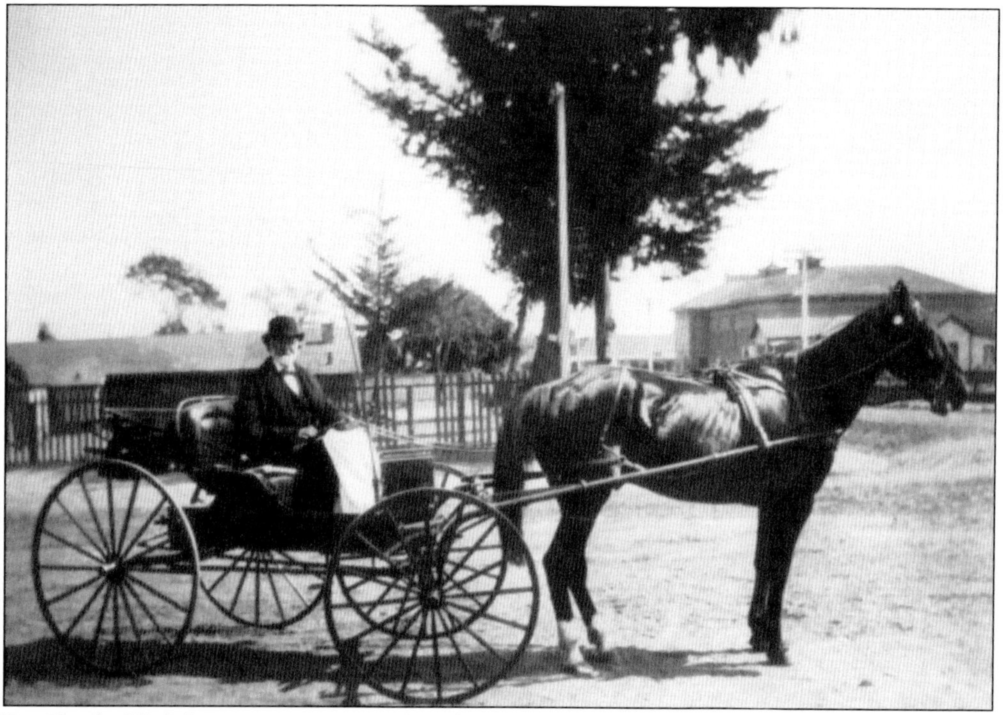

Dr. Charles W. Schoenemann practiced medicine in his native Germany and then France before traveling to California about 1853. He set up practice in Stockton but soon moved to Lancha Plana and then on to Ione. After practicing here for a number of years, he continued to Mokelumne Hill and then on to Tulare, where he died in 1912.

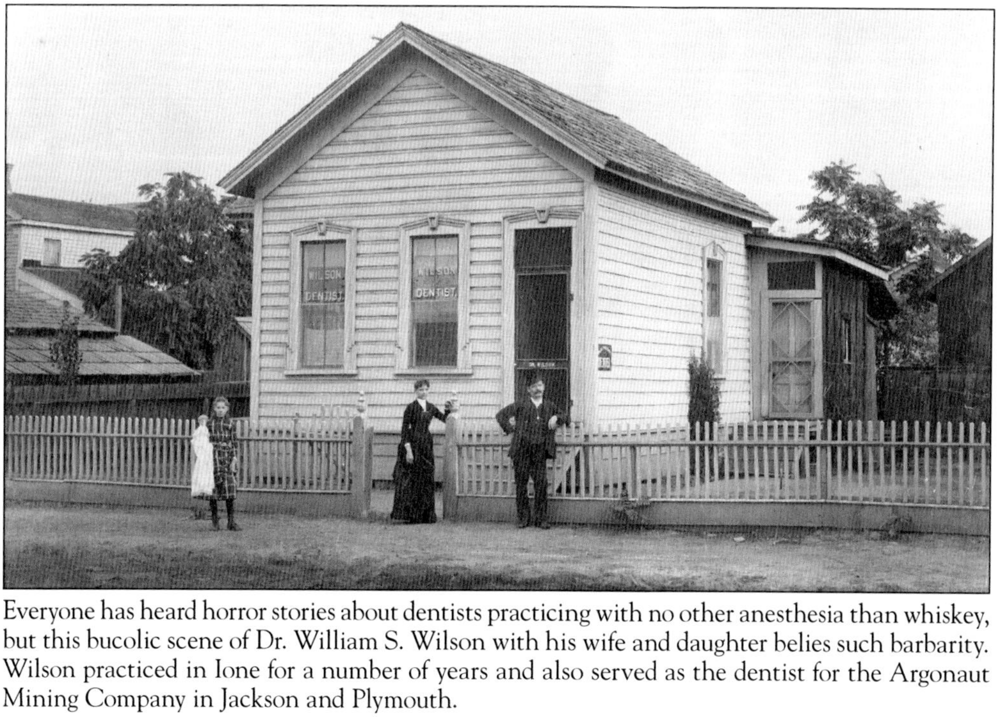

Everyone has heard horror stories about dentists practicing with no other anesthesia than whiskey, but this bucolic scene of Dr. William S. Wilson with his wife and daughter belies such barbarity. Wilson practiced in Ione for a number of years and also served as the dentist for the Argonaut Mining Company in Jackson and Plymouth.

Clarence Warren Swain—carpenter, architect, and contractor—was well known in Ione and as well as in all quarters of Amador County. The bridge that once spanned Sutter Creek in Ione, pictured below, is a display of his handiwork. Swain is also known for designing and building the Pitt Street bridge in Jackson, the two-story brick school that once stood in Jackson, and the county hospital, which was built in 1890. He also tried his hand at mining in the 1860s, when he leased the Oneida mine. History records that he lost as much in one year at the mine as the previous owner had made in profits in 10 years.

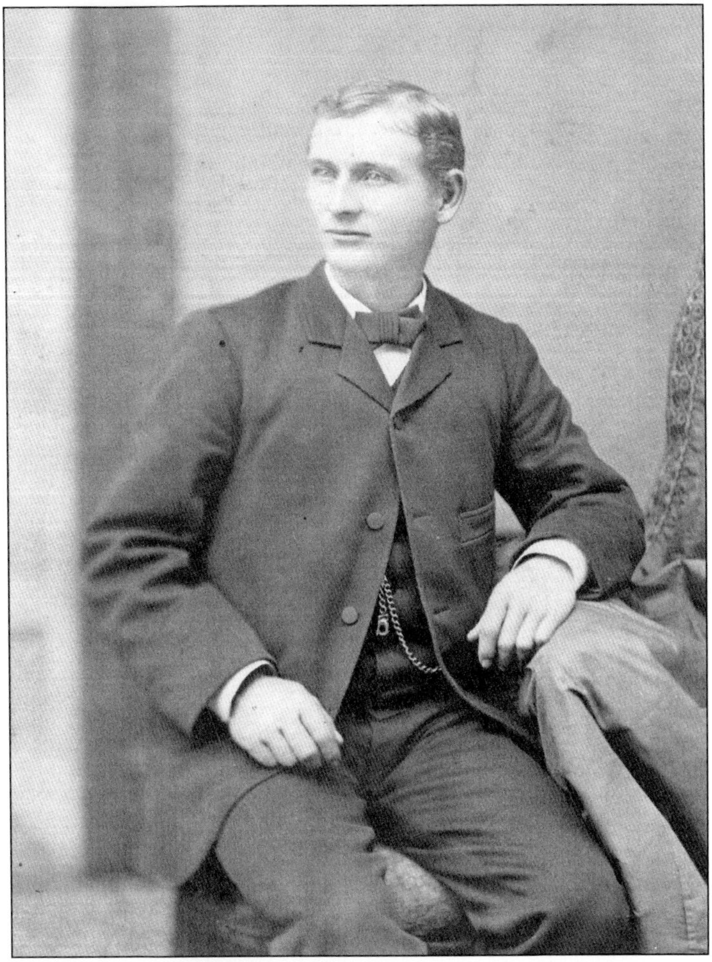

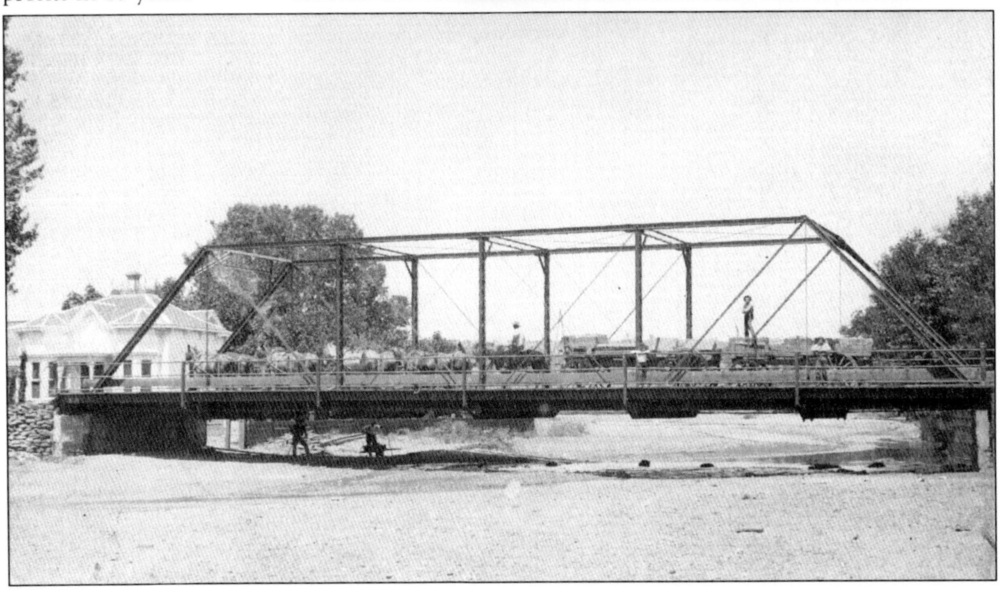

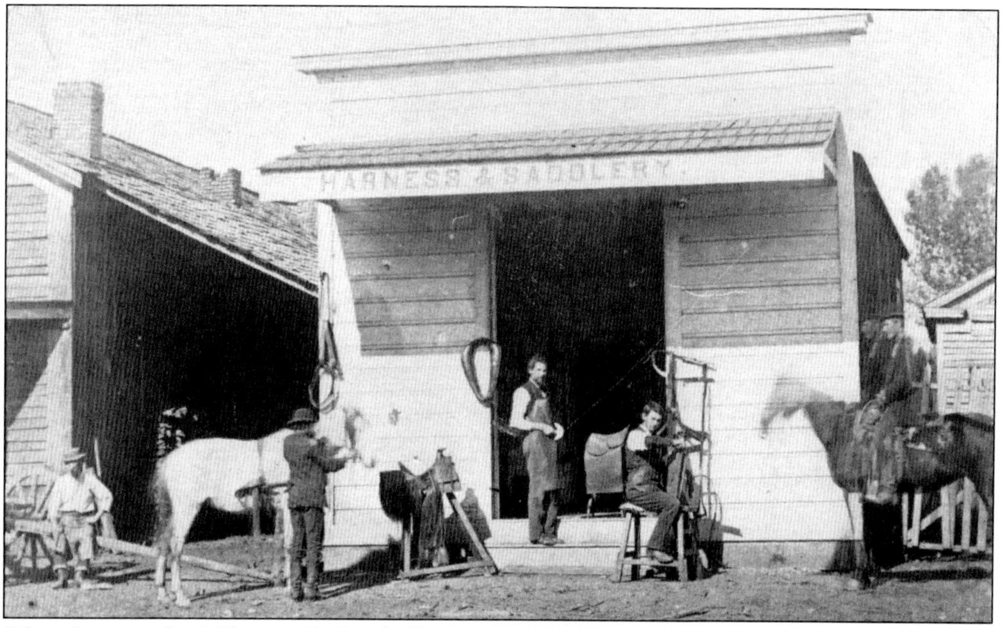

.This photograph of Thomas Richards Harness and Saddlery, taken by Ione photographer Eliza W. Withington, catches everyday life in Ione in the 1870s. In contrast to the livery stable, which served as a blacksmith, boarded horses, and hired out teams and buggies, the saddlery produced and repaired the equipment needed for those horses and teams. When Richards's wife died, he left the wilds of California to return to his native England.

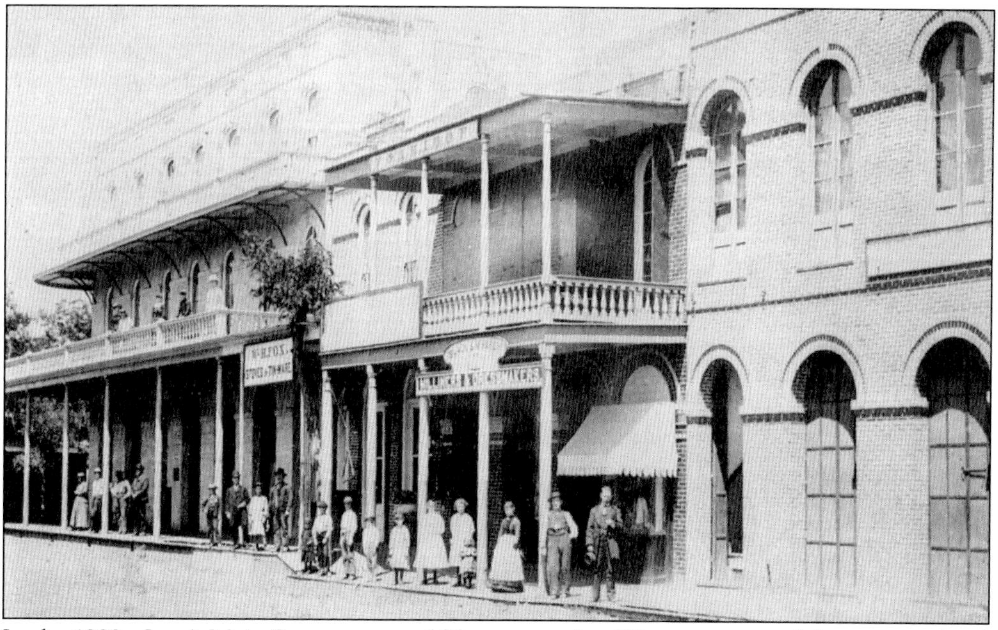

In the 1880s, Ione's Main Street appeared like many other Western towns of the time, with all manner of goods and services available. This photograph provides a view of the buildings along the north side of the street. Among the businesses pictured are, from left to right, the Commercial Hotel, the store of William H. Fox, the local tinsmith, and a millinery and dress shop. Note the fraternal meeting rooms in the top story.

The Commercial Hotel once stood on the corner where the Ione City Hall is now located. Built in 1884 by James McCauley, it stood for over four decades until a major portion was destroyed by fire in 1930. The surviving ground floor was remodeled and then occupied by a bank for a number of years. In the 1960s, it was purchased by the City of Ione to serve as city hall.

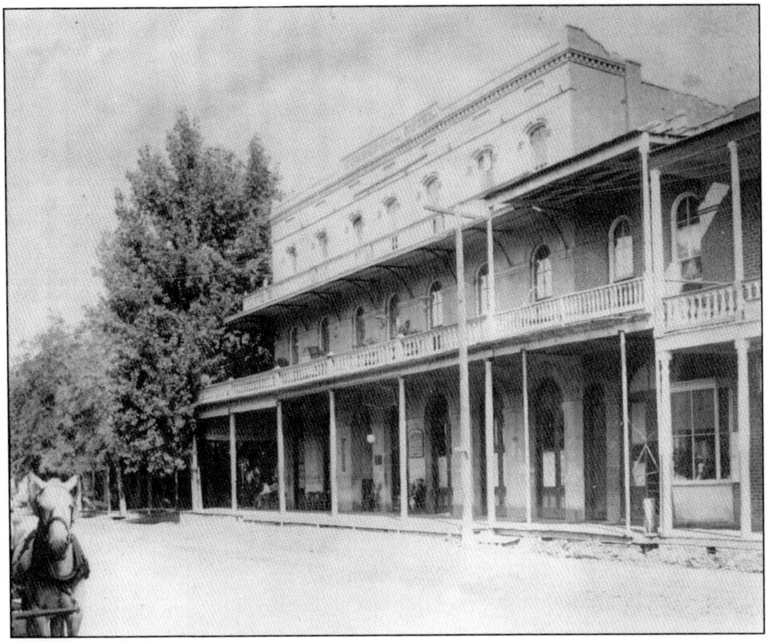

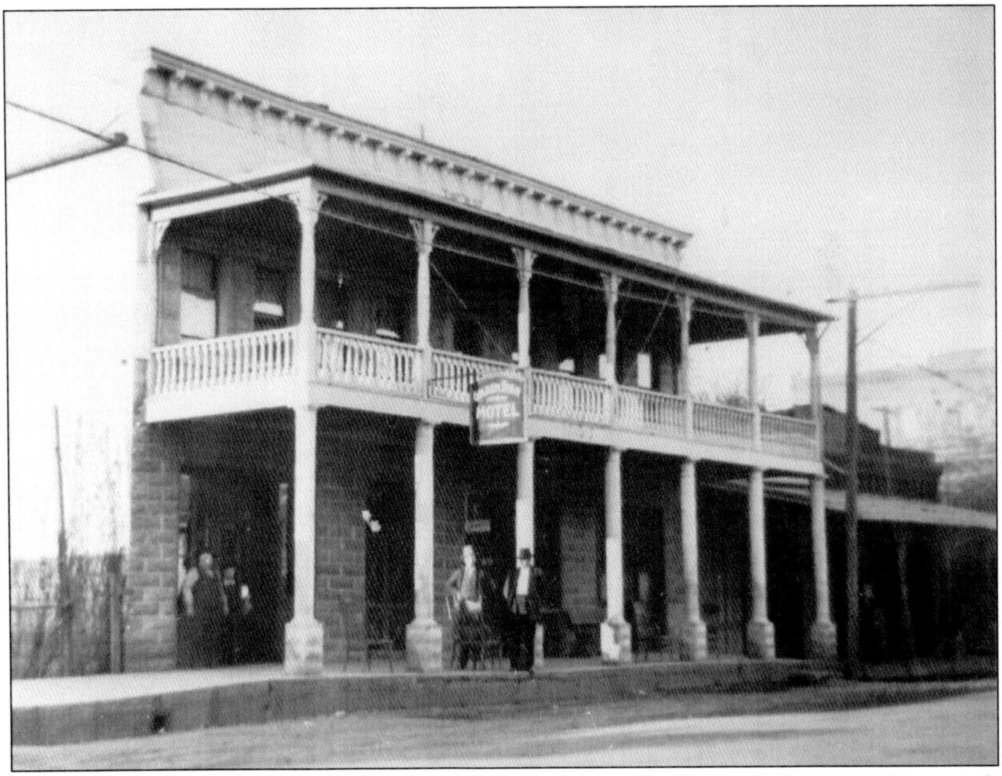

The Golden Star Hotel was constructed by the Tonzis in 1910, after a fire destroyed their wood-frame hotel. The concrete blocks of the building were manufactured at a blacksmith shop standing at the corner of Main Street and Preston Avenue. The Tonzi family sold the hotel in 1971. It has been through several owners and was remodeled after a 1988 fire.

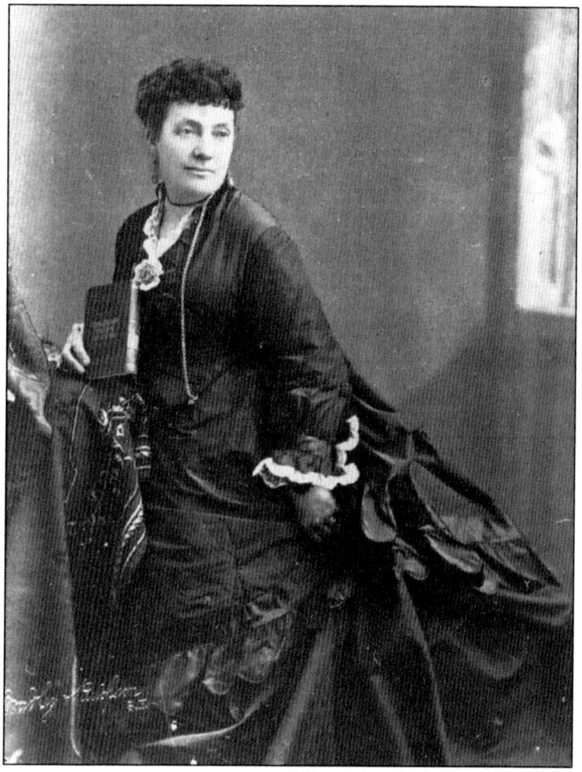

Many women left their mark on the history of Ione, but none more so than photographer Elizabeth Kirby Withington, better known simply as Eliza. She was married in Michigan in 1845 and had three children with her husband, George. In 1849, George came to California, where he was joined by Eliza and the children in 1852. Eliza learned the business of ambrotypes, opening a studio on Main Street. Standard portrait photography was much of her fare; however, she set herself apart from other female photographers when she traveled into the Sierra Nevada to photograph settlements and scenery, as seen in the stereoviews below of the Kirkwood Dairy and a family camp in the mountains. Many other photographs seen throughout this book are her work.

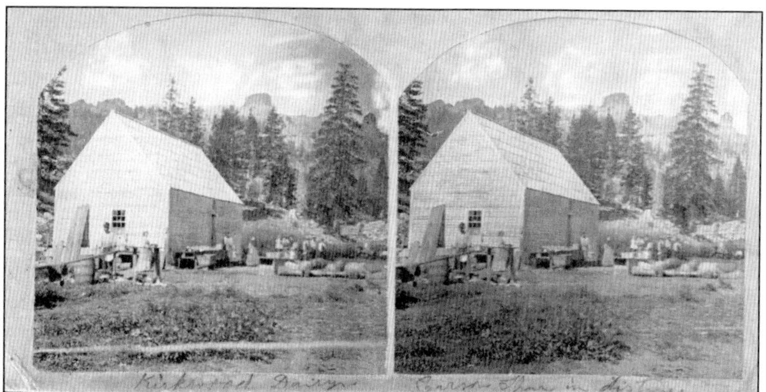

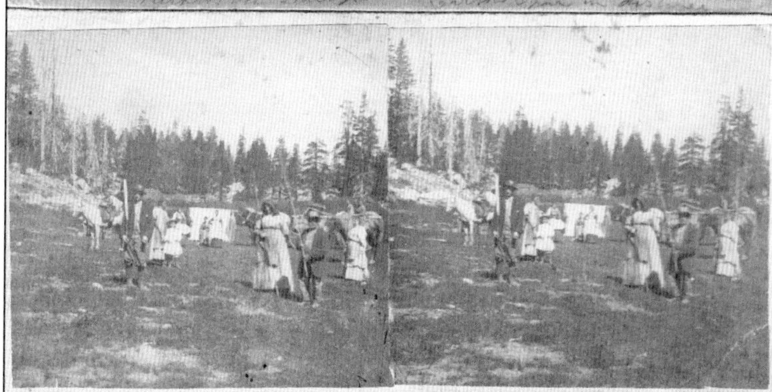

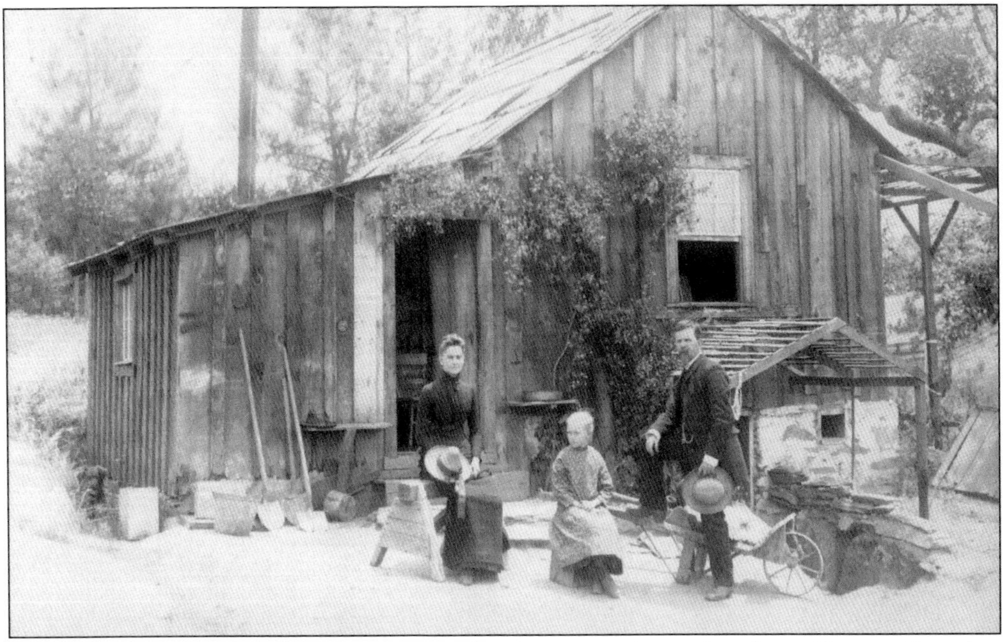

Eliza Withington was not the only photographer practicing the trade in Ione. Clement Sutterley, pictured above at a mountain cabin with his wife and daughter, also set up a studio in town. Unlike Withington, Sutterley was experienced when he arrived in the early 1880s, his trade spanning many years and locations, including one of the largest galleries in Virginia City, Nevada. He was also in business with his brother J. K., traveling throughout a number of Western states. His studio in Ione was spacious, with rooms fitted for reception, dressing, photographic sitting, and developing. The photograph below, depicting Ione's Main Street, was taken around 1890 by Sutterley, as were many other scenes and portraits herein.

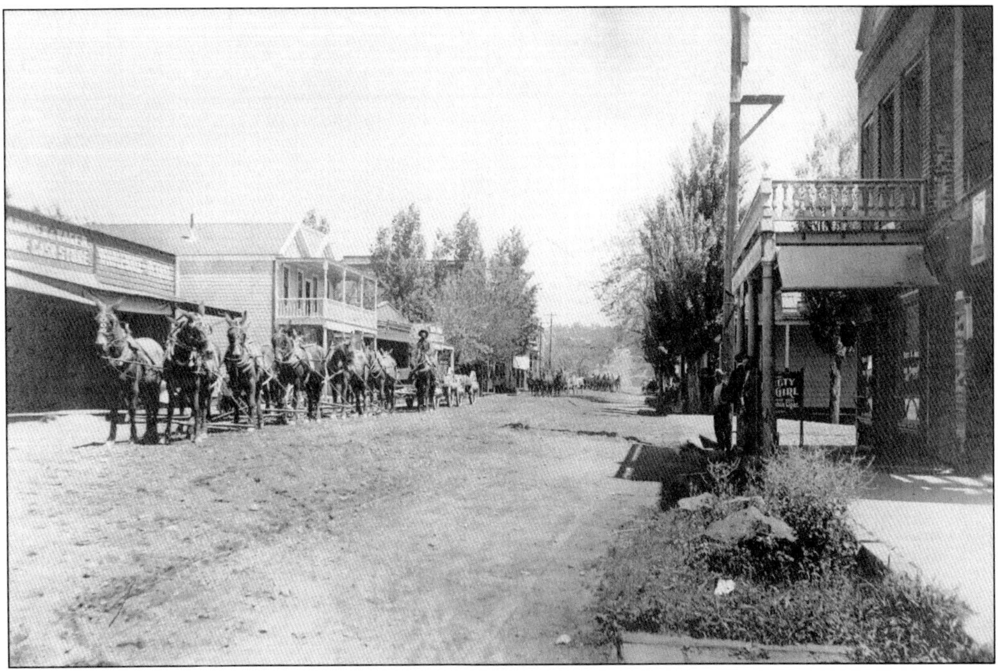

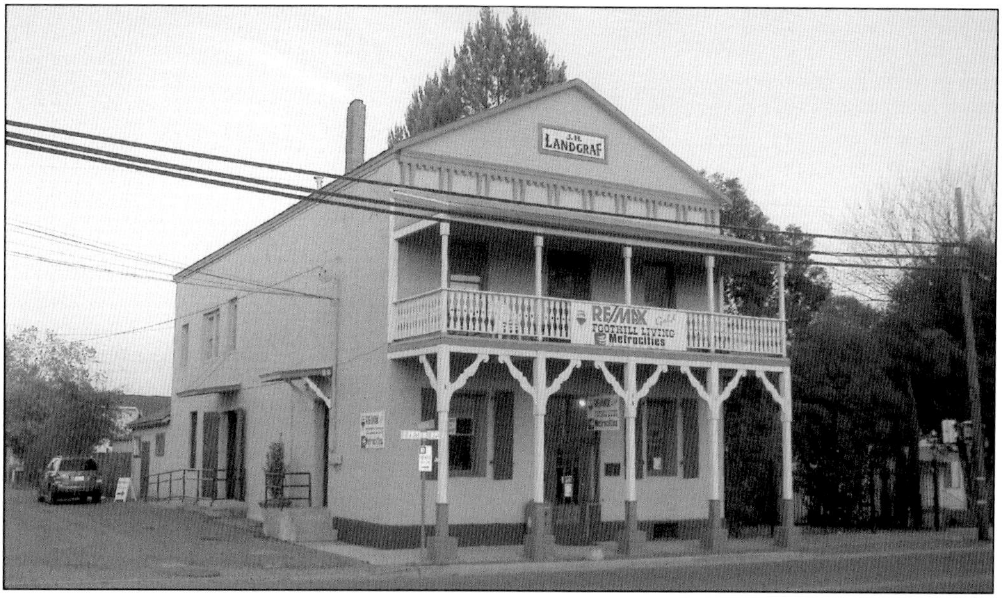

The Ione Brewery, also known as the Ice House Brewery, was built on this site in 1860. Many gallons of beer, brewed from barley and hops grown in the Ione Valley, were produced in this building. In 1891, a creamery operation began on the site because state law prohibited the brewery following construction of the nearby Preston School of Industry, a state prison. Eventually, an ice works was added to the creamery. (Author's collection.)

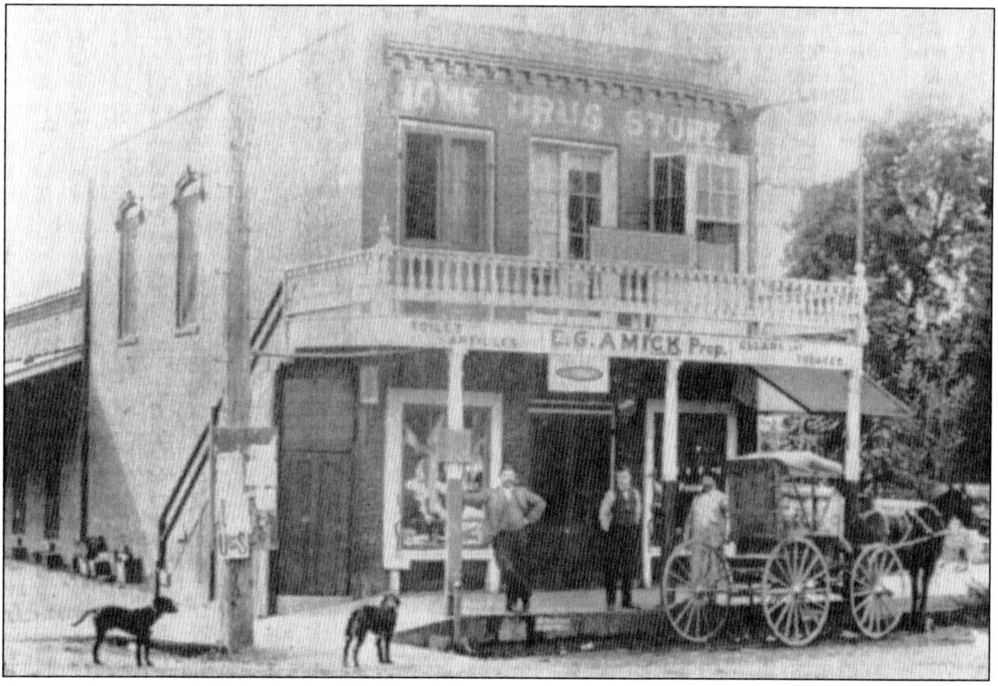

Pictured here are the Ione Drug Store and the Arcade Hotel. The hotel was built around Ione's first log house. In December 1889, the building caught fire, and several businesses were lost in addition to the drugstore and hotel. Mack Amick (left), J. P. Horton (center), and A. L. Adams pose in front of the building, along with Barney the horse.

A well-known name around Ione from the early days was Alfred J. Amick. Along with his wife, Nancy Phillips Amick, he came to California from Missouri in the early 1850s. The couple's son Wesley, pictured here, grew to become a prominent businessman in the town, operating a livery stable on Main Street and serving as county supervisor from Ione in 1900–1907 and 1912–1920.

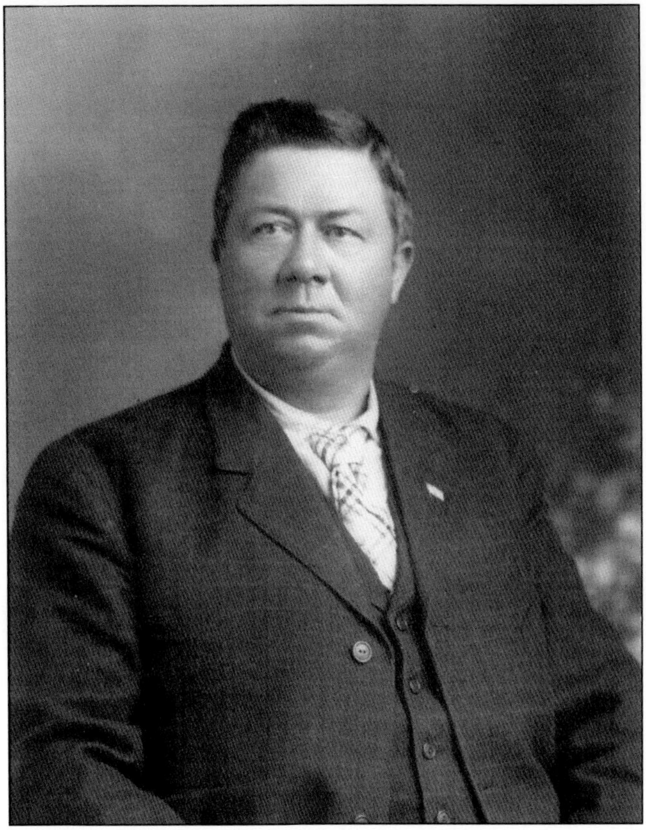

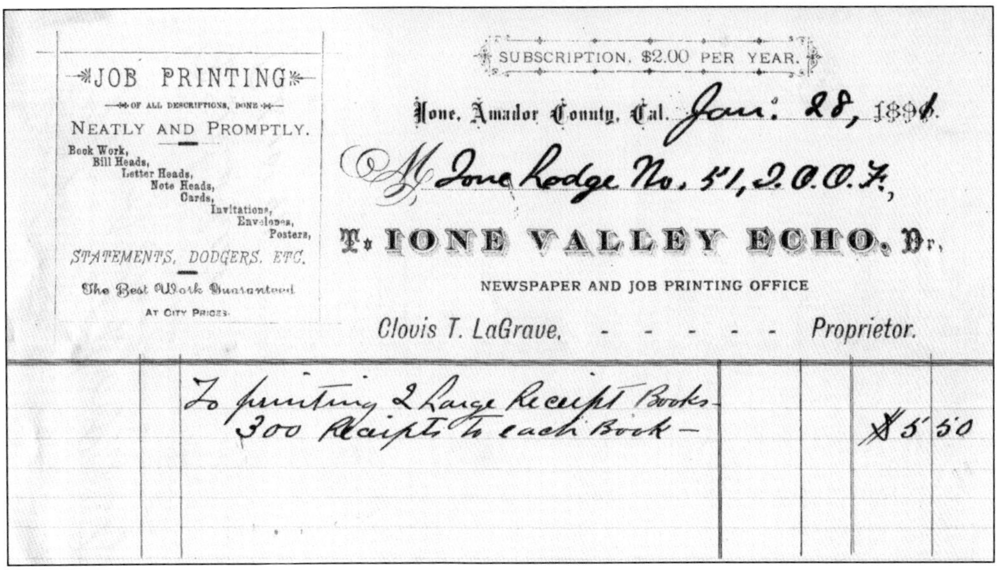

JOB PRINTING
OF ALL DESCRIPTIONS, DONE
NEATLY AND PROMPTLY.
Book Work,
Bill Heads,
Letter Heads,
Note Heads,
Cards,
Invitations,
Envelopes,
Posters,
STATEMENTS, DODGERS, ETC.
The Best Work Guaranteed
AT CITY PRICES.

SUBSCRIPTION, $2.00 PER YEAR.

Ione, Amador County, Cal. Jan: 28, 1896.

M Ione Lodge No. 51, I.O.O.F.,

To IONE VALLEY ECHO, Dr.,

NEWSPAPER AND JOB PRINTING OFFICE

Clovis T. LaGrave, - - - - - - Proprietor.

To printing 2 Large Receipt Books — 300 Receipts to each Book — $5.50

Ione has been the home of several newspapers. In 1861, a weekly paper was established by Folger and Company; it only lasted a few months and then moved to Alpine County. Another, started in 1877 by Haley and Company, had a longer life of about three years. By far the longest-running newspaper for the town was the *Ione Valley Echo*, which operated under various owners from the late 19th century until 1943.

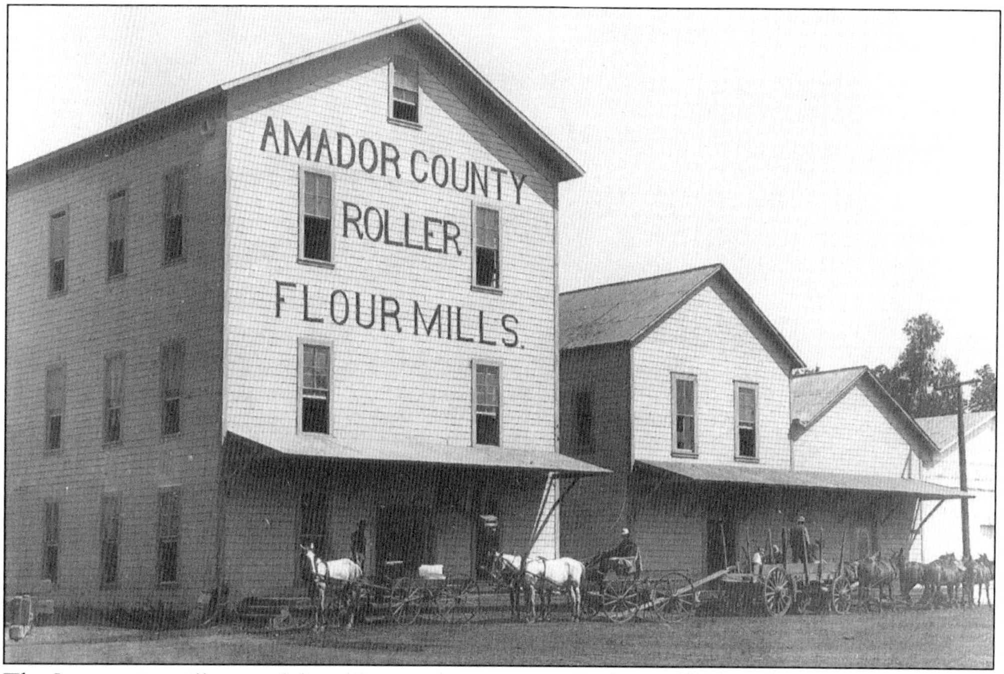

The Ione grain mill, one of the oldest in the state, was built in 1856 by Thomas Rickey. Rickey sold the mill to H. T. Hall and M. Helfron, who improved the property. By 1876, it was grinding a yearly average of over 3,500 tons of grain, making flour and livestock feed. By 1934, the mill had closed down and the Ione Lumber Yard acquired the property.

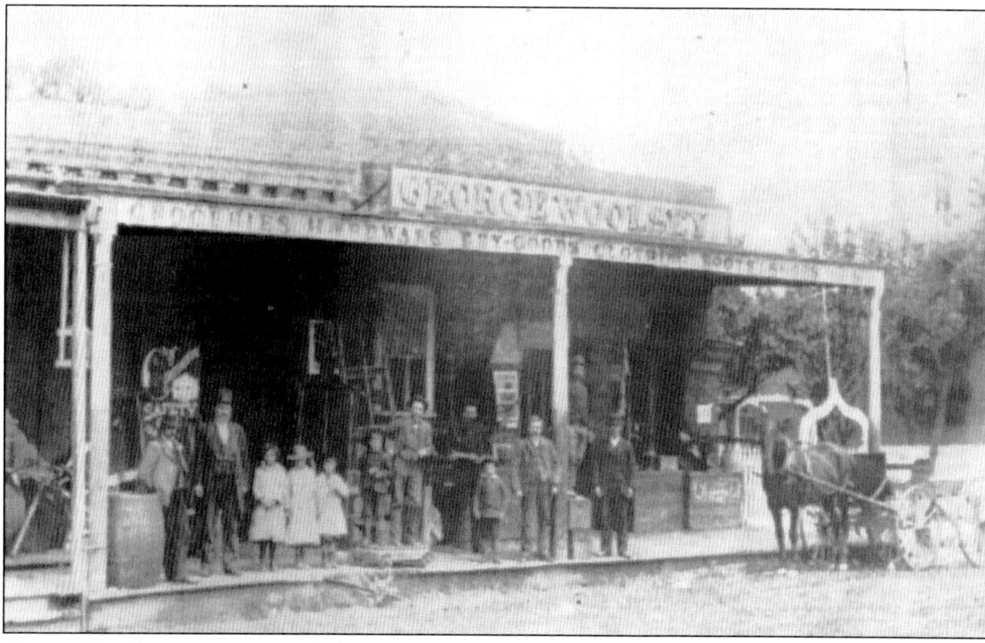

George Woolsey's store provided goods to the citizens of Ione for a number of years. Woolsey arrived in California in 1856 and set up his first store in partnership with J. P. Palmer at Lancha Plana. Also the owner of the Q Ranch in the Ione Valley, he was known for the wonderful fruit and vegetable crops he raised.

John Dabney Perkins, known to his friends as J. D., came to California in 1850 with his uncle on a wagon train that brought 1,500 pounds of tobacco to the goldfields. Upon his arrival, he tried his luck at mining at Murphys, Chili Gulch, and Michigan Bar and then ran a teaming operation. In 1876, Perkins settled in the Ione Valley and entered the business of brick making. He was then appointed postmaster of Ione and, within four years, purchased the drugstore on Main Street. (Courtesy Rick Smith, great-grandson of J. D. Perkins.)

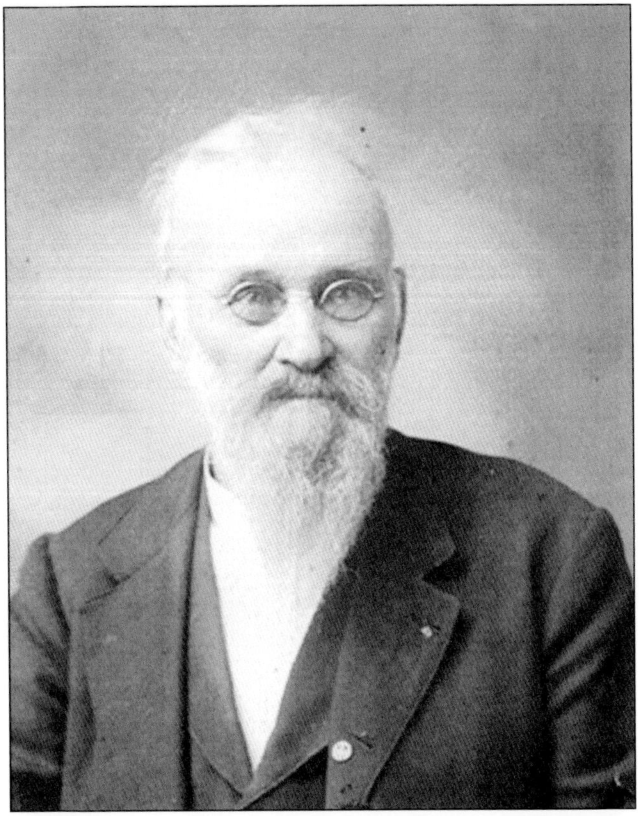

Just as in most small rural California towns, sweets were a welcome delight during a visit to Ione. Pictured here is the interior of the Ione Ice Cream Parlor and Candy Store, which once operated on Main Street.

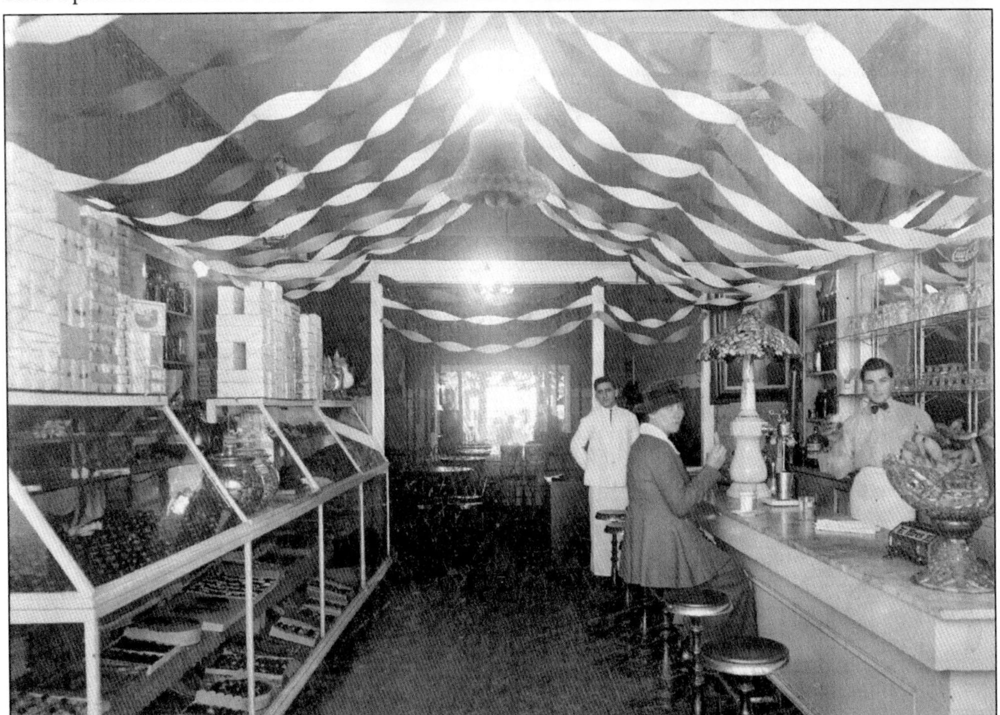

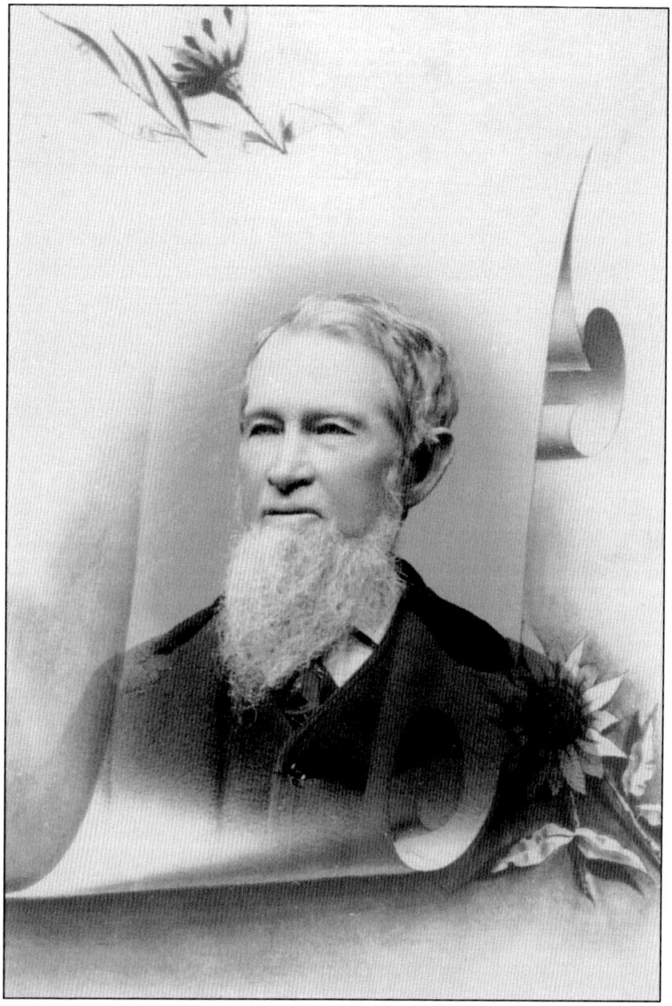

Another patriarch of the Ione business community was Daniel Stewart, who first came to California in 1850 and settled at Ione in 1852. Along with his brother Thomas, he built the first brick store in Ione in 1856. It was constructed from bricks whose clay was mined and baked at nearby Muletown. Stewart's first wife, who arrived in California in 1852, died in 1866. Two years later, he married Tabitha Forker of Mercer, Pennsylvania; altogether, five sons and two daughters were born to Stewart and his two wives. Stewart was a prominent member of the Odd Fellows and a trustee of the Ione Public School. The Stewart Store served the citizens of Ione for more than 50 years. During the early years of operation, it was known as the Daniel Stewart Store; in 1899, it was reorganized as the D. Stewart Company. The store building is now California State Historic Landmark No. 788.

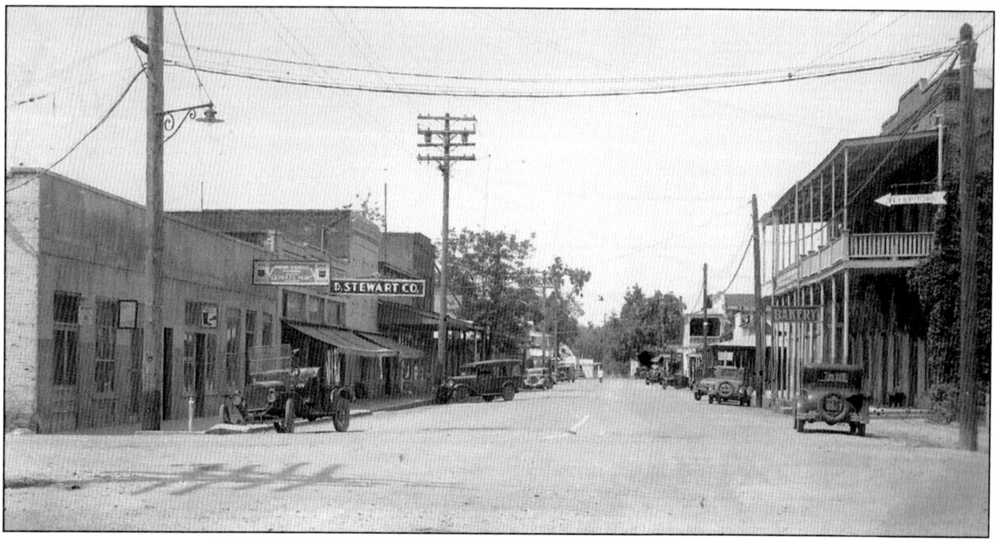

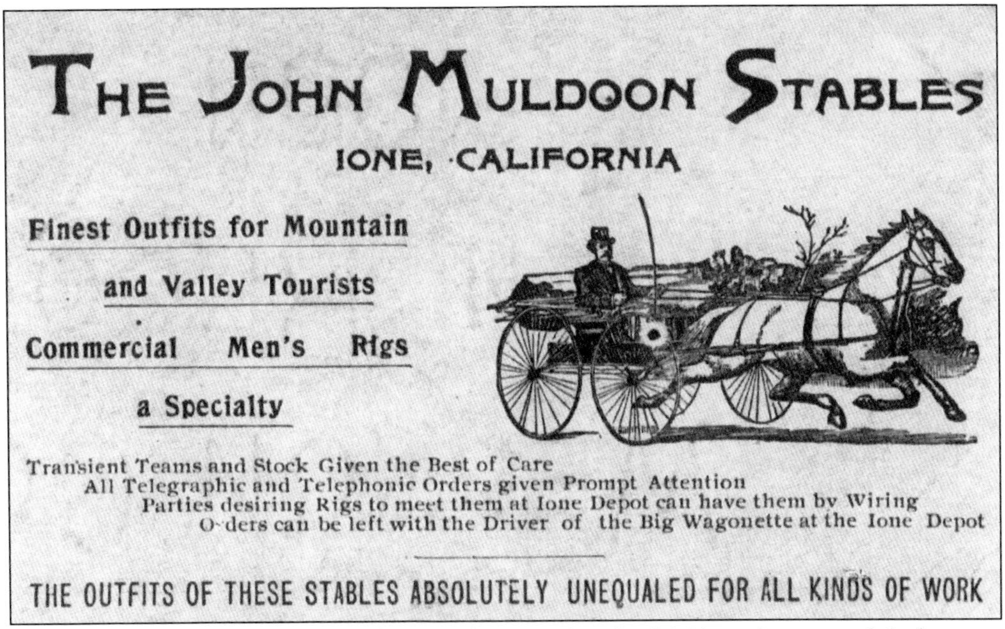

The John Muldoon Stables operated in Ione for many decades. Muldoon first opened the business under the name of the Veranda Livery in partnership with a man named Peak. When Peak left, Muldoon continued until the early 1900s, when he moved to Berkeley and worked in real estate until his death in 1933.

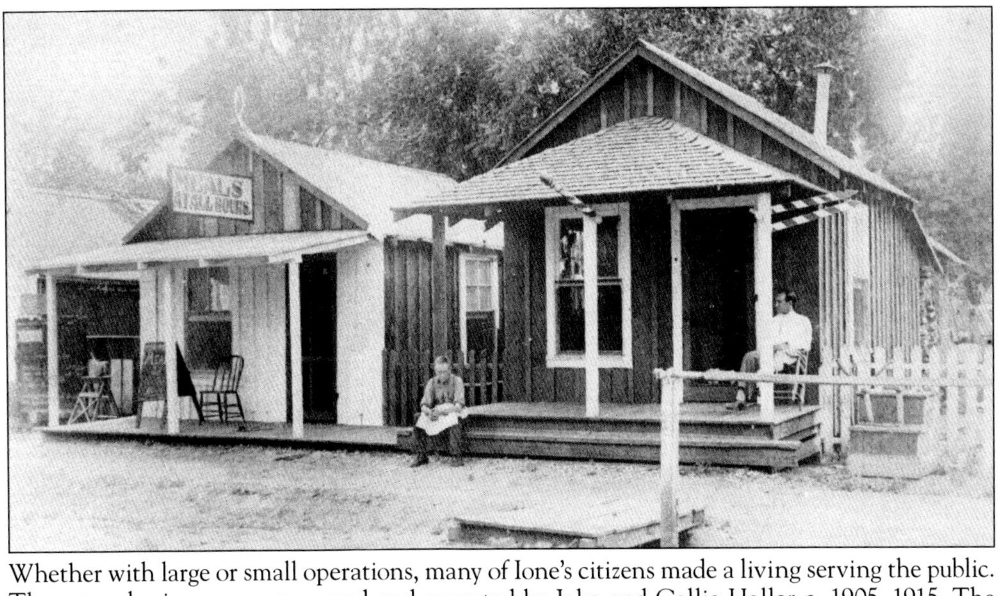

Whether with large or small operations, many of Ione's citizens made a living serving the public. These two businesses were owned and operated by Jake and Callie Haller c. 1905–1915. The husband and wife team cooked and served meals out of the building on the left. Jake also had a dray wagon he used to haul freight from the railroad depot to stores in Ione. On the right is the barbershop of Jim Haller, Jake's brother.

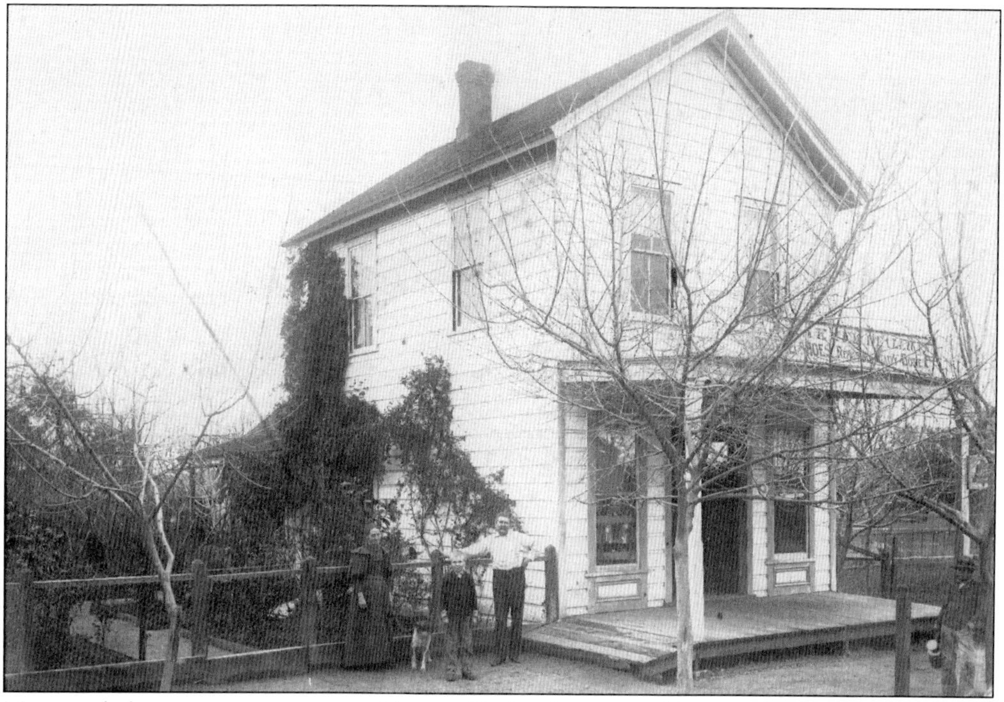

Many early business proprietors could not afford to keep a building separate from their home but often used a portion of their living space to accommodate their establishment. This large, commodious home served as both residence and shop for Ione's cobbler. The people posing in front of the home are unidentified.

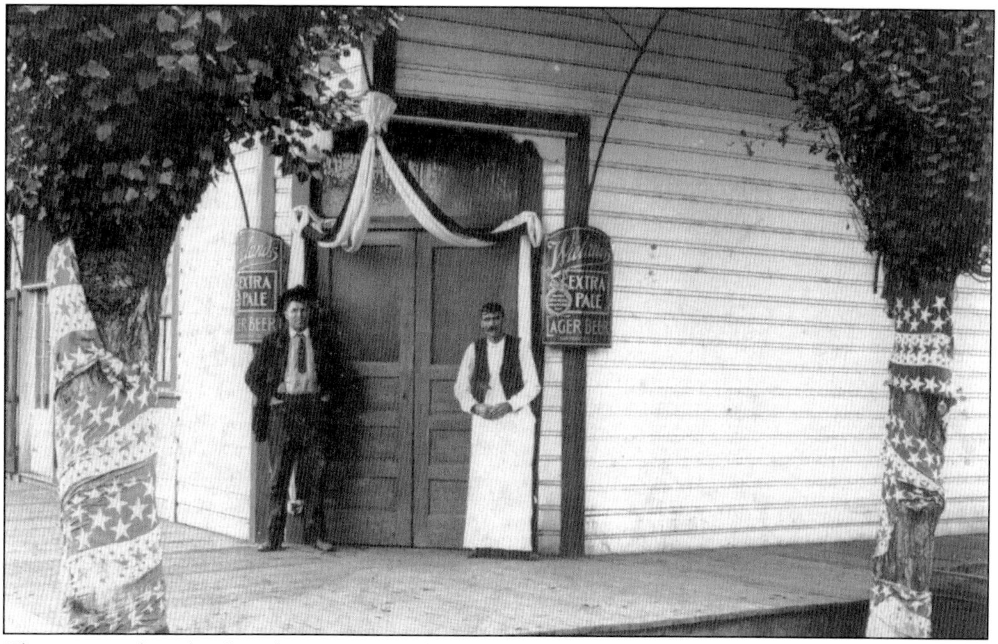

The corner saloon has long been a retreat for relaxation since the early days of the Gold Rush, when many were hastily erected pole-and-canvas tents. In this photograph, two men stand in front of Neil Hamm's establishment. The building has been remodeled and serves as retail space today.

Four

A Place to Call Home

The glory of riches lured the Argonauts to California—not only gold, but the promise of owning a piece of land or having one's own business to escape whatever bounds existed from whence they came. To the 49ers, making it to California meant "seeing the elephant," and success meant finding gold, but for many others simply finding a new place to call home was all they sought. All across the golden state, from the central valleys to the coastal tidewaters and the foothills to the high Sierra, pioneers trickled in until the influx of newcomers suddenly turned into a flood. As the settlers poured into California, young towns sprung up everywhere. Many newcomers settled in for the long haul, while others moved on. Those who stayed built the institutions, established education, formed churches and aid societies, and made this state their own.

Ione City was somewhat settled by the mid-1850s and continued to flourish into the later part of the 19th century. Several religious denominations built churches. Although citizens throughout Amador County had provided for numerous grammar schools to educate their young, Ione was the first to have a high school.

Many of the settlers that came to the Ione area will never be known, having left no lasting mark. They departed when their luck ran dry, moving on to find greener pastures. The stories told in this chapter are of those who persisted against a wild frontier and occasional disaster to make Ione what it is today. They are the pioneers of this story, their homes the footprint of the town, and their cultural institutions the framework of the community. Among them are several famous personages associated with the town. If only there was enough space in this volume, then the author could tell the story of all the pioneers who gave us the "home sweet home" town of Ione.

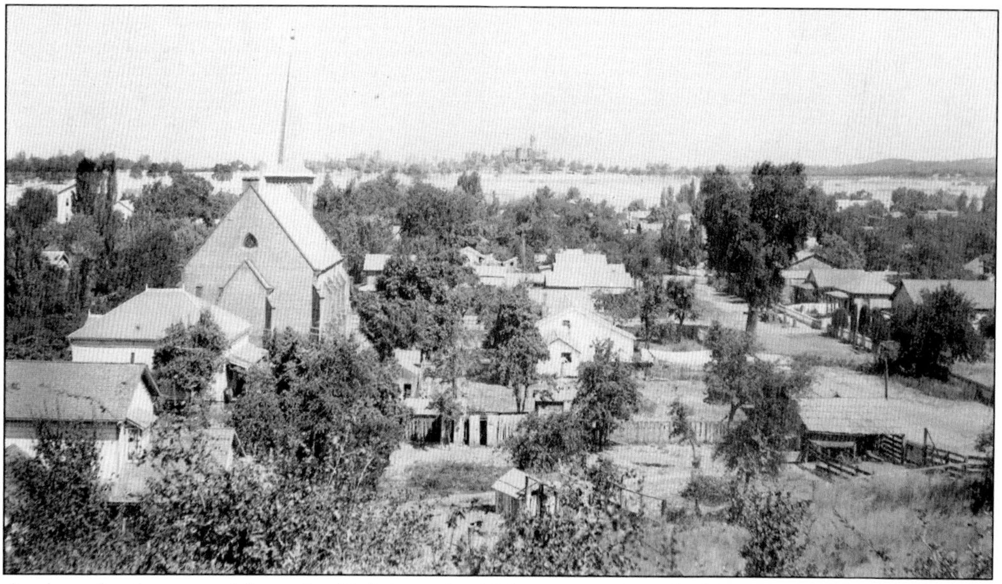

As the calendar turned from the 19th into the 20th century, Ione had become a prosperous town. This photograph, taken around 1895, provides a bird's-eye view of the berg with the towering citadel of the Preston School of Industry in the distance. The expanse of open land situated between the tree line and Preston is now occupied by homes.

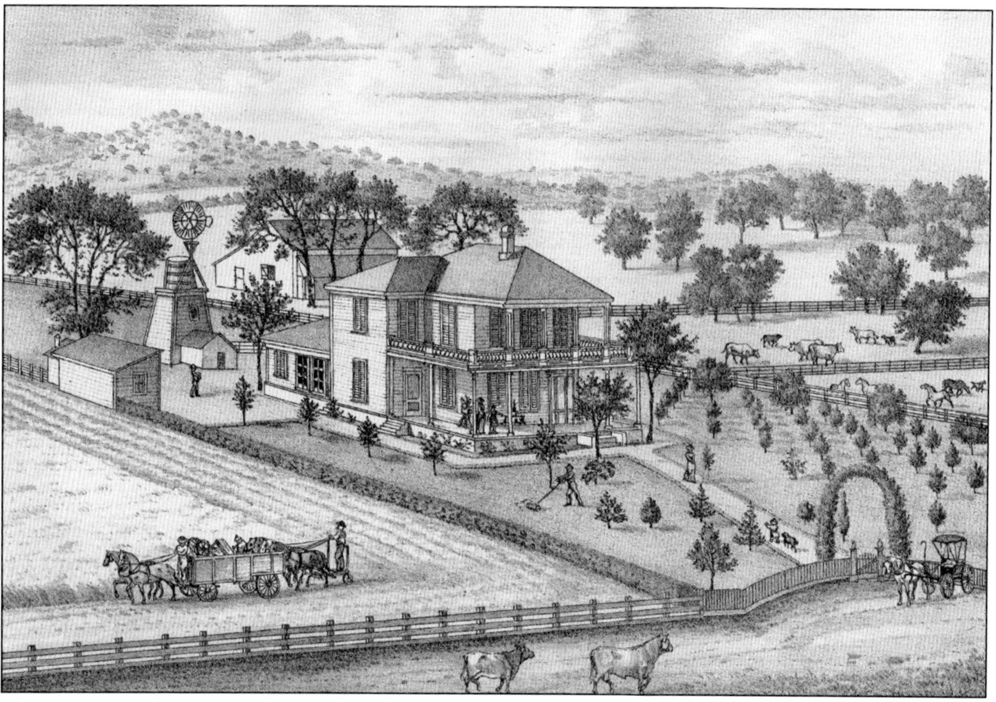

Shown here is the home of one of Ione's better-known sons, Alexander Sheakley. After his arrival in 1853, he worked as a blacksmith for a decade and then became the proprietor of the Arcade Hotel on Main Street. When it was built, this home was considered out of town and stood amid 180 acres farmed by Sheakley. In 1864, Sheakley married the widow A. E. Montandon. (Author's collection.)

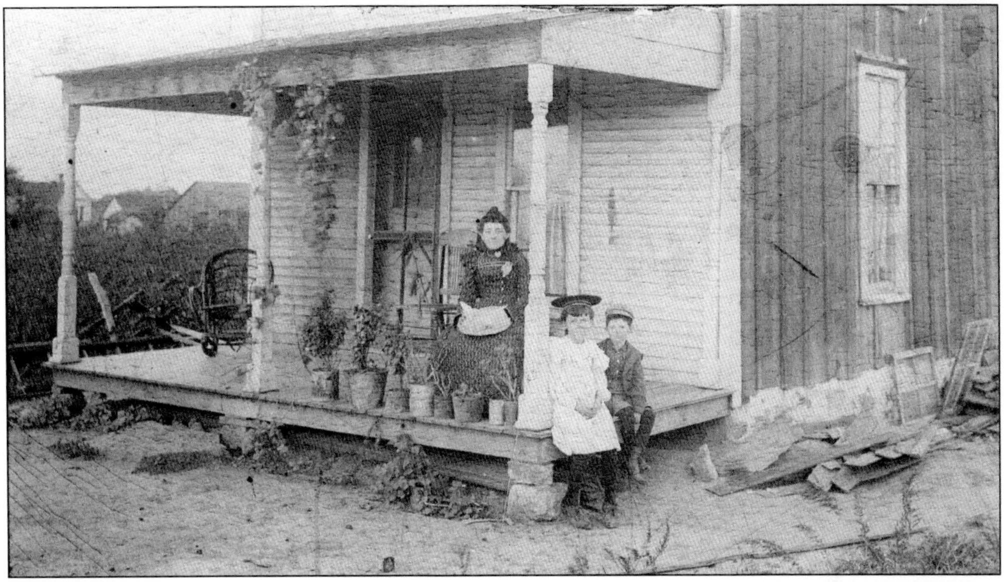

Settlers of modest means lived in small frame dwellings and often improved upon them as finances allowed. An Ione mother and children pose on their somewhat picturesque porch, displaying turned decorative posts and potted flowers attached to a simple structure on a stone foundation. Note the construction materials and old windows lying next to the building.

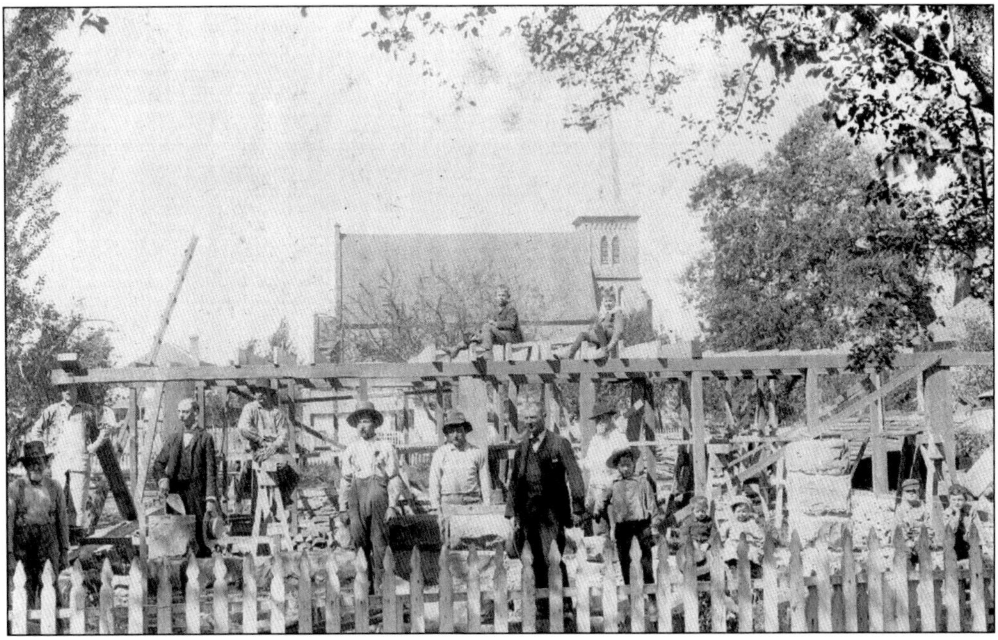

As the population of the town grew, so did the need for housing. Here a construction crew, most likely a group of neighborhood men, builds a home on Church Street. Today one can still see the picket fence, as well as the spire of the Methodist church over the roof of this extant home. The man in the suit at the center is Ione builder C. W. Swain.

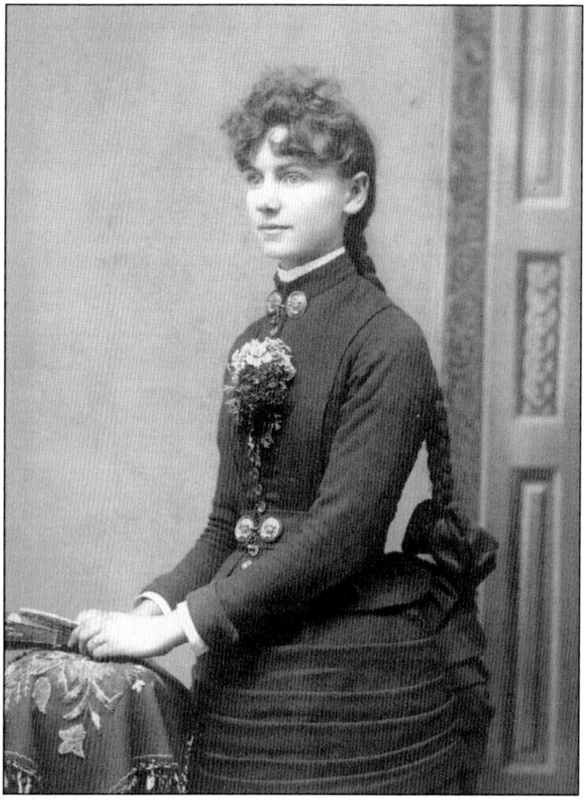

Early on, the refined civility of the fairer sex permeated the society of Ione. In 1857, a local newspaper reporter known as "the Traveler" was visiting Ione and commented on the women of the town, noting that the "order-loving citizens are surely worthy of commendation, to say nothing of its accomplished ladies—Where all are so charming." Charm and refinement can be seen in this portrait of Jane Mullen, taken about 1880.

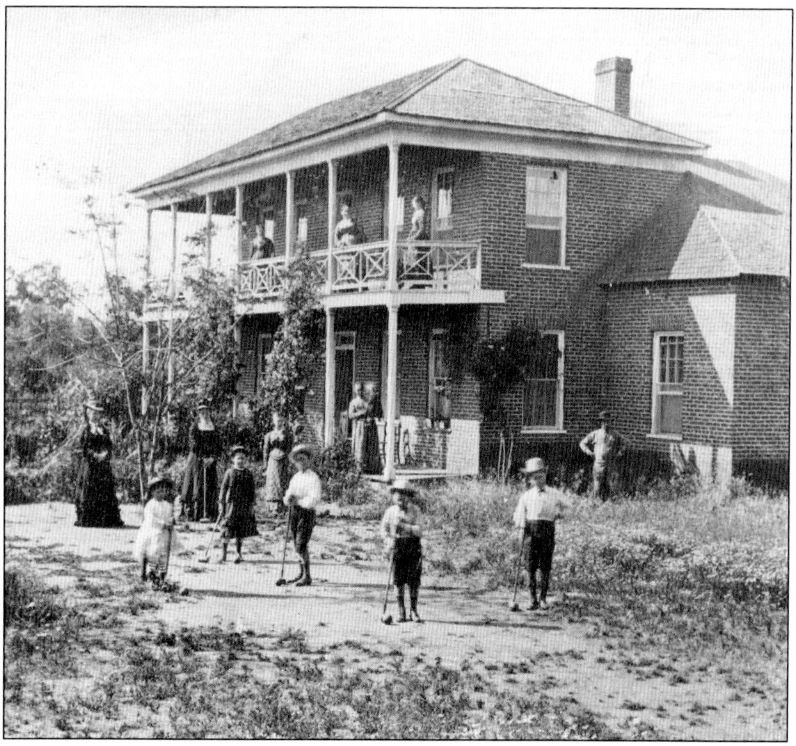

Children engage in a game of croquet in front of the home known as the Grant House, which has stood for over 150 years and has been occupied by various managers of the Arroyo Seco Rancho. This photograph was taken by Eliza Withington around 1875, when she and her husband, George, lived in the home.

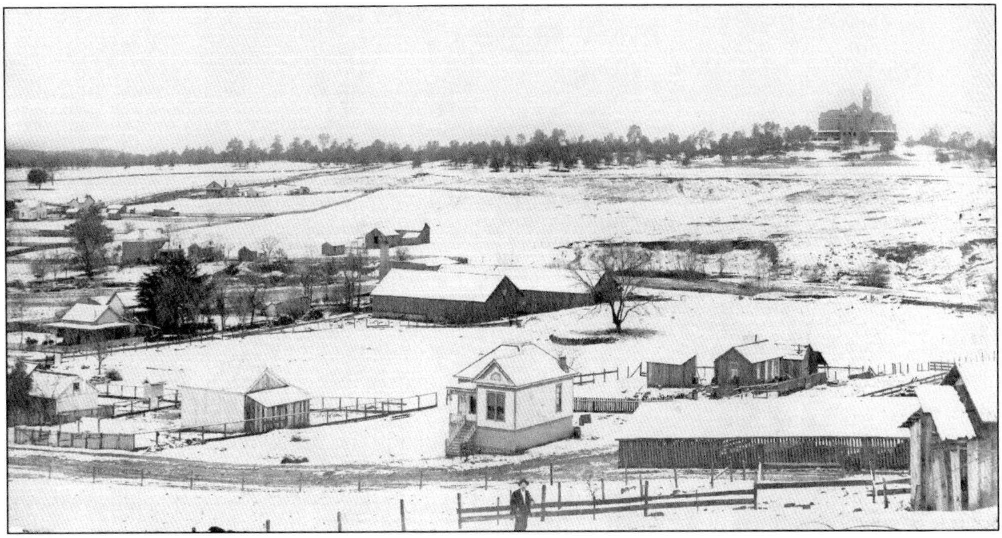

The residents of Ione have suffered several disasters, such as floods and fires and occasional weather extremes, but have persevered. Here a rare snowfall blankets the town at the start of the 20th century. Preston School can be seen in the background.

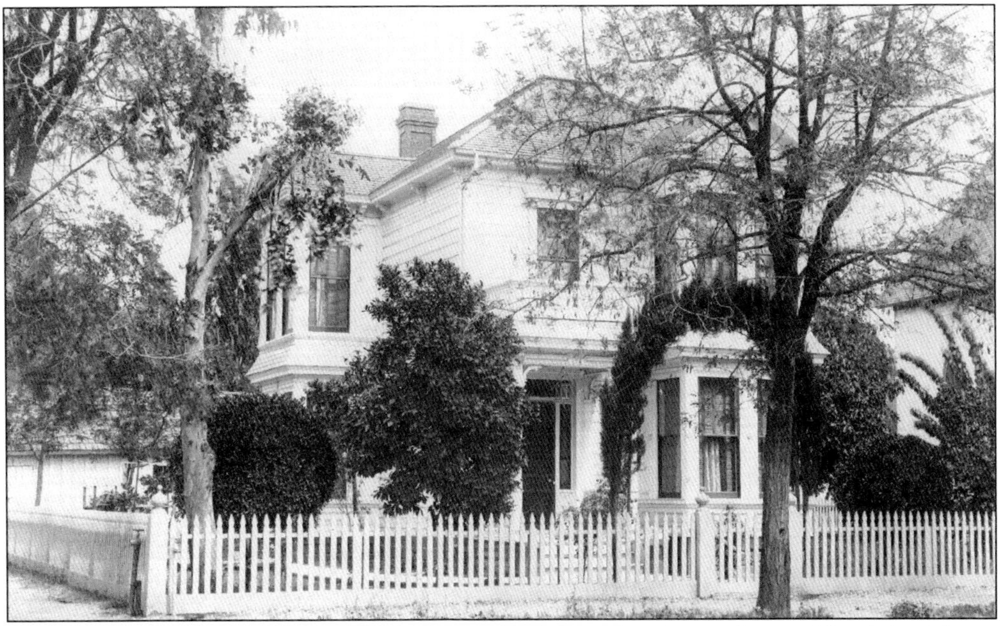

This beautiful Victorian home, still standing in Ione, served as the residence of Dr. A. L. Adams, who also owned a drugstore on Main Street. Adams was remembered by one citizen as a man with the peculiar habit of eating only "hot" bread with his meals. He is also recognized as one of the trustees that helped build the Ione Academy, the first high school in Amador County.

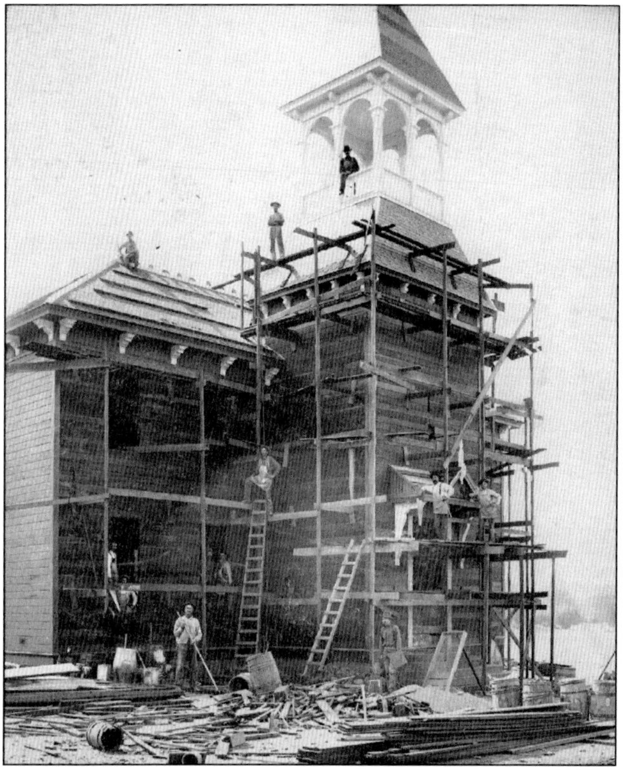

The Ione Academy, Amador County's first high school, is shown here under construction and when finished. The academy was established in 1902, and the first classes were held in the Baptist church until this building was completed the following year. In 1905, a class of seven students became the first to graduate from the school. After the railroad between Martell and Ione was completed, many students from around the county were able to attend because they could use the train instead of making the long trip by wagon.

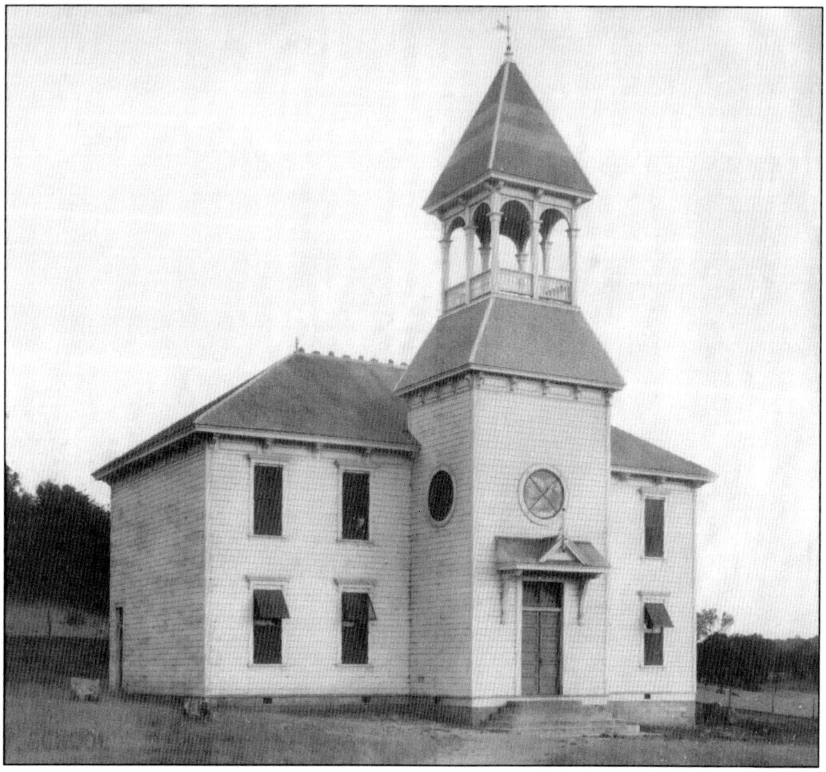

Sports were a popular pastime for both boys and girls. These students composed the 1908 Ione High School girls' basketball team. Pictured from left to right are the following: (first row) Violette Woods, Ida Williams, and Olive Gordon; (second row) Hilda Winter, Bessie Scott, and Margaret Marchant.

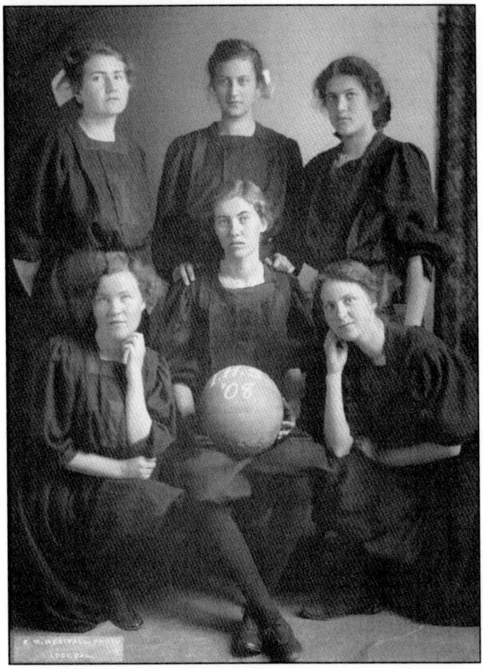

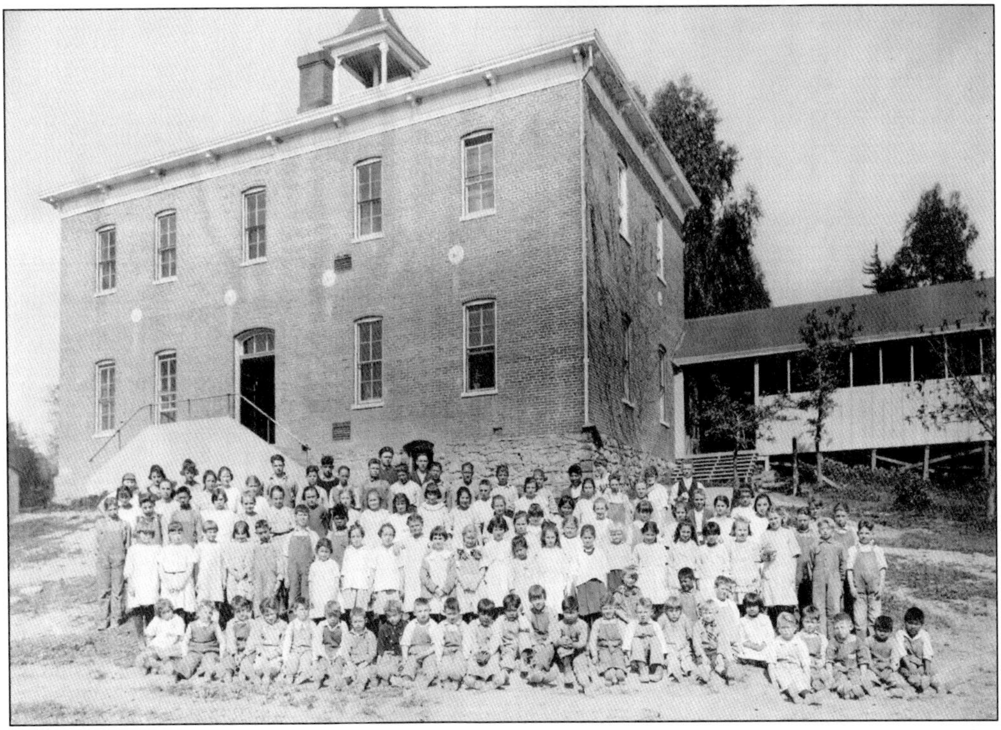

Constructed in 1882, the Ione Grammar School was originally built by the Ione Masonic Lodge as a meeting place; however, seeing the need for a schoolhouse, the group allowed the district to use the ground floor for classes, while the second floor was reserved for meeting rooms. In 1952, a new grammar school was completed, and this building became home to the Veterans of Foreign Wars. The second story was removed some time ago.

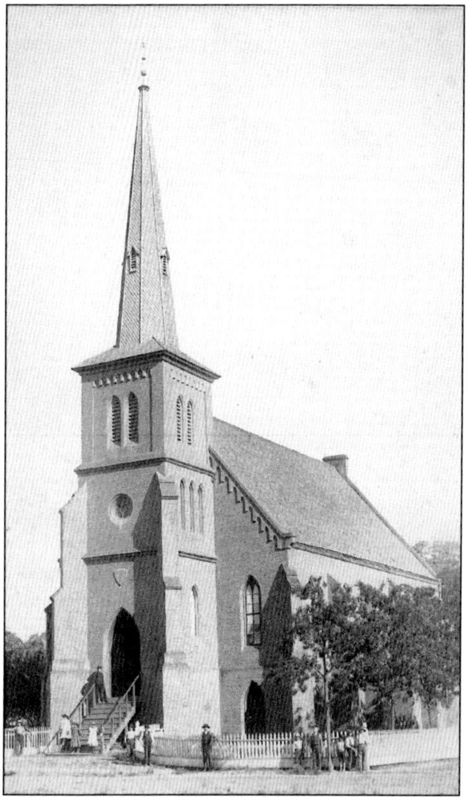

The spire of the Community Methodist Church of Ione marks a high point in the subtle skyline of this small town. The cornerstone for this beautiful brick building was laid in 1862. Constructed of locally mined and fired brick, the church was completed in 1866. Known as the "Cathedral of the Mother Lode," it has been designated California Historic Landmark No. 506.

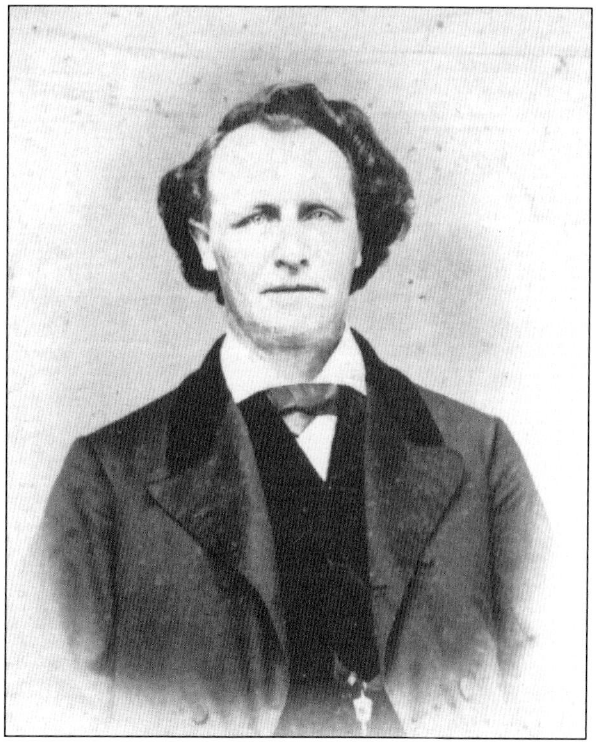

Rev. Isaac B. Fish was one of the ministers serving the Methodist community of Gold Rush–era Ione City. Although he is better known for preaching in the barrooms of Jackson and founding and building the Methodist church in that town, he also shared ministerial duties in Ione in 1854 and 1863.

Sacred Heart Catholic Church stands on a hill at the southern edge of Ione. It was built in 1874 under the direction of Fr. Joseph Sadoc Alemany, the first archbishop of San Francisco. For a number of years, the church was attended by the priests from Jackson. In 1931, Fr. Caroll Lawson, who had been the assistant to Fr. Meceal Carney in Jackson, became the first resident priest at Sacred Heart. Pictured at right is Father Gleason, who ministered to Ione's Catholic community for 17 years, from 1895 to 1912. Several other priests have since ministered at Sacred Heart. Today the congregation is served by the Rev. Thomas Relihan.

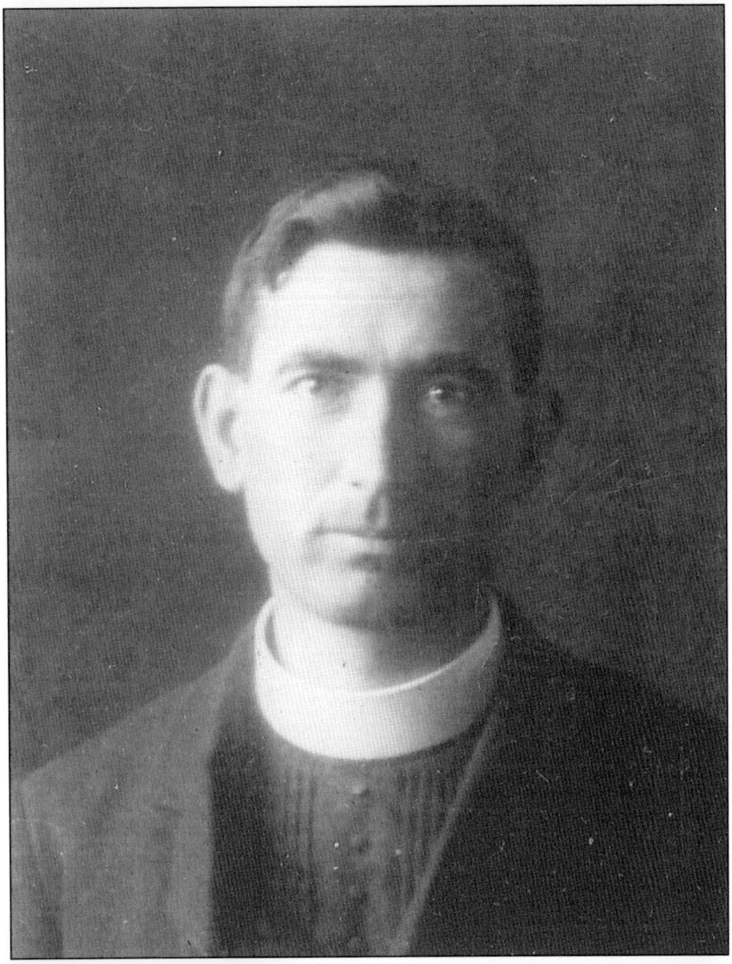

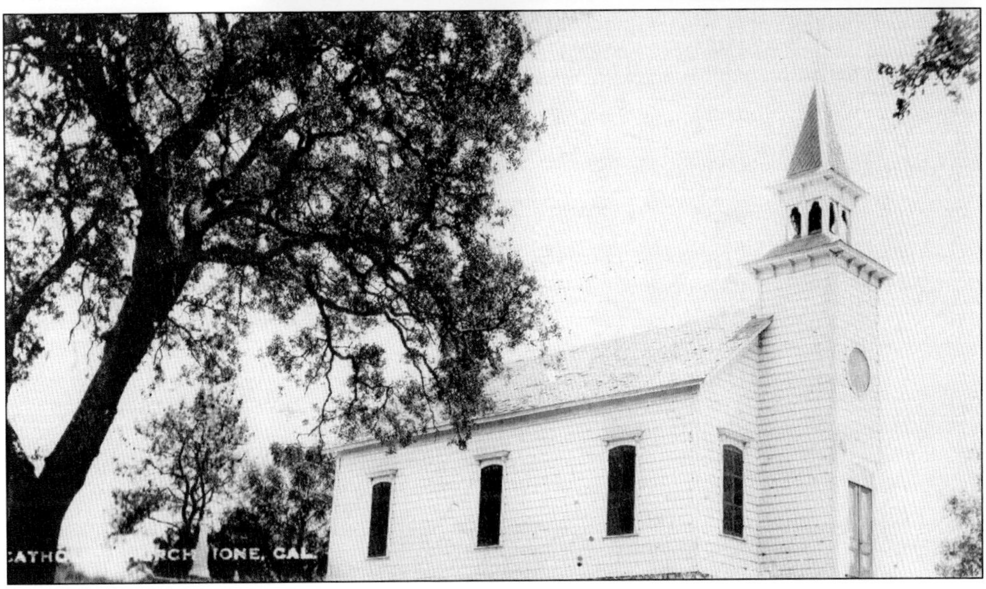

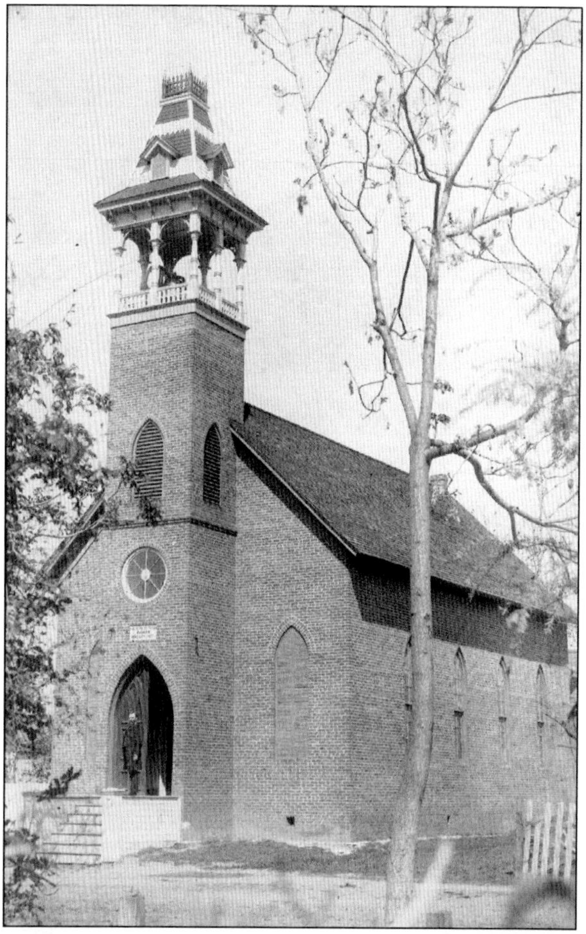

Pictured at left is the First Presbyterian Church of Ione. Built in 1877, it once stood on the lot that is now home to the Cornerstone Church of Ione. A Presbyterian following was first organized in Ione in 1861 under the direction of Rev. William C. Mosher of Jackson. For more than a century, this building was home to the Presbyterians of Ione until the congregation dwindled; it then became the property of the Baptist Church. When bricks in the church began to crumble, it was razed and replaced by the Cornerstone Church, so named for the time capsule *casquet* discovered when the old building was torn down. Seen below are members of the Ladies Aid Society of the Presbyterian church. The group was instrumental in organizing social events and performing benevolent work throughout the county.

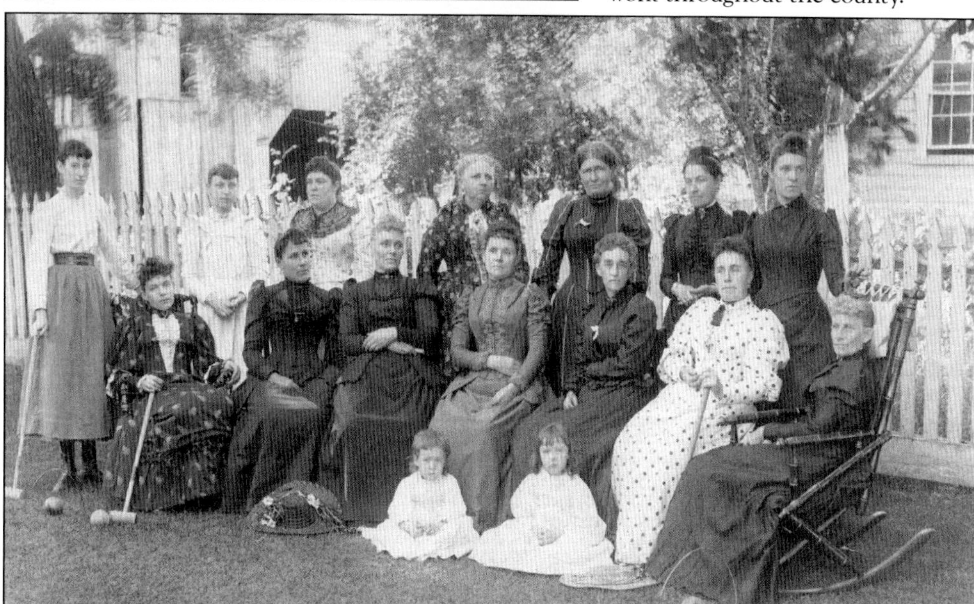

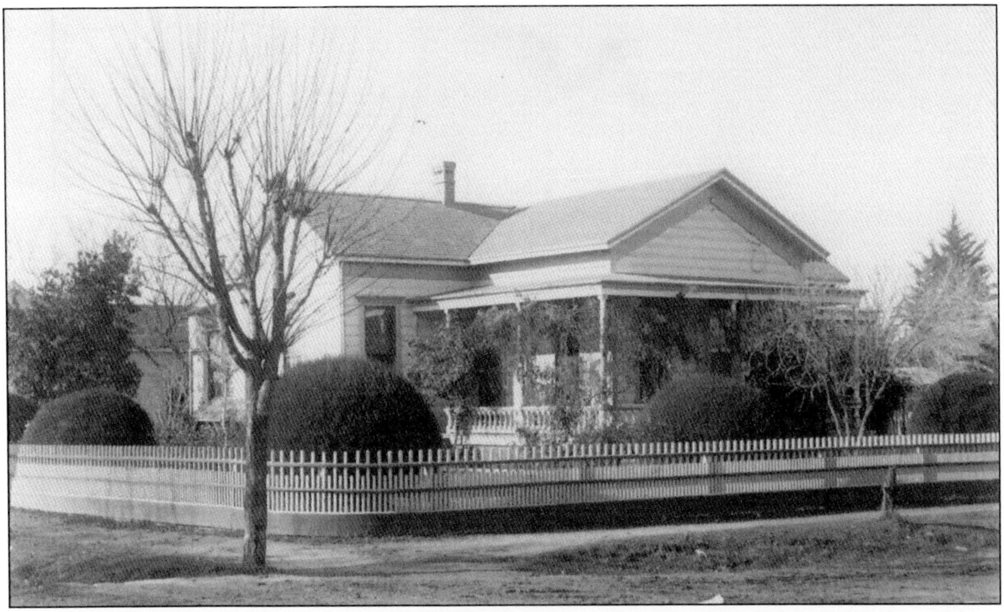

John Fairfield Wharff, whose home is seen here, came to Ione in 1890. Wharff family members included the following, from left to right: (first row) Keith Emmert; Francis Emmert; Wallace Emmert; and Elmer Vanderbilt; (second row) Charles Josiah Emmert, holding Charles John Emmert; Merilyn Bagley; William Hatch Wharff; Lois Bagley; Corinne Emmert (in front of Lois); the patriarch, John Fairfield Wharff; his wife, Olive Washburn Wharff, holding Janice Bertha Lowell; John Vanderbilt; Warren Vanderbilt (in front of John); and Joseph Wharff; (third row) Ethel Wharff Emmert; Olive Vanderbilt Bagley; Dr. Walter Lowell; Bertha Vanderbilt Lowell; Ruth Williams Vanderbilt; Ira Vanderbilt; Bertha Wharff Vanderbilt; Mildred Vanderbilt; and Ella Vanderbilt.

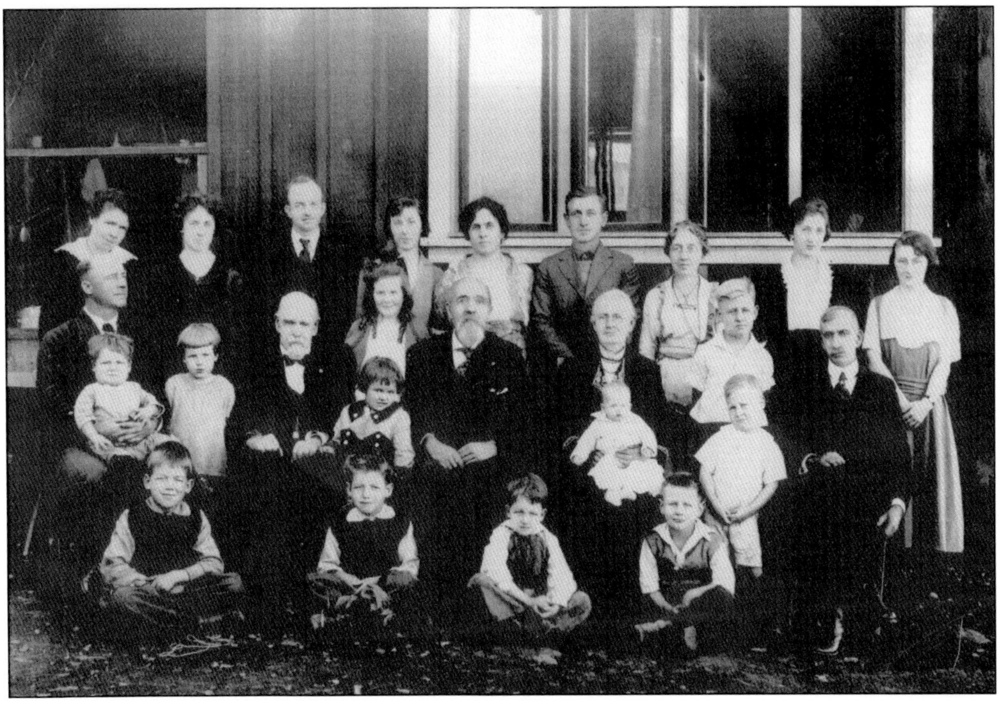

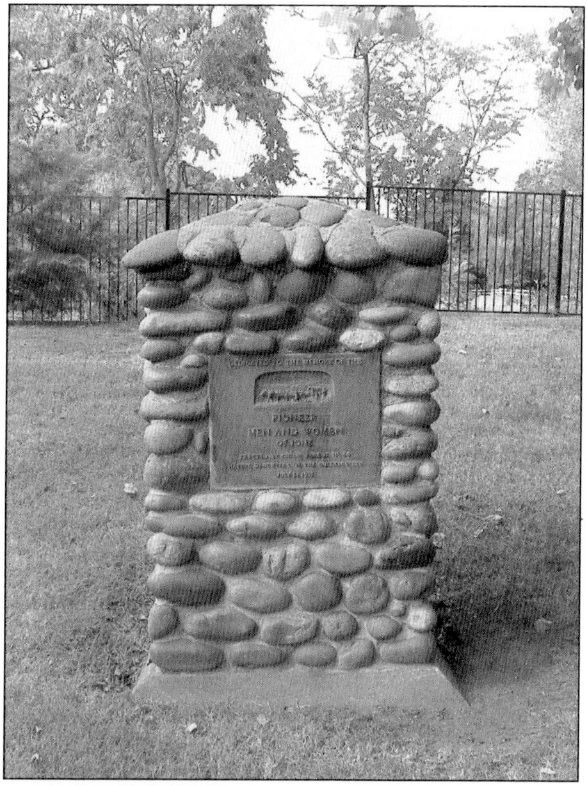

As in many other towns throughout California, residents in Ione proud of their heritage have dedicated several memorials and plaques to commemorate the accomplishments of their forebearers. This monument, dedicated to the pioneer men and women of Ione, stands in the community park behind city hall. It was dedicated in 1999 by the Native Daughters of the Golden West Monument. (Author's collection.)

Most of those who lived and died in Ione are buried in the Ione City Cemetery. Many of the grave sites found here are creative and ornate, displaying remembrances of the lifestyle, accomplishments, and environment of the deceased. The grave house of W. N. Garland is composed of local brick and reflects a higher station in life than that of Nat Cecil, onetime slave, whose gravestone is pictured on page 20. (Author's collection.)

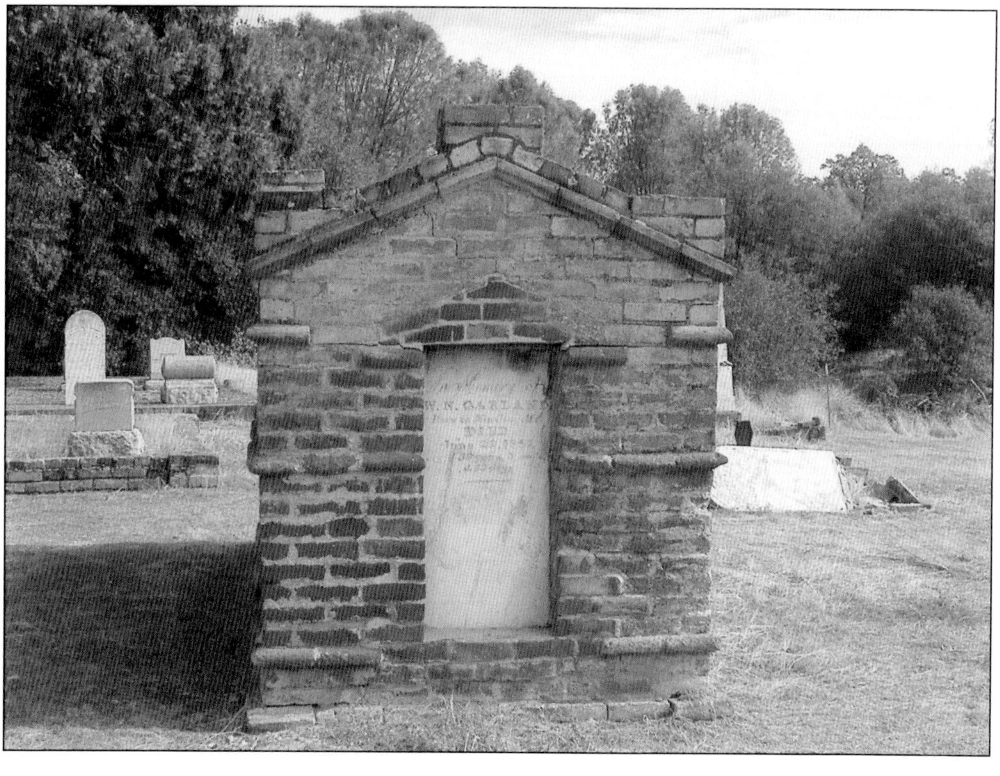

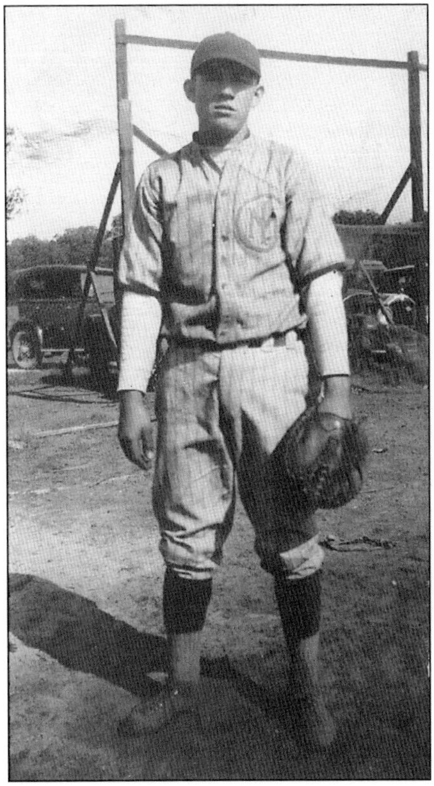

The DuFrene family has for generations lived in the Ione and Jackson Valleys. Ralph DuFrene, seen here in his baseball uniform, was the catcher for the famed Yankees pitcher Ernie Bonham when the two attended high school in Ione.

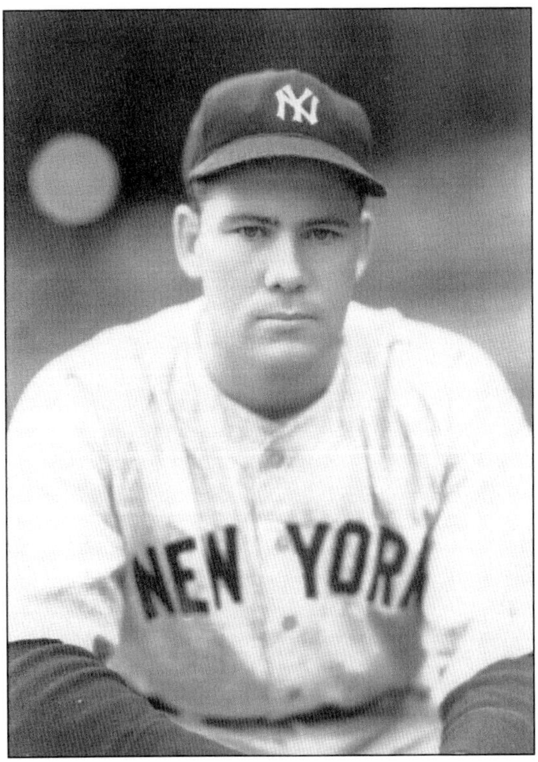

The name Bonham is well known throughout Amador County, and Ernie Bonham is probably the most famous of Ione's sons, having played professional baseball for a number of years. The first pitcher to successfully use the forkball, Bonham led the American League with a 1.90 ERA as a rookie in 1940. His untimely death in 1949 at the age of 37 resulted from complications of appendicitis surgery.

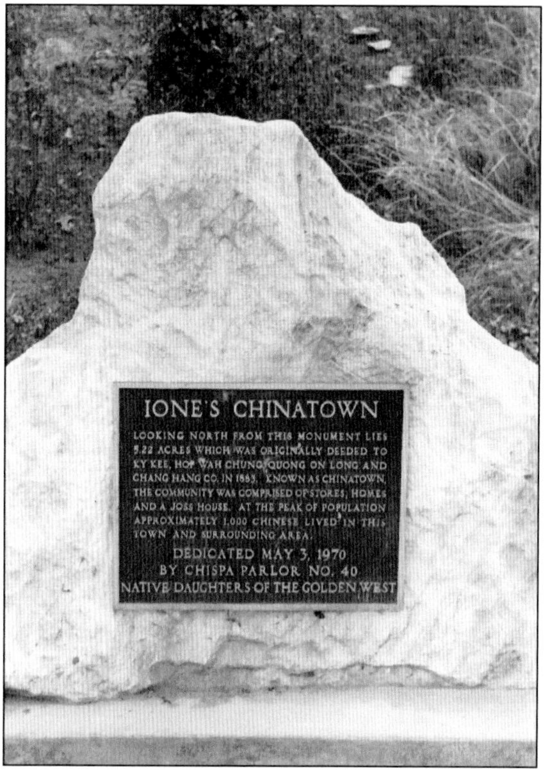

Ione's Chinatown was located to the east of the center of town, on North Summit Street. Four to five businesses and a least one laundry thrived here, while a joss house offered a social gathering place for the citizens. In 1898, a match factory was opened, offering employment for the Chinese. When this plaque was dedicated in 1970, a festival was held and descendants of former Celestial residents attended the ceremonies.

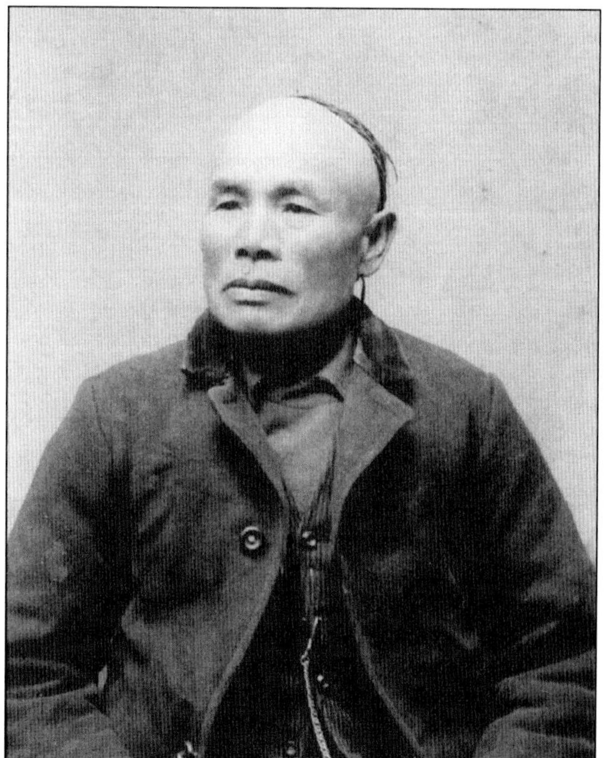

Gum San, or Golden Mountain, was the name the Chinese gave to California. Large numbers of Chinese came to work at making a fortune in gold but soon found that dream elusive. Many returned to their homeland; others remained and worked in the community. Sadly discrimination led to a nameless future for most. This unidentified Chinese man represents many anonymous laborers who toiled to make our country great but whose stories will never be known.

Members of the Moey family of Ione gathered for this photograph about 1915. Pictured from left to right are the following: (first row) Willie, Fannie, and Joseph; (second row) Mary Ah Moey and Big Chung Ho Moey.

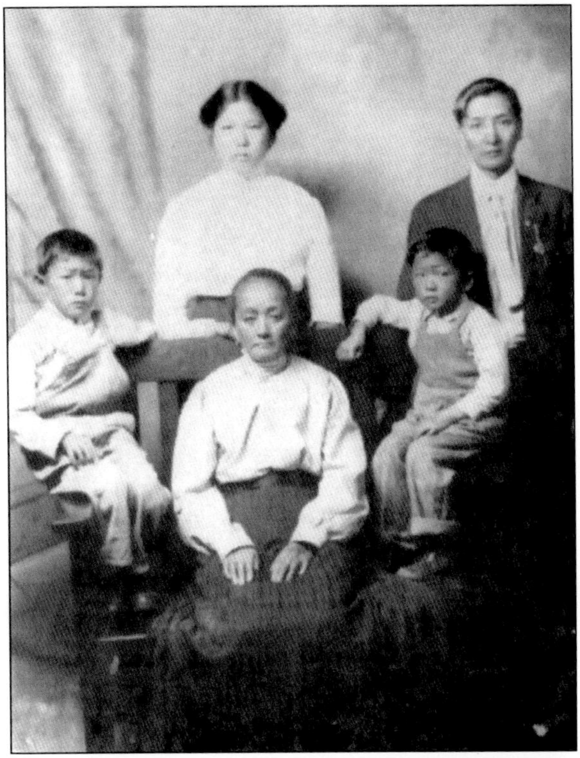

At its peak, Ione's Chinatown boasted about 1,000 residents. These immigrants, like most ethnic groups, found comfort in close association with others of the same culture. The Chinese were proud of their heritage and held fast to their traditions and customs. Celebrations like this parade down Main Street in Ione (possibly to celebrate the Chinese New Year) reinforced their identity in this foreign land.

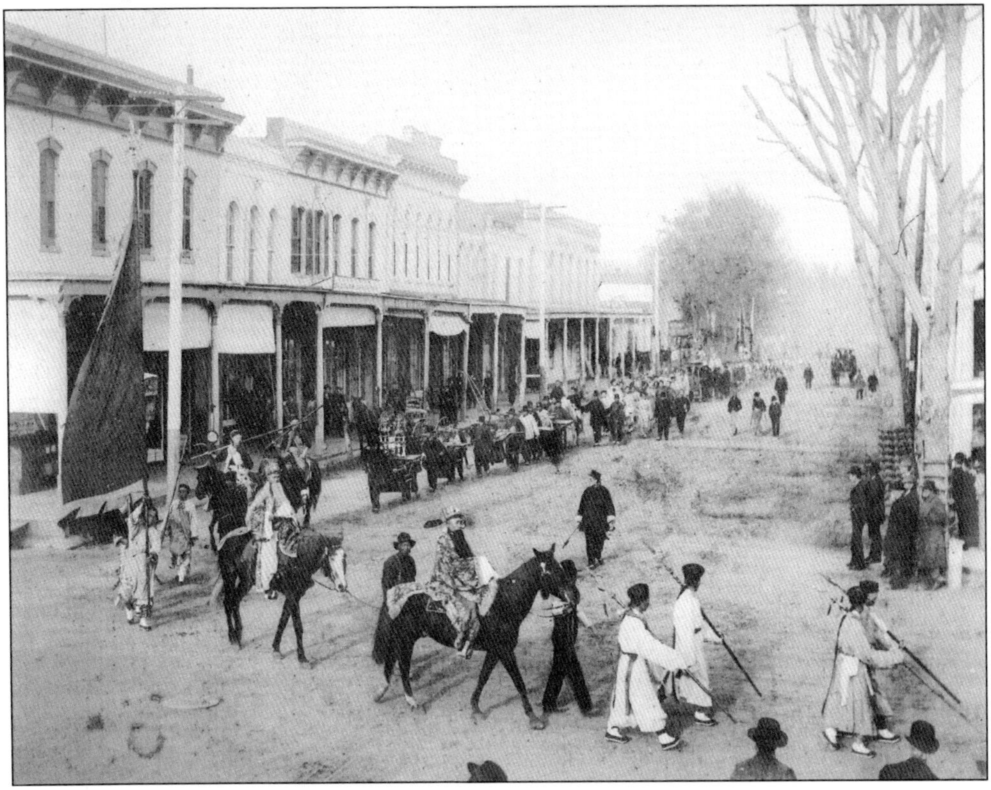

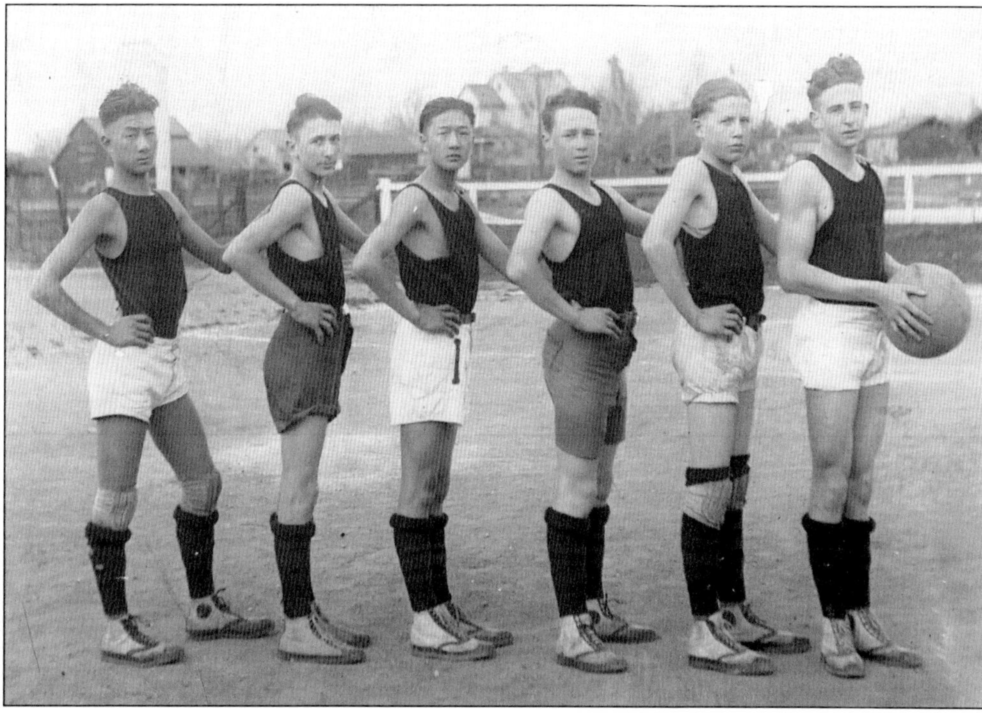

In 1900, a fire nearly destroyed Ione's Chinatown. The area was never completely rebuilt, but many Chinese residents stayed on and assimilated into the community. When this photograph of the Ione High School basketball team was taken around 1925, two Chinese boys played on the team. Joseph Won (third from left) was the last Chinese child born in Ione's Chinatown, in 1909.

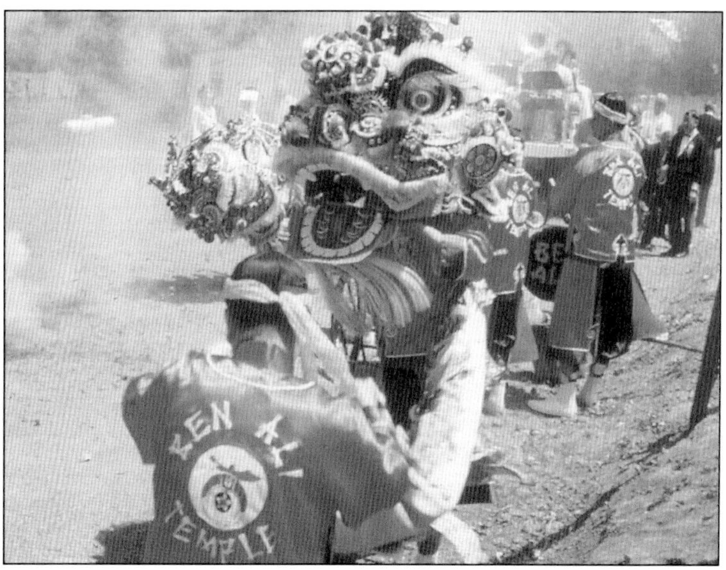

In 1970, when the plaque was placed at Chinatown by the Native Daughters of the Golden West, a large festival was held. Joseph Won attended the ceremonies, as did other descendants. Perpetually recognized as the symbol of good fortune, the grand tradition of the dragon leading the parade was carried on by members of the Ben Ali Temple.

Five

Law and Order in a Small Town

The identity of a town is often defined by its prominent institutions. Just as the cotton industry became an identifying feature of the small mill towns in the Southern United States, so have crime and punishment somewhat defined the character of Ione. As one approaches Ione from any direction, the towering citadel of the Preston School of Industry's administration building comes into view. If approaching from the west, upon arriving at the outskirts of town, the visitor will first see Mule Creek State Prison to his left and then the campus of Preston surrounding that tall building, known locally as "the Castle."

During Ione's youthful years, law enforcement consisted of a justice of the peace. After the affray concerning the Arroyo Seco Grant, foremost in the settlers' minds was protecting hearth and home. In 1865, men of Ione and the surrounding rural area formed the Ione City Guards, a local militia. The regular law was the county sheriff and his deputies, more than a few of whom came from the Ione Valley. The circuit court of the West is a well-known feature of early justice, whereby judges or magistrates traveled between towns meting out justice; however, the Amador District, County, and Superior Courts for the most part conducted business at the county seat in Jackson. Likewise, the jail, a county institution, was situated in Jackson.

It was not until 1894, when the Preston School of Industry was built, that the town became associated with the criminal justice system. Then, nearly 100 years later, in 1987, the California Department of Corrections built Mule Creek State Prison near Preston. Both of these institutions are inextricably linked to the history and personality of Ione, offering employment to local citizens and also drawing newcomers to work in Ione. In turn, the influx of new residents offered a boost in the economy and increased the size of the sleepy town. Today the Castle and the prison stand as symbols of law and order in Ione, while the city's police department stands at the corner of Main and Church Streets, providing safety and security to the small town.

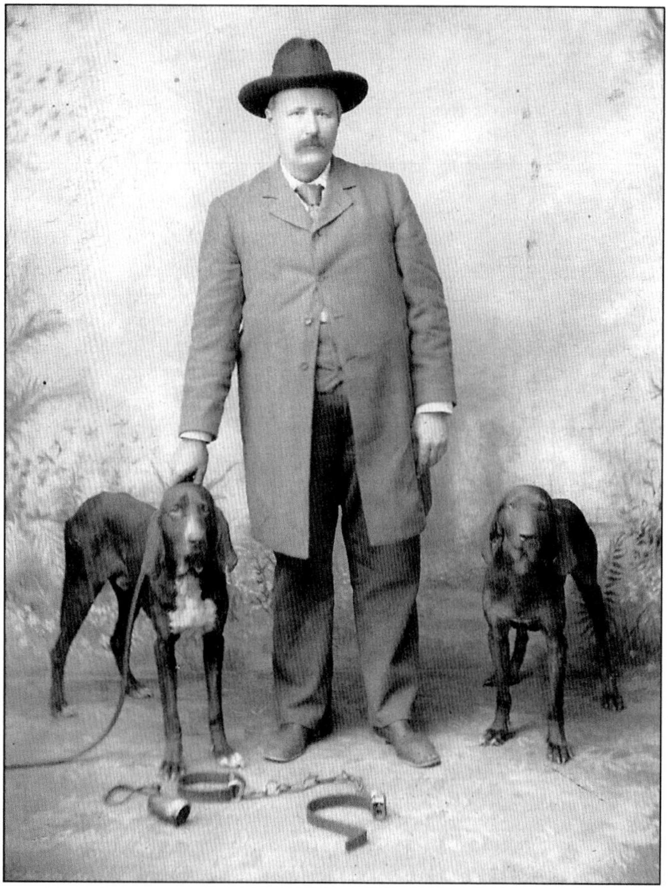

One of the better known early law enforcement officers of Amador County was U. S. Gregory, who was from Ione and is pictured here with his hounds. Gregory came to Ione in 1866, serving as county sheriff from 1892 to 1902. Gregory was the sheriff in charge when Wells Fargo messenger Mike Tovey was murdered on the road from Ione to Jackson.

In 1865, men in Ione and the surrounding area formed a local militia known as the Ione City Guards. Although an independent group, they were also recognized as the 4th Brigade of the California State Militia. That militia is now known as the California division of the National Guard.

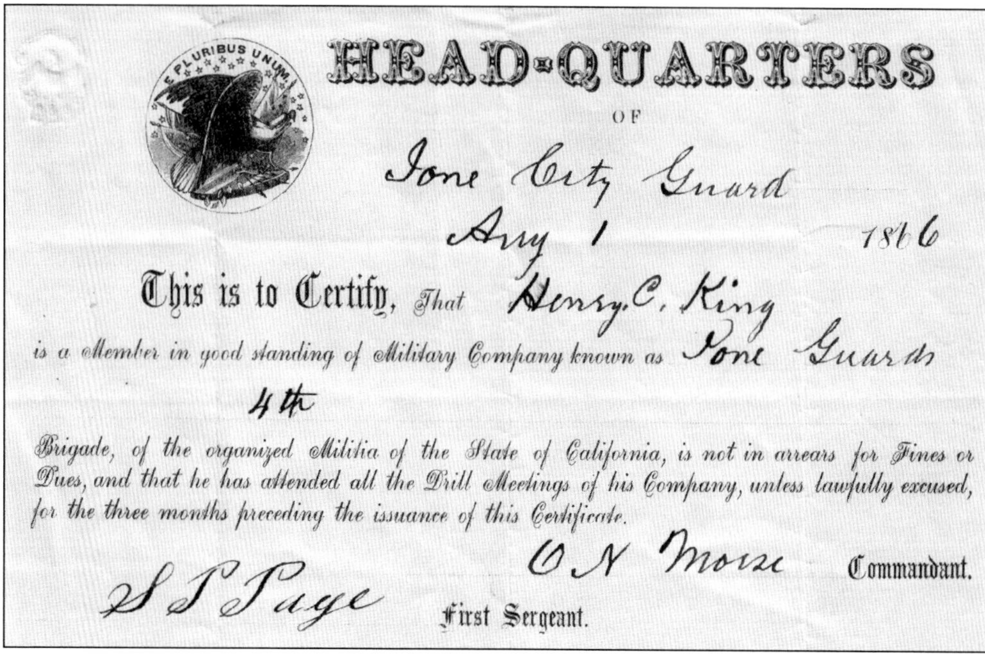

E PLURIBUS UNUM

HEAD-QUARTERS

OF

Ione City Guard

Aug 1 1866

This is to Certify, *That* Henry C. King

is a Member in good standing of Military Company known as Ione Guards

4th

Brigade, of the organized Militia of the State of California, is not in arrears for Fines or Dues, and that he has attended all the Drill Meetings of his Company, unless lawfully excused, for the three months preceding the issuance of this Certificate.

O N Morse Commandant.

S P Page First Sergeant.

Early on, Ione became a crossroads for travelers and commerce—and thus a main stage stop on routes from Sacramento to Jackson. Michael Tovey, an express messenger for Wells Fargo on the Ione-Jackson route, was murdered during an attempted robbery of the stagecoach on June 15, 1893. A stone monument stands near the spot at the top of the ridge between Jackson and Ione where he lost his life. Tovey is buried in the Jackson City Cemetery.

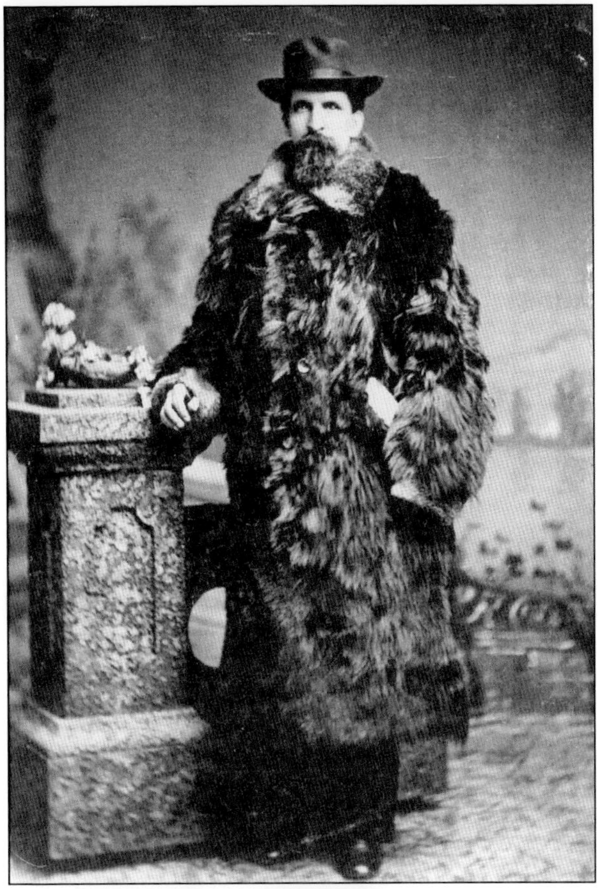

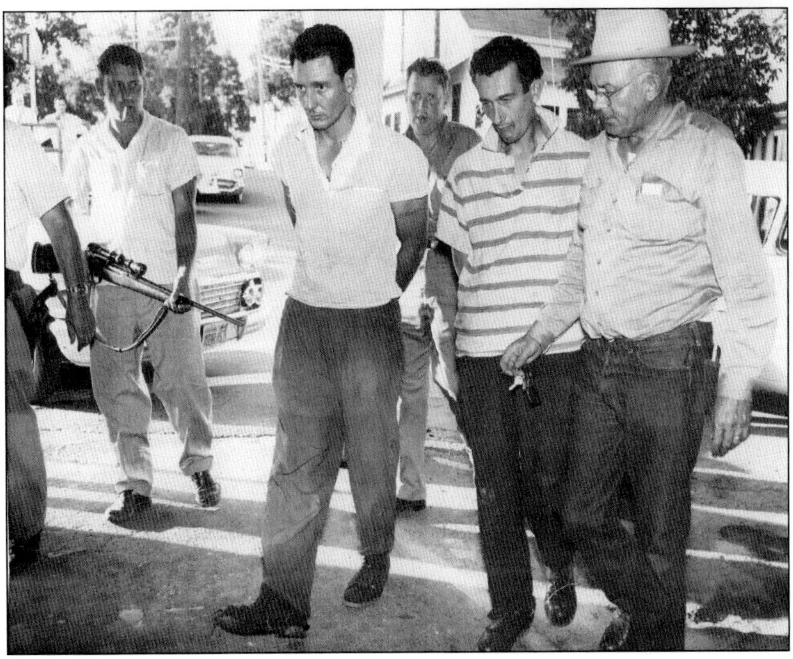

Another of Ione's native sons to serve as Amador County sheriff was Karl Joses (far right). With the assistance of deputies, Joses escorts two escaped Folsom Prison inmates to the county jail. The Joses name is well known throughout the county as a longtime Ione family.

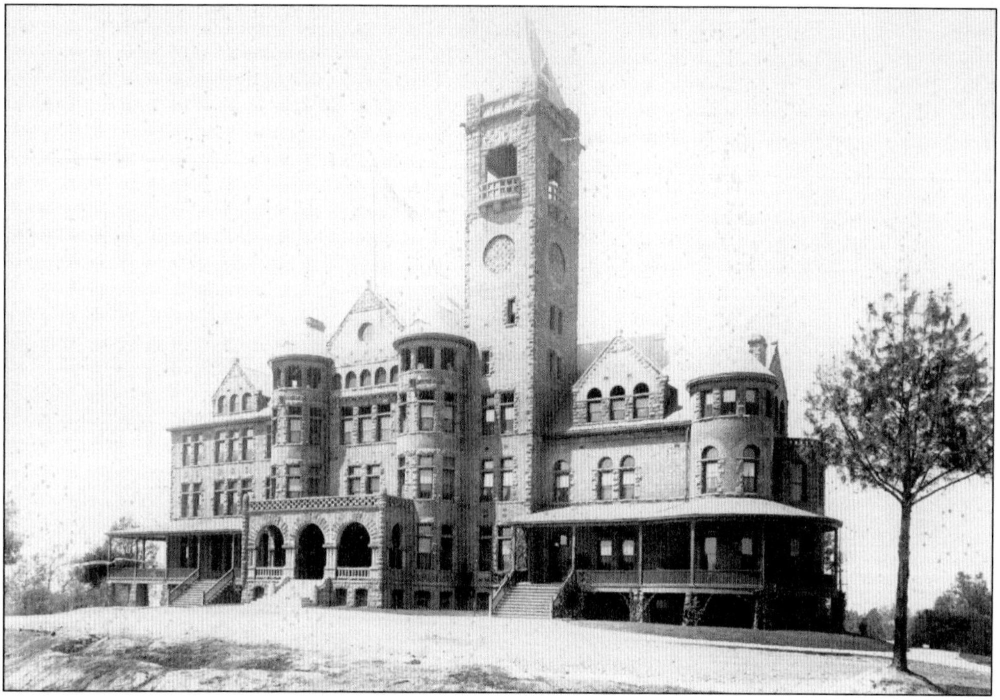

The story of Preston began when Sen. E. M. Preston of Nevada County, California, introduced a bill to the state senate in 1889 proposing an act to establish a state reform school to house young offenders. The large administration building, known as the Castle, was built of locally produced brick and took about three years to complete.

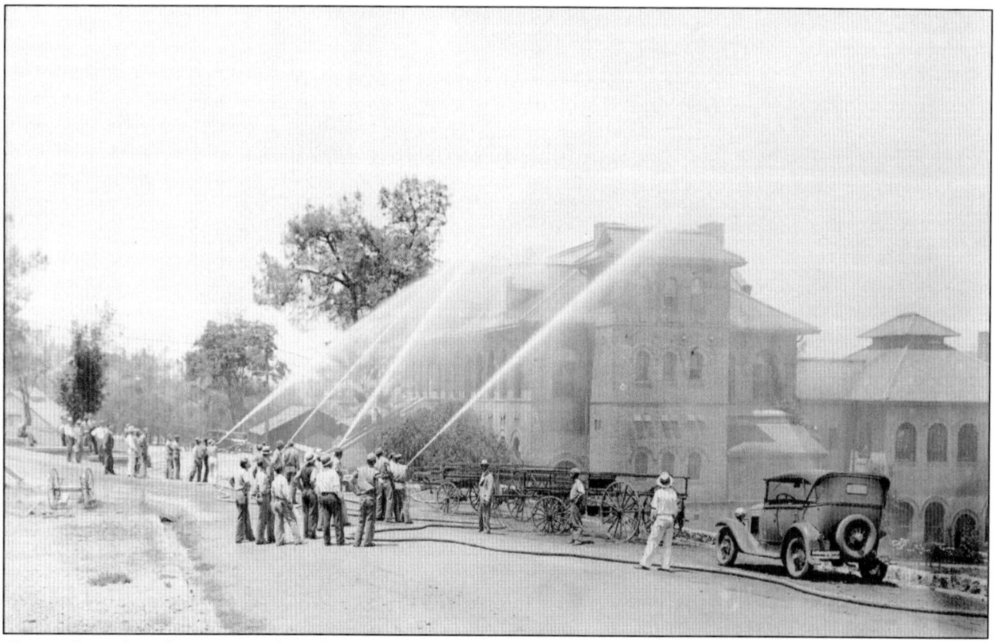

Once the school was completed and inmates were settled into the school, Preston became more or less a self-sufficient community. Here the Preston Fire Department runs a practice exercise in the use of hoses. Note the old wagon-style hose carts still in use at the time.

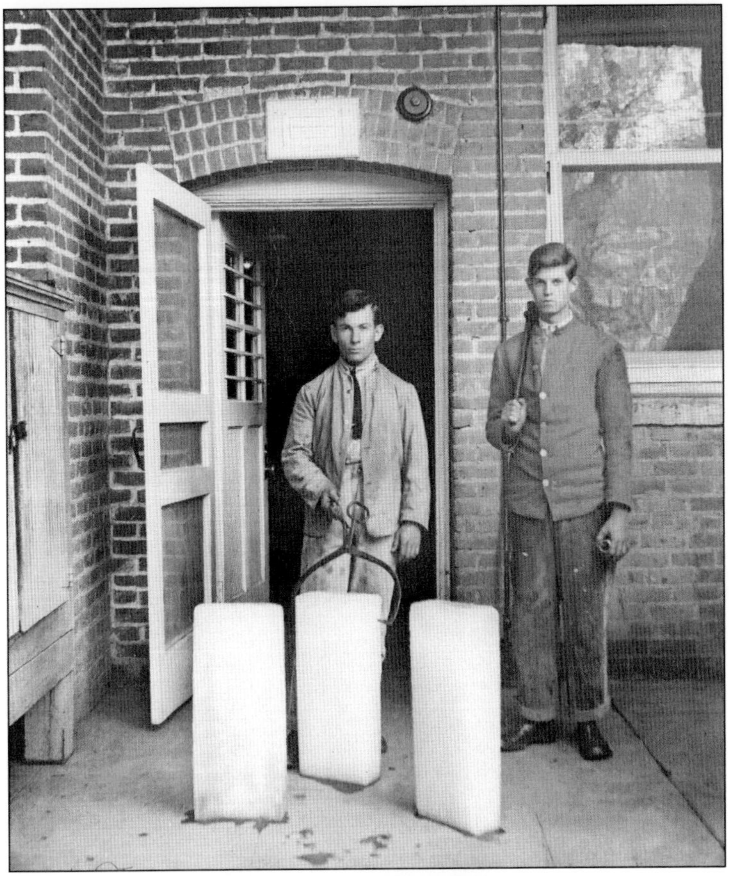

The youth offenders housed at Preston were known as wards. The first seven arrived at the school from San Quentin Prison on June 13, 1894. Because the school was for the most self-sustaining, all wards were expected to perform some type of work duty. Here, two unidentified young men pause from their duty of moving ice to pose for a photograph.

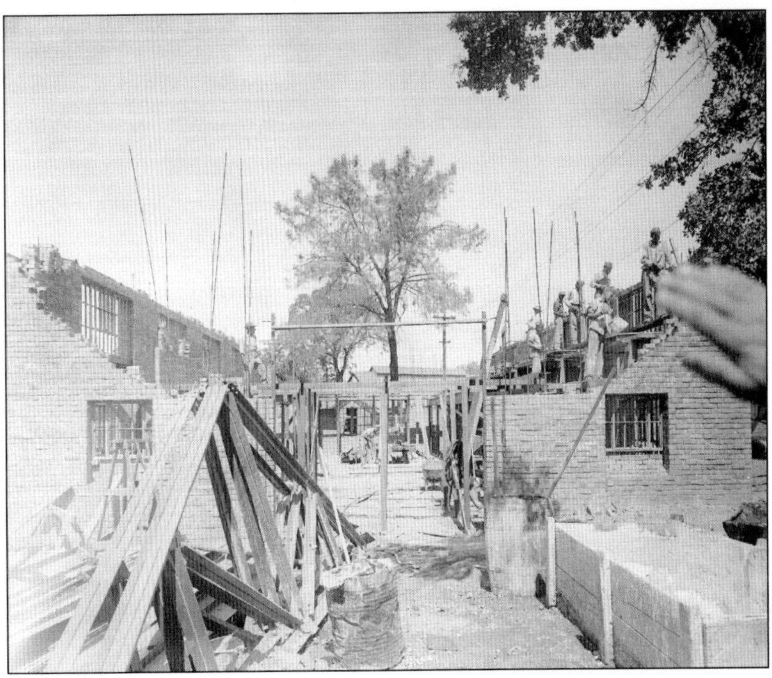

Because the Preston School of Industry was considered a reform school, it offered the ward various ways to reform his life, including the learning of a trade. Training covered the construction trades as well as photography, printing, auto repair, tailoring, plumbing, and machine shop skills. Here wards work to construct a brick building at the school.

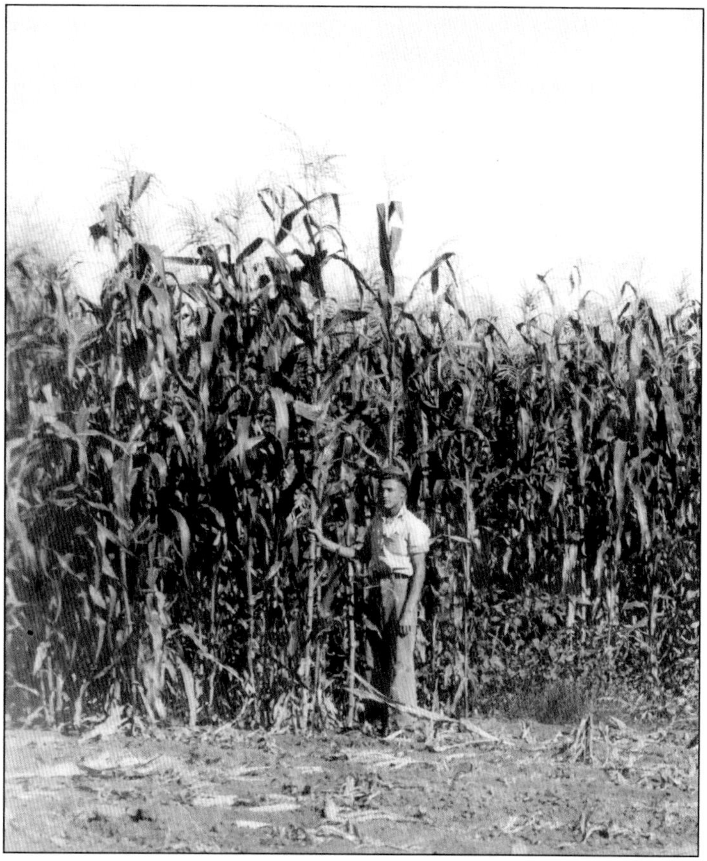

The wards also learned farming and animal husbandry. The rural setting and large tract of land taken in by the school allowed the institution to provide for nutritional needs of the staff and inmates. Both livestock and crops, such as the corn seen in this photograph, were tended by the wards.

Below several wards ride horse-drawn apparatus, mowing and plowing a field. In addition to edible crops, hay and grain were grown on the grounds to feed livestock raised for meat to be consumed at the school. In 1906, more than 20,000 bushels of oats and barley were grown and threshed on the farm.

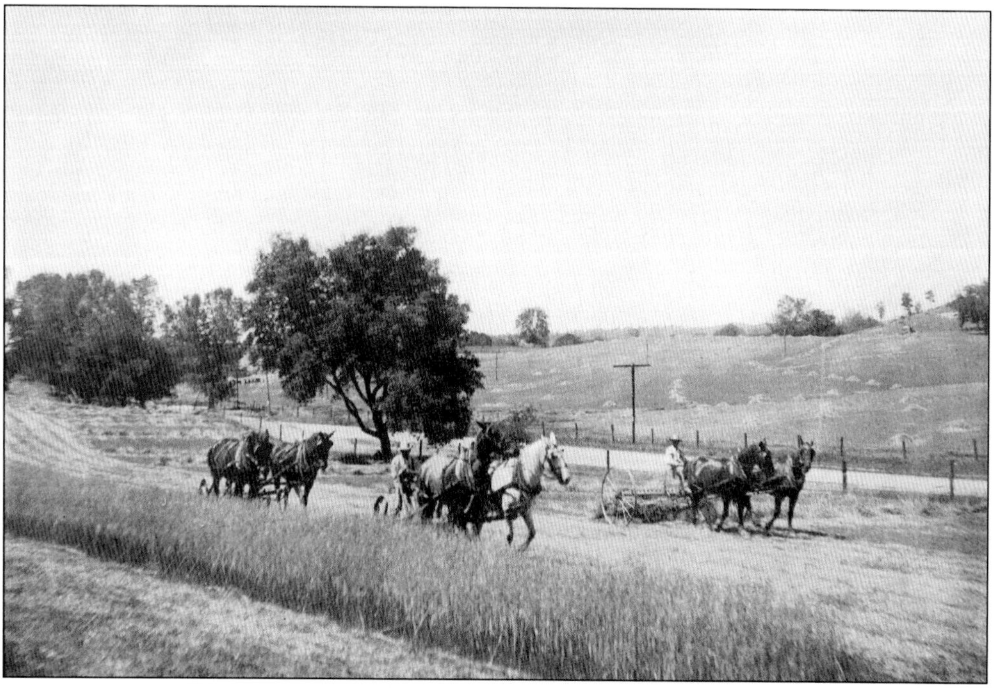

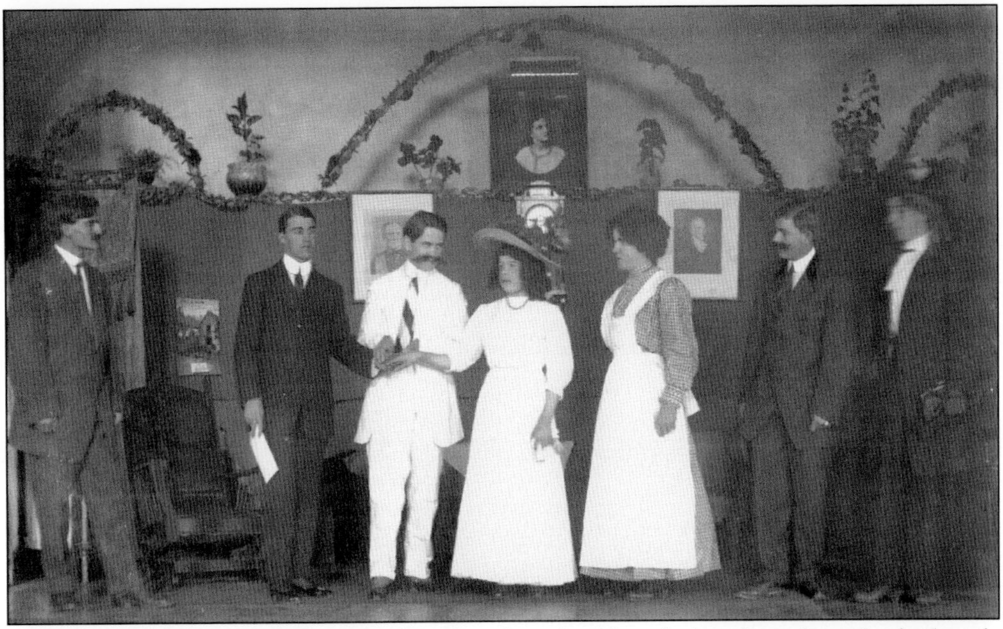

Being a ward at Preston did not mean all work and no play. Here the boys have dressed as both male and female to put on a stage play during the 1911 Christmas Pageant. This photograph was taken by a Mr. Greenough, who served as the official school photographer during the early 20th century.

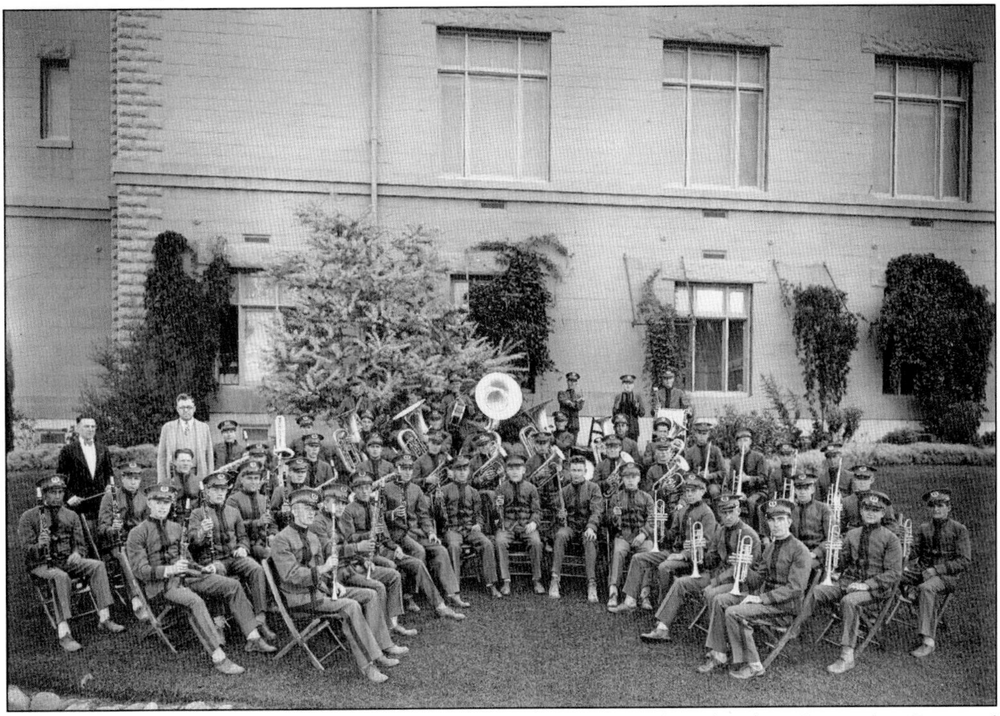

Cultural studies like drama and art were just as important at the school as the trades. Pictured here is the Preston Military Band, which participated in many local events and always performed at visitor days and other special gatherings. In 1915, the band left the school and traveled on an extended concert trip, playing at 14 towns in central California.

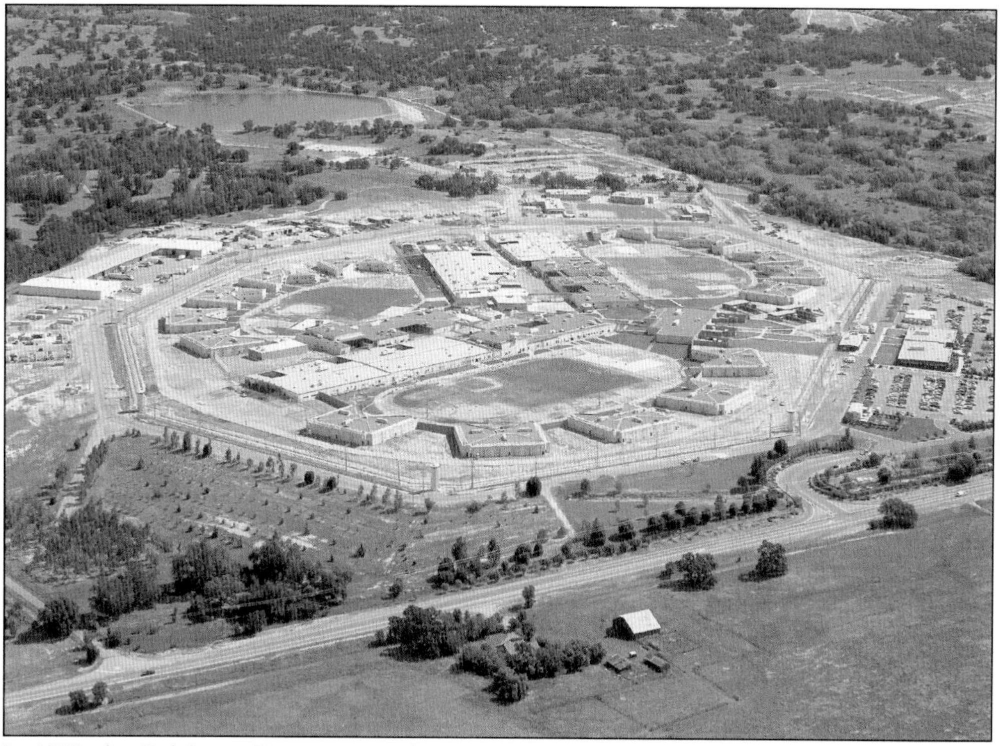

In 1987, the California Department of Corrections built Mule Creek State Prison just a few long blocks west of the Preston campus. Once again, local residents found employment at a correctional facility; however, many folks also moved to Ione from other towns and cities to work at the prison.

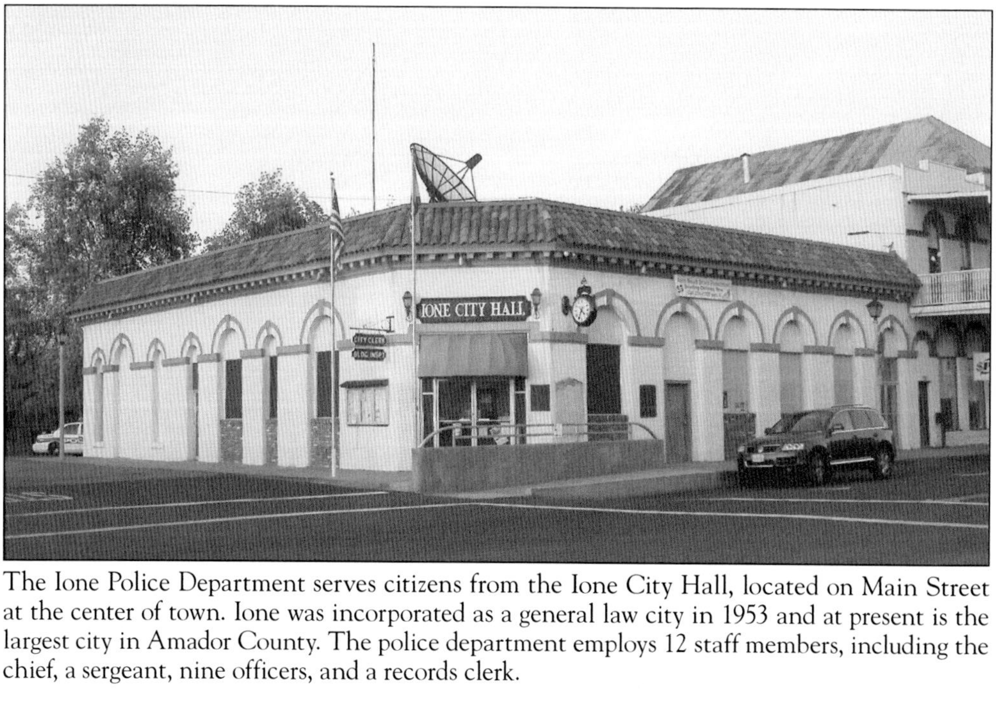

The Ione Police Department serves citizens from the Ione City Hall, located on Main Street at the center of town. Ione was incorporated as a general law city in 1953 and at present is the largest city in Amador County. The police department employs 12 staff members, including the chief, a sergeant, nine officers, and a records clerk.

Six

Around the Ione Valley

Stretching beyond the limits of Ione City is the Ione Valley, and beyond that are the rolling hills and valleys that were once the location of numerous mining camps and hamlets now lost to time. How the town and valley obtained their name has long been a matter of discussion. Some sources state that they were named after Bulwer's heroine from *The Last Days of Pompeii.* Others say that Billy Hicks stood up one day and named the valley with a sweep of his hand, claiming, "I own it." This author has often wondered if it was for Ione Harnett, the first white child born in the valley in 1852. What we do know is that the valley was named first.

Before Ione City was well settled, travelers through the region recognized that the valleys on the western edge of Amador County were easily accessible and marked with trails long used by the Native American Miwok people. During the decade preceding the Gold Rush, several Mexican expeditions reportedly passed through the area. Then, with the explosive influx of Argonauts to the region, numerous mining camps, small towns, and public inns sprang up along creeks, streams, and roads, and ranchers and farmers took up large tracts of land raising livestock and grain. Early on, both the Ione and Buckeye Valleys became important in the production of agricultural goods.

At the onset of the Gold Rush, many way stations and inns were crude lean-tos covered with hides. As a sense of permanency spread across the area, many of these became solid frame buildings with comfortable accommodations to serve the traveling public. In some cases, small towns grew up around what began as simply a stop on the road. Around the Ione Valley, places such as Doschville, Quincy, Muletown, Boston Store, Alabama House, and Carbondale seemed to spring up overnight, stay for not much longer than three years, and then return to the unobstructed landscape from whence they came.

In this chapter, the reader will learn about a few folks from around the valley and get a glimpse of those bergs that are no more.

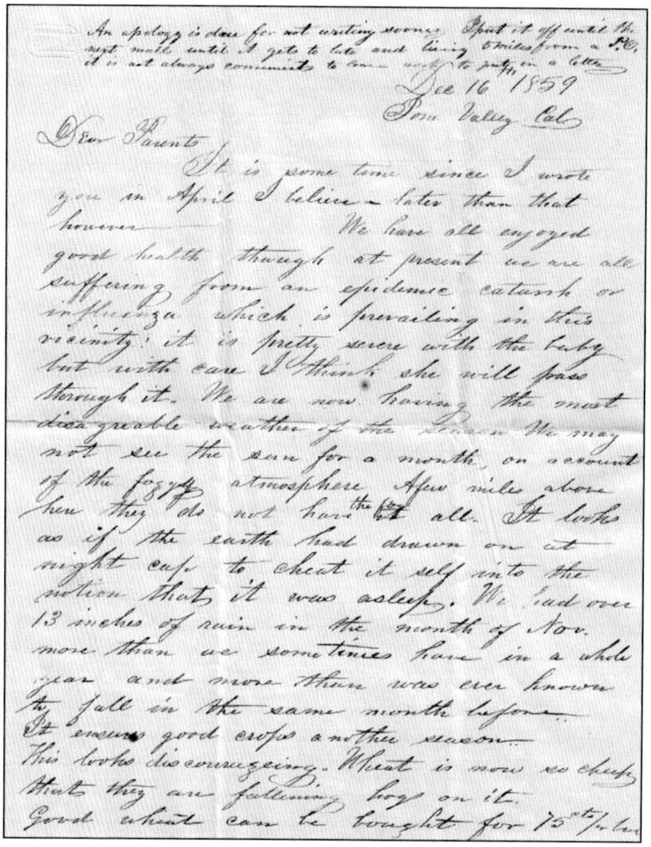

An apology is due for not writing sooner. I put it off until the next mail until it gets to late and living 5 miles from a P.O. it is not always convenient to [illegible] [illegible] to put it in a letter

Dec 16 1859
Ione Valley Cal

Dear Parents

It is some time since I wrote you in April I believe – later than that however. We have all enjoyed good health though at present we are all suffering from an epidemic catarrh or influenza which is prevailing in this vicinity: it is pretty severe with the baby but with care I think she will pass through it. We are now having the most disagreeable weather of the season. We may not see the sun for a month, on account of the foggy atmosphere. A few miles above here they do not have the fog at all. It looks as if the earth had drawn on a night cap to cheat itself into the notion that it was asleep. We had over 13 inches of rain in the month of Nov. more than we sometimes have in a whole year and more than was ever known to fall in the same month before. It ensures good crops another season. This looks discouraging. Wheat is now so cheap that they are fattening hogs on it. Good wheat can be bought for 75cts/pr bu

In 1859, Jesse Dimon Mason, author of the 1881 *Amador County History*, penned this letter and mailed it to family in his native Vermont. As with much correspondence written during the Gold Rush era, it describes the weather, crops, and happenings of the Ione Valley, including the 13 inches of rain that fell that November.

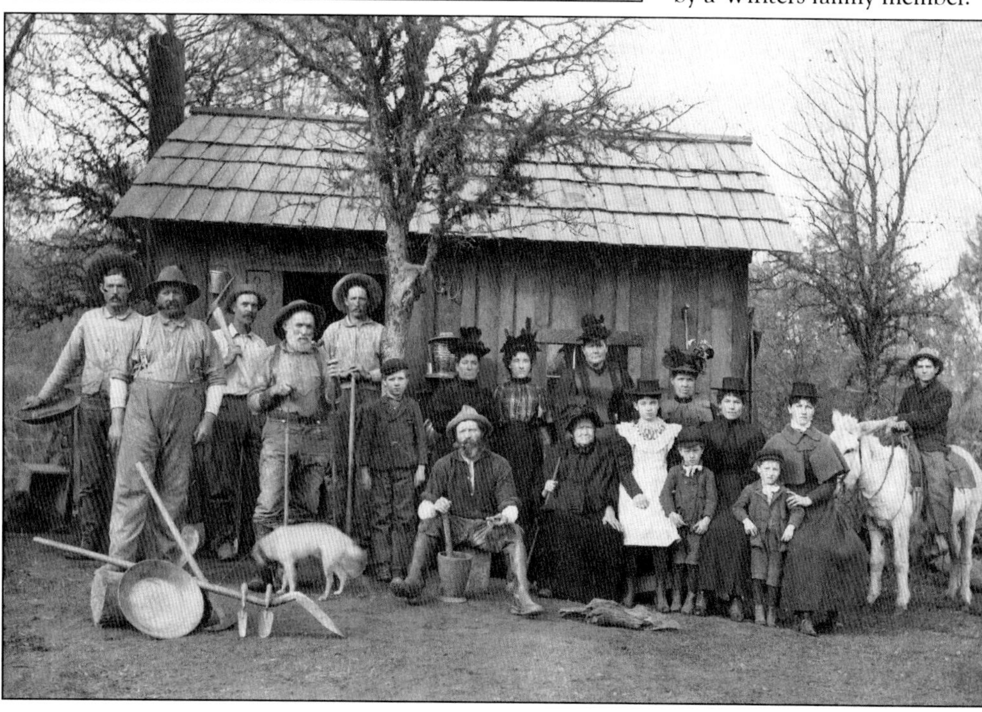

Many extended families moved West together, recognizing that there was strength in numbers given the harsh environment of 19th-century rural California. These unidentified subjects, showing off their mining implements, are likely members of the Winters family, as this photograph was given to the Amador archives by a Winters family member.

A young Thomas Henry Gartlin is pictured here with his mother, Alice. Known as "Judge" Gartlin, he worked at various professions around the Ione Valley, including engineer at a copper mine, hired hand on the Arroyo Seco Ranch, clerk in the store of Charles Dosch, hydraulic miner at Irish Hill, and head farmer at the Preston School. He also served as justice of the peace in Ione for over 16 years.

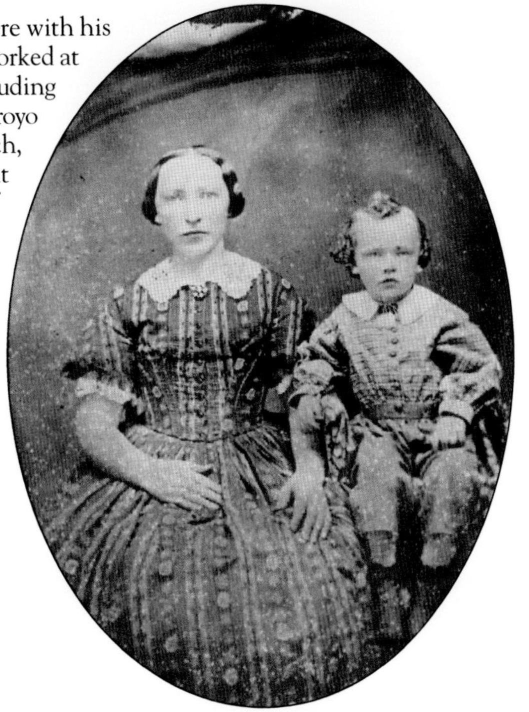

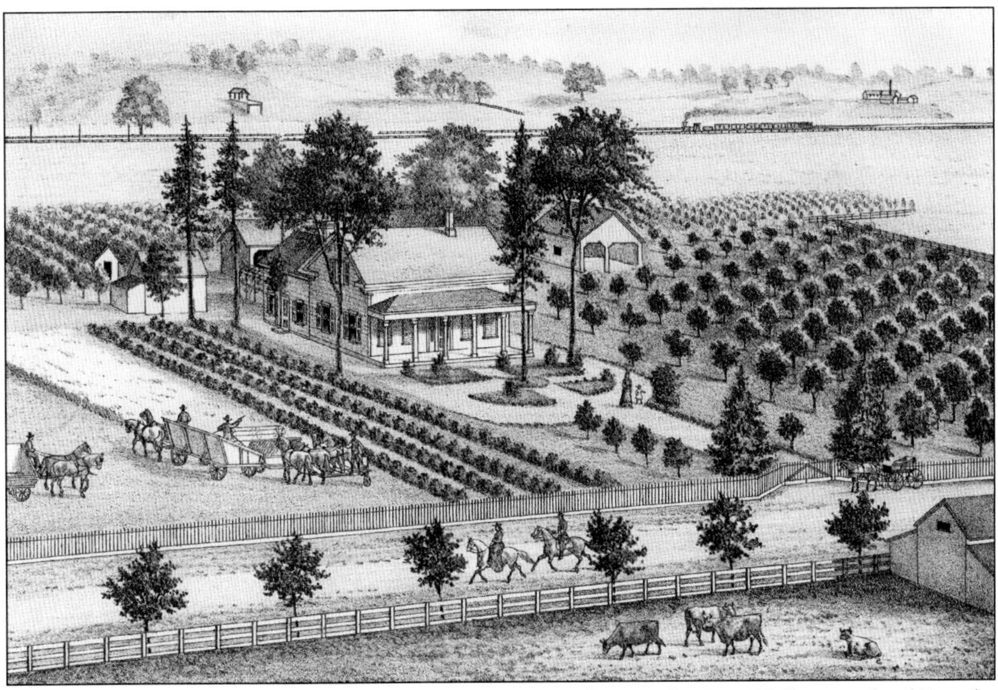

This lithograph from the 1881 *Amador County History* depicts the Ione Valley ranch of Dwight Younglove, who came to California from Massachusetts in 1864. The ranch took in 233 acres of ground and was described in the history as being laid out in "European style with drives and graveled walks bordered with flowers and fragrant herbs . . . being the most artistically improved place in Amador County."

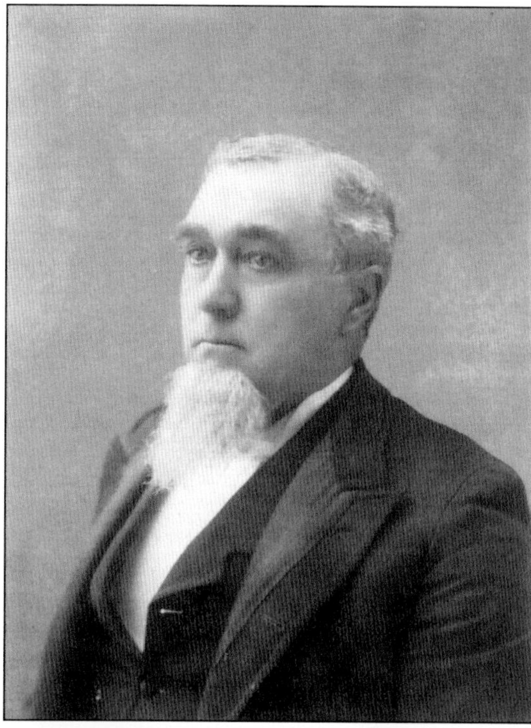

Olney N. Morse was for a time the owner of the locally famous Q Ranch, so named after military Company Q. Morse traveled to California in the 1850s and entered into farming at the Q Ranch in the early 1860s. After losing his home, a barn, and livestock to two different fires, he sold the ranch. Morse ran for state office against A. H. Rose when Sen. G. W. Seaton was killed in the explosion of the steamship *Yosemite*.

The Q Ranch was known far and wide as one of the larger ranches in the Ione Valley and a source of fine livestock and produce. Here both fresh and preserved fruits and vegetables are displayed at a fair or exposition during a centennial celebration of the nation's founding. George Woolsey, who owned ranch in 1876, also ran a general store in Ione.

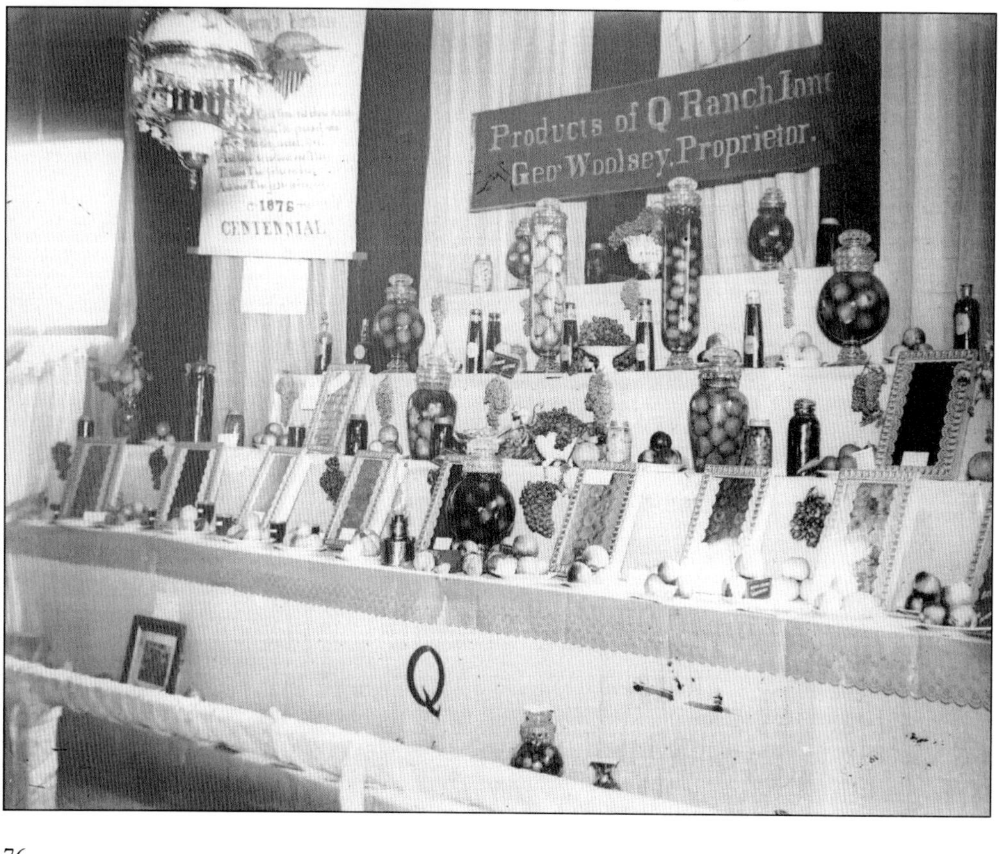

Charles Henry Hoover (left) is seen here with a friend. He was born in the Ione Valley in 1860 to pioneers Daniel Wayne Hoover and Mary Potter Hoover, who came to California in 1853 via wagon train from Pope County, Kentucky. As an adult, Charles worked on Ione ranches for a number of years, but by the age of 40 he had moved on to cowboy in Shasta County, where he died in 1939.

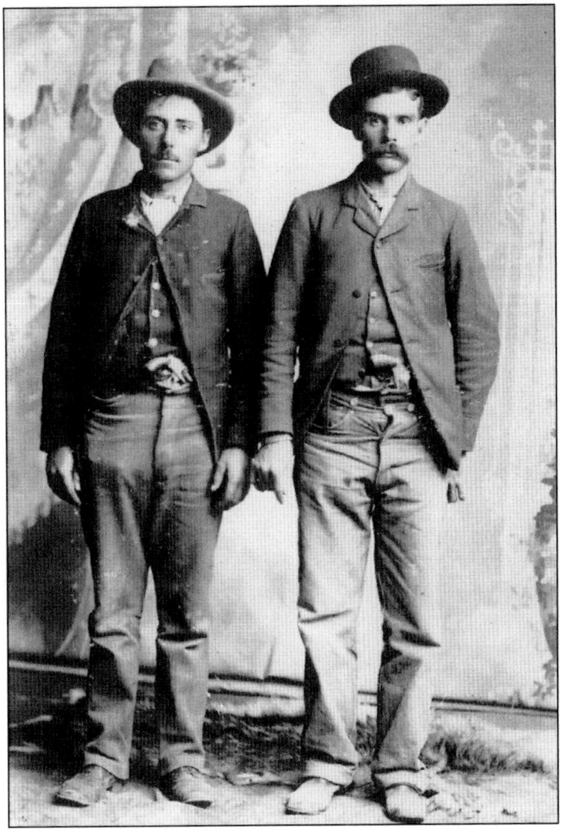

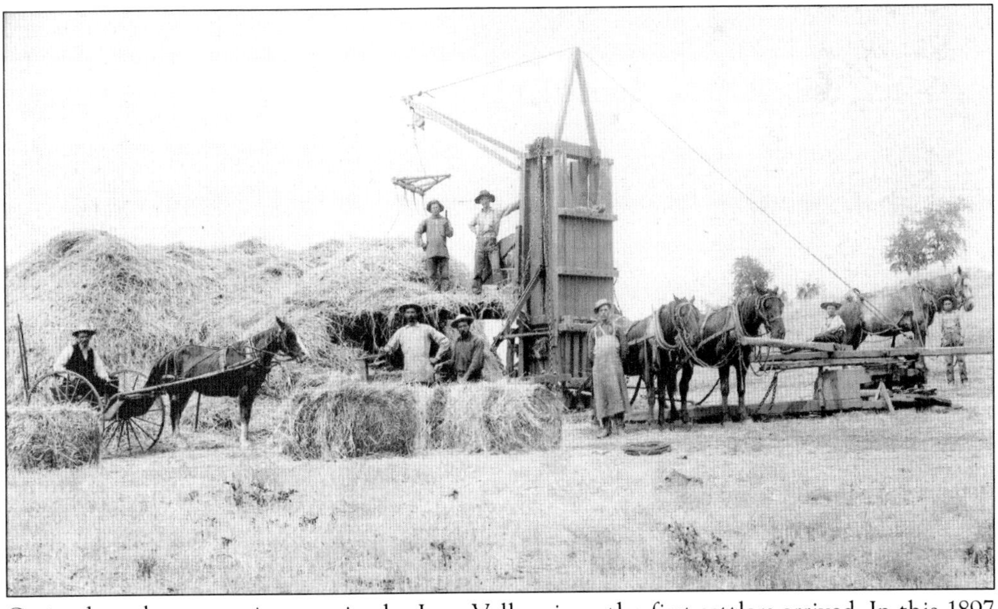

Grains have been a major crop in the Ione Valley since the first settlers arrived. In this 1897 photograph, men are baling hay. "Grandpa" Blodgett stands in the cart, Fred Grover is at left on the ground, Tom Carpenter is at right on the baler, and Bert Grover rides on the turntable. The other three men are unidentified.

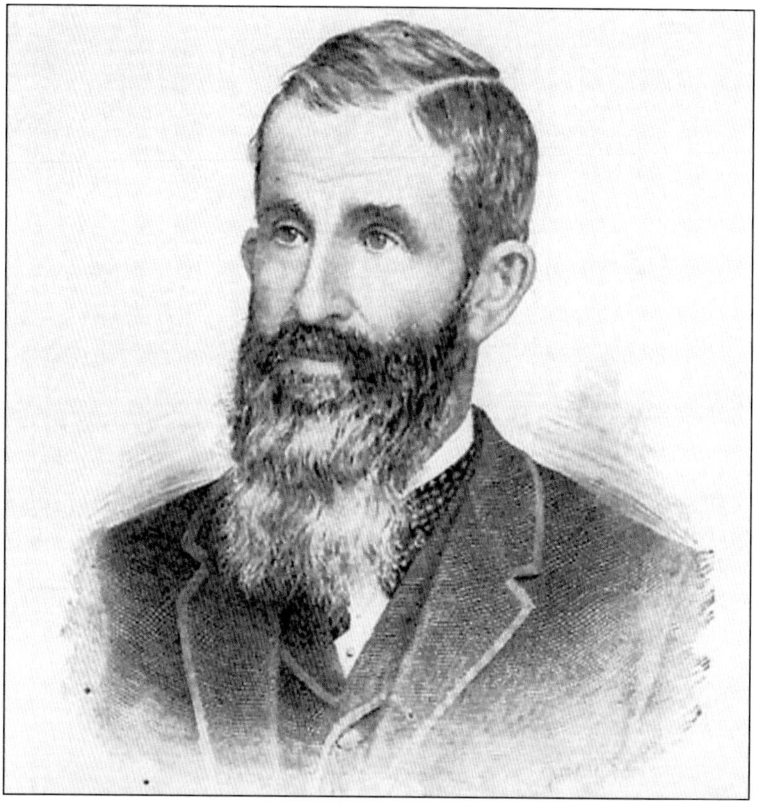

John S. Harbison has long been recognized as California's first and leading beekeeper. What is not well known is that Harbison first engaged in his calling in 1852 in the Ione Valley, where he resided for over a decade until relocating to San Diego in 1869. There, in partnership with R. G. Clark, he arrived with 110 colonies of bees and set up shop. Within seven years, Harbison had become the largest producer of honey in the world.

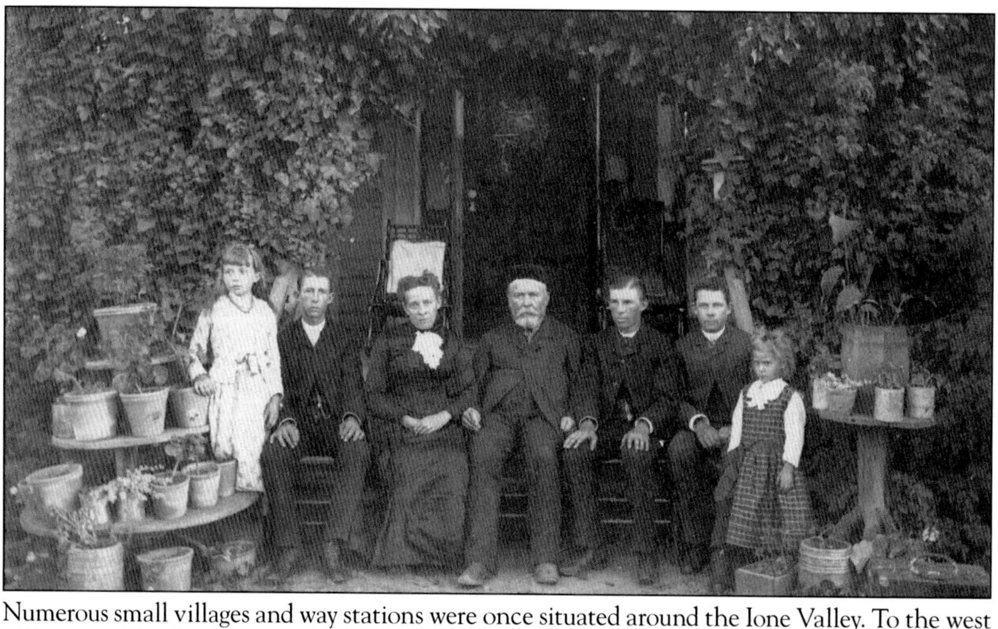

Numerous small villages and way stations were once situated around the Ione Valley. To the west of Ione was Doschville, named for Charles Dosch, pictured here with his family. Not only was it a stage stop with a store, but the town also included a blacksmith shop, a nearby clay mine, and several small farms. Seen from left to right are Annie, Charles Jr., Louisa (their mother), Charles Sr. (their father), Walter, George, and Lottie.

Several small, short-lived mining towns once existed near Ione but were abandoned when the placer gold played out. These included Quincy, its neighbor Muletown on Mule Creek, and Boston Store. Here Quincy residents Sam Allcar (left) and George Folger don blackface and mask to portray theatrical personas of an "Americanized" Native American man and woman. Folger later became the postmaster of Jackson.

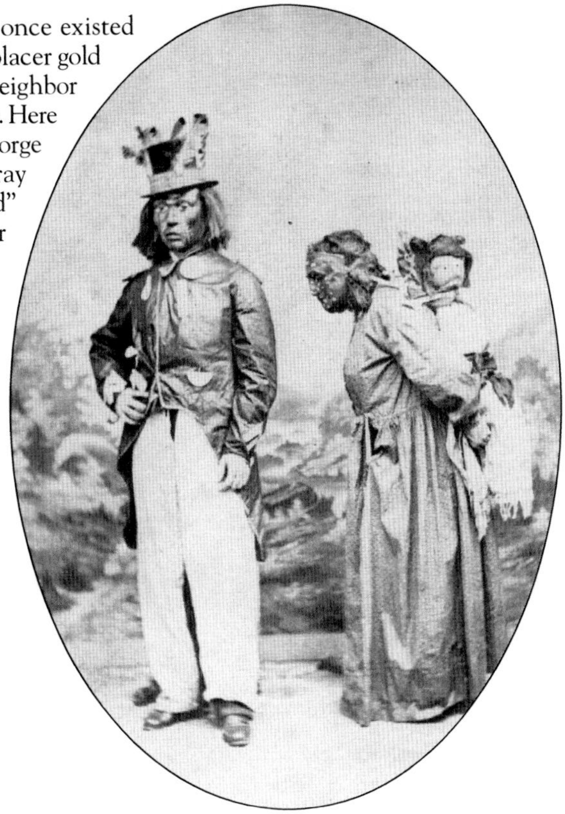

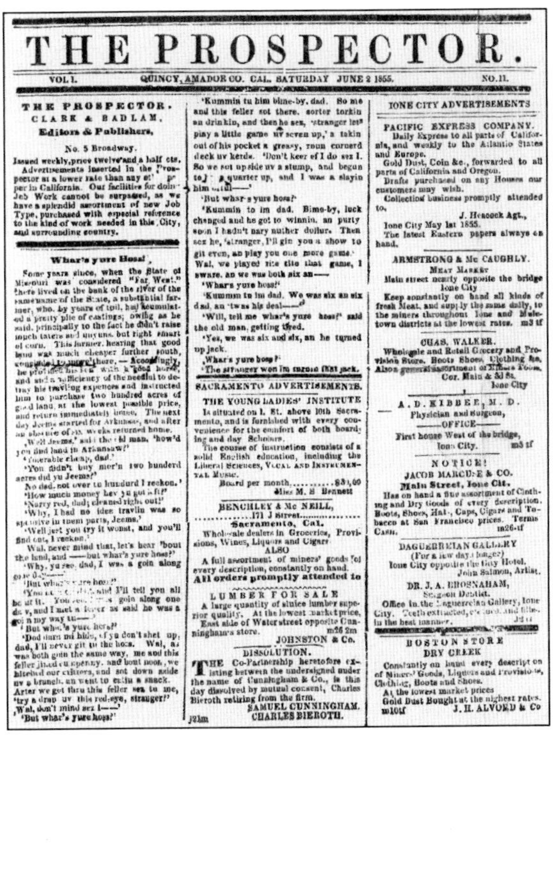

THE PROSPECTOR.

VOL. I. QUINCY, AMADOR CO. CAL. SATURDAY JUNE 2 1855. NO. 11.

THE PROSPECTOR.
CLARK & BADLAM,
Editors & Publishers,

No. 5 Broadway.

Issued weekly, price twelve and a half cts.
Advertisements inserted in the Prospector at a lower rate than any ot[illegible] paper in California. Our facilities for doin[illegible] Job Work cannot be surpassed, as we have a splendid assortment of new Job Type, purchased with especial reference to the kind of work needed in this City, and surrounding country.

Whar's yure Hoss!

Some years since, when the State of Missouri was considered "Far West," there lived on the bank of the river of the same name of the State, a substantial farmer, who, by years of toil, had accumulated a pretty pile of castings; owing as he said, principally to the fact he didn't raise much taters and unyuns, but right smart of corn. This farmer, hearing that good land was much cheaper further south, [illegible] there. — Accordingly, he pro[illegible] his [illegible] with a good horse, and [illegible] a sufficiency of the needful to defray his travling expences and instructed him to purchase two hundred acres of good land, at the lowest possible price, and return immediately home. The next day Jeems started for Arkansas, and after an absence of six weeks returned home.

'Well Jeems,' said the old man, 'how'd you find land in Arkansaw?'
'[illegible]erable cheap, dad.'
'You didn't buy mor'n two hunderd acres did yu Jeems?'
'No dad, not over tu hundurd I reckon.'
'How much money hev yu got left?'
'Narry red, dad; cleaned right out!'
'Why, I had no idee travlin was so [illegible] in them parts, Jeems.'
'Well just you try it wonst, and you'll find out, I reckon.'
'Wal, never mind that, let's hear 'bout the land, and —— but whar's yure hoss?'
'Why, yu see, dad, I was a goin along one day——'
'But whar's yure hoss?'
'You [illegible] and I'll tell you all bout it. You see, I was goin along one day, and I met a feller as said he was a goin my way tu——'
'But whar's yure hoss?'
'Dod darn mi hide, if yu don't shet up, dad, I'll never git to the hoss. Wal, as was both goin the same way, me and this feller jined cumpenny, and bout noon, we hitched our critters, and sot down aside uv a branch, an went to eatin a snack. Arter we got thru this feller sez to me, 'try a drap uv this red-eye, stranger!' Wal, don't mind sez I——'
'But whar's yure hoss?'
'Kummin tu him bime-by, dad. So me and this feller sot there, sorter torkin an drinkin, and then he sez, 'stranger let's play a little game uv seven up,' a takin out of his pocket a greasy, roun cornerd deck uv kerds. 'Don't keer ef I do sez I. So we sot up side uv a stump, and begun to [illegible] a quarter up, and I was a slayin him [illegible]——'
'But whar's yure hoss?'
'Kummin to im dad. Bime-by, luck changed and he got to winnin, an purty soon I hadn't nary nuther dollur. Then sez he, 'stranger, I'll gin you a show to git even, an play you one more game.' Wal, we played rite tite that game, I sware, an we was both six an——
'Whar's yure hoss?'
'Kummin tu im dad. We was six an six dad, an 'twas his deal——'
'Will, tell me whar's yure hoss!' said the old man, getting tired.
'Yes, we was six and six, an he turned up jack.
'Whar's yure hoss?'
'The stranger won im turnin that jack.

SACRAMENTO ADVERTISEMENTS.

THE YOUNG LADIES' INSTITUTE
Is situated on L St. above 10th Sacramento, and is furnished with every convenience for the comfort of both boarding and day Scholars.
The course of instruction consists of a solid English education, including the Liberal Sciences, Vocal and Instrumental Music.
Board per month............$3[illegible],00
Miss M. S Bennett

BENCHLEY & Mc NEILL,
............171 J Street.................
Sacramento, Cal.
Wholesale dealers in Groceries, Provisions, Wines, Liquors and Cigars
ALSO
A full assortment of miners' goods of every description, constantly on hand.
All orders promptly attended to

LUMBER FOR SALE
A large quantity of sluice lumber superior quality. At the lowest market price, East side of Water street opposite Cunningham's store. m26 2m
JOHNSTON & Co.

DISSOLUTION.
THE Co-Partnership heretofore existing between the undersigned under the name of Cunningham & Co., is this day dissolved by mutual consent, Charles Bieroth retiring from the firm.
SAMUEL CUNNINGHAM.
CHARLES BIEROTH.
j2lm

IONE CITY ADVERTISEMENTS

PACIFIC EXPRESS COMPANY.
Daily Express to all parts of California, and weekly to the Atlantic States and Europe.
Gold Dust, Coin &c., forwarded to all parts of California and Oregon.
Drafts purchased on any Houses our customers may wish.
Collection business promptly attended to.
J. Heacock Agt.,
Ione City May 1st 1855.
The latest Eastern papers always on hand.

ARMSTRONG & Mc CAUGHLY.
Meat Market
Main street nearly opposite the bridge
Ione City
Keep constantly on hand all kinds of fresh Meat, and supply the same daily, to the miners throughout Ione and Muletown districts at the lowest rates. m3 tf

CHAS. WALKER.
Wholesale and Retail Grocery and Provision Store. Boots Shoes, Clothing &c. Also a general assortment of [illegible]
Cor. Main & 3d St.
Ione City

A. D. KIBBEE, M. D.
Physician and Surgeon,
——OFFICE——
First house West of the bridge,
Ione City. m5 tf

NOTICE!
JACOB MARCUSE & CO.
Main Street, Ione Cit.
Has on hand a fine assortment of Clothing and Dry Goods of every description. Boots, Shoes, Hats, Caps, Cigars and Tobacco at San Francisco prices. Terms Cash. m26-tf

DAGUERREIAN GALLERY
(For a few days longer)
Ione City opposite the City Hotel.
John Salmon, Artist.

DR. J. A. BROSNAHAM,
Surgeon Dentist.
Office in the Daguerreian Gallery, Ione City. Teeth extracted, [illegible] and filled in the best manner. [illegible]

BOSTON STORE
DRY CREEK
Constantly on hand every description of Miners' Goods, Liquors and Provisions, Clothing, Boots and Shoes.
At the lowest market prices
Gold Dust Bought at the highest rates.
m10tf J. H. ALVORD & Co

Quincy even boasted a newspaper, the *Prospector*, which was founded in 1855 by Alexander Badlam, M. B. Clark, and W. I. Wallace, who printed the weekly on an outdoor press. A limited number of issues were published, and like the town itself, the paper was just a memory by 1856, when all inhabitants had moved away.

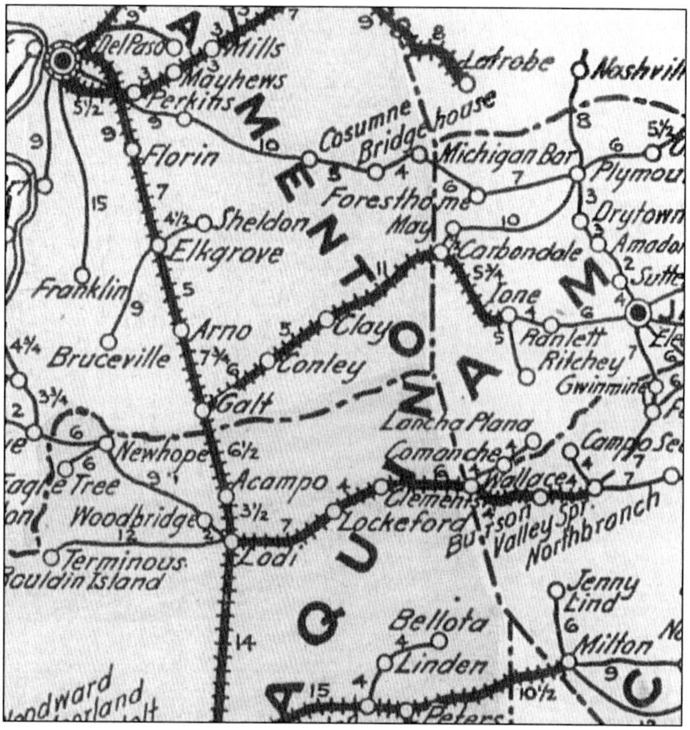

In 1876, the Central Pacific Railroad built the Amador Branch Railroad, a 27.2-mile line from Galt to Carbondale, and then extended it into Ione. This now-defunct line connected to the main line in the Sacramento Valley and was first used to haul coal for locomotives on the Central Pacific. In 1904, the Ione and Eastern Railroad was built into Martell, extending rail service into Central Amador County.

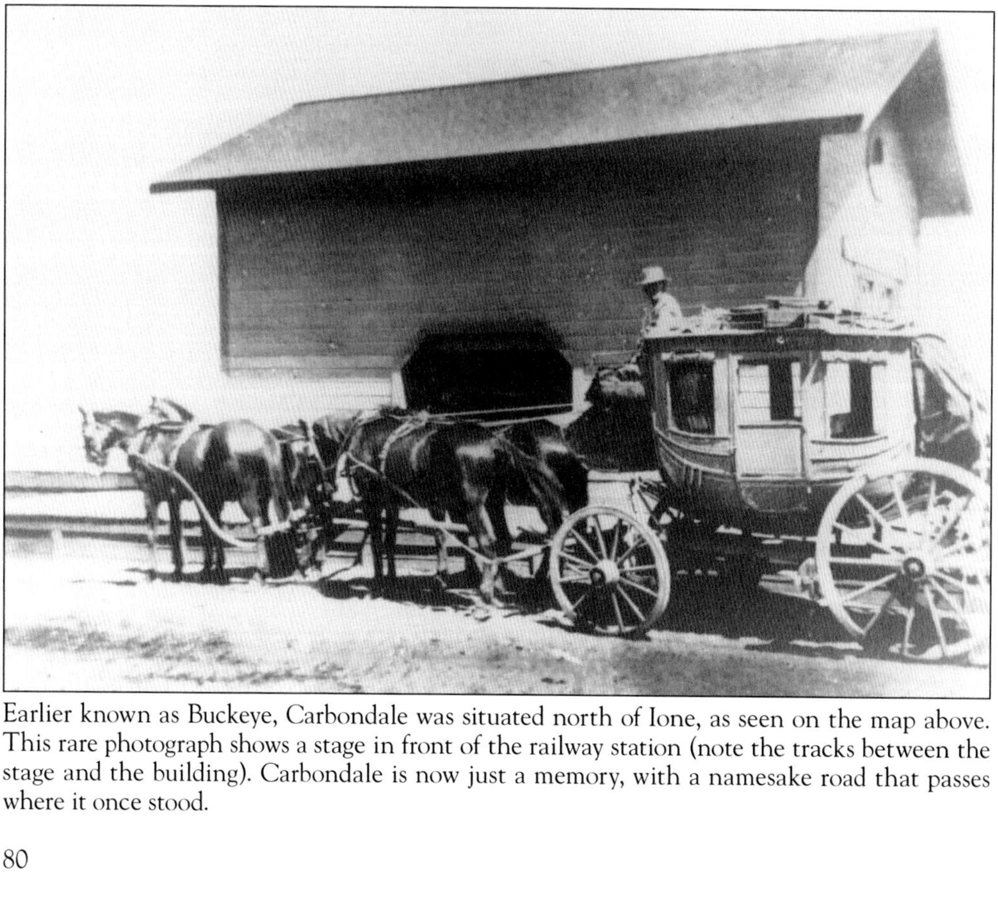

Earlier known as Buckeye, Carbondale was situated north of Ione, as seen on the map above. This rare photograph shows a stage in front of the railway station (note the tracks between the stage and the building). Carbondale is now just a memory, with a namesake road that passes where it once stood.

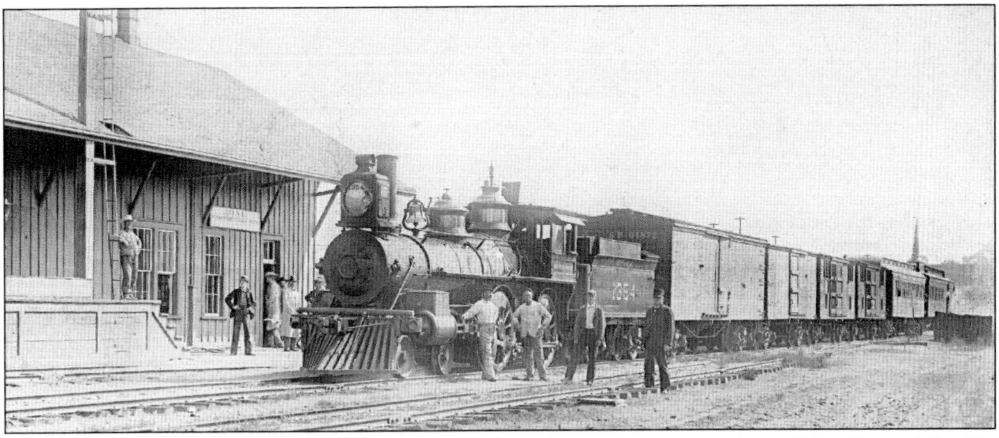

The Ione railroad station was a bustling place when the trains were running. The Central Pacific Railroad Company operated the Amador Branch Railroad from 1876 through 1885, when it was taken over by Southern Pacific. In 1888, the line was consolidated into the Northern Railway but eventually again became part of the Southern Pacific system.

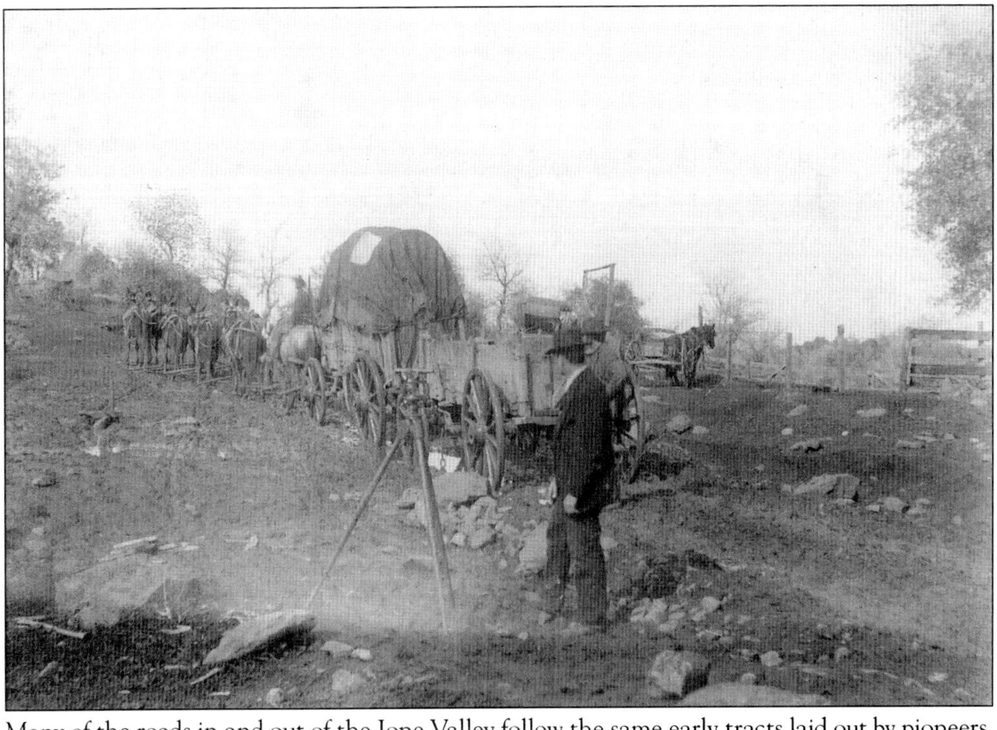

Many of the roads in and out of the Ione Valley follow the same early tracts laid out by pioneers. The main route to Jackson, the Ione-Jackson Road (now State Route 88), has been in use since the 1850s. In this 1860s photograph, a crew surveys the route of the road over the ridge known as Hurricane Hill.

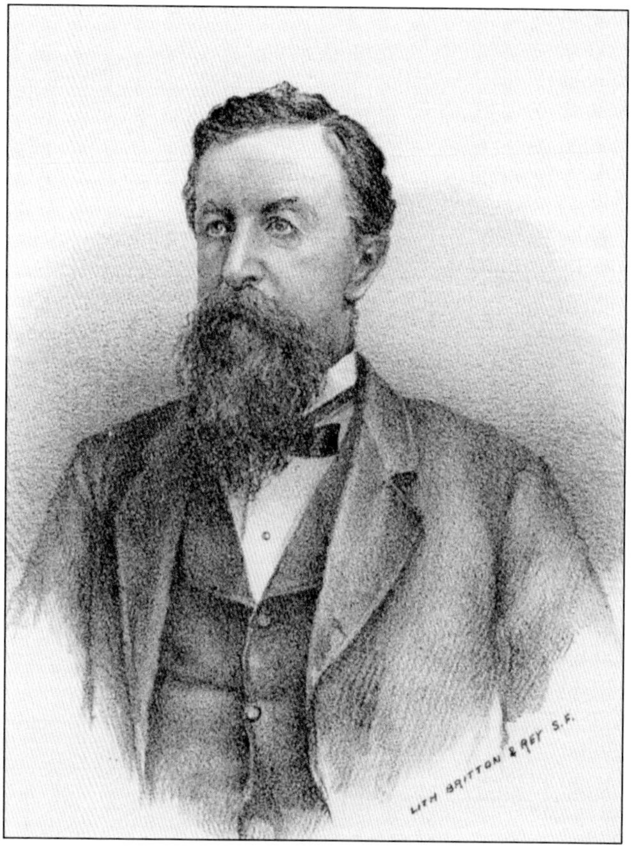

John Vogan came to California in 1849 and engaged in the stage line business with William Green, who had purchased the Q Ranch in 1853. The business was called the Forest Line but was known locally as the Ione Valley Stage Lines, running from Sacramento to Sonora via the Q Ranch. Vogan also served successive terms as sheriff from 1875 to 1882.

A hollow stone shell is all that remains of the Bonham family's statuesque home, which stood among the rolling hills of the Mount Echo District, just beyond the Ione Valley. Here James Bonham raised five children with his first wife, Amanda Melvin Fenwick Bonham. Nearby are the remnants of a stone lime kiln built and operated by Bonham.

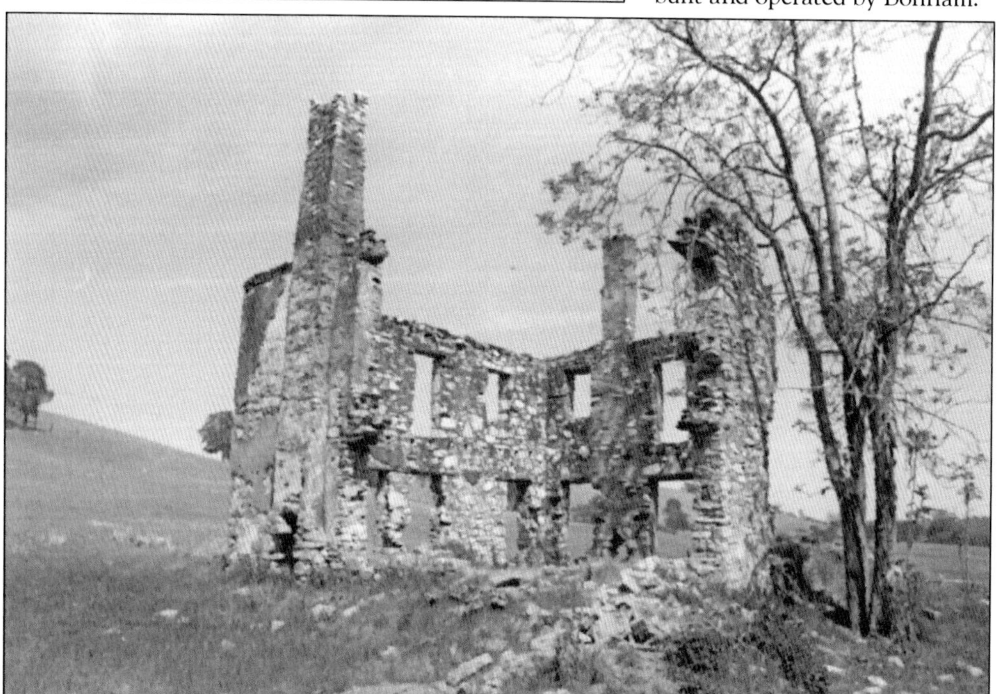

Seven

Traditions and Amusements

There is nothing quite as fine as a picnic in the park, a parade down Main Street, or simply lounging around on a warm afternoon in the shade of a big oak tree. Since the beginning of recorded history, people have sought fraternization, entertainment, and relaxation to ease the stresses of life. From the rural farm community to large cities, membership in fraternal organizations and social clubs give people a sense of belonging. Special occasions celebrated on a community level fulfill people's desire to participate in culture socially and provide another stitch in the tapestry that weaves humans' lives together.

At the onset of the Gold Rush, people from around the globe flocked to California, bringing with them traditional ways to celebrate various occasions; however, upon arrival, they found that many of the old ways would not fit into their new home, and so they formed new traditions. Likewise, many had the desire to belong in some way—beyond simply living in a new community—and thus formed their own chapters of fraternal organizations and benevolent societies. Ione had both Odd Fellows and Masonic Lodges, as well as burlesque groups, such as the Knights of the Assyrian Cross and E. Clampus Vitus. Many of the annual celebrations and festivals were supported by these organizations. In Ione, the annual homecoming picnic, which began as a centennial celebration of our nation's independence, is now a traditional event every spring. Holidays and other special occasions are also marked by the community throughout the year.

From the time when traveling troupes of actors made brief stops in Gold Rush towns to the heyday of the cowboy western on the silver screen, the citizens of Ione and the surrounding area have known how to entertain themselves. Every year, on the first Sunday in June, the town invites all to sit on the sidewalk and watch the homecoming parade entries pass by, and each December the young and old delight in all the bright lights of Christmas that glow along "Candy Cane Lane," a few blocks from the business district. Ione is truly a place of tradition and amusement.

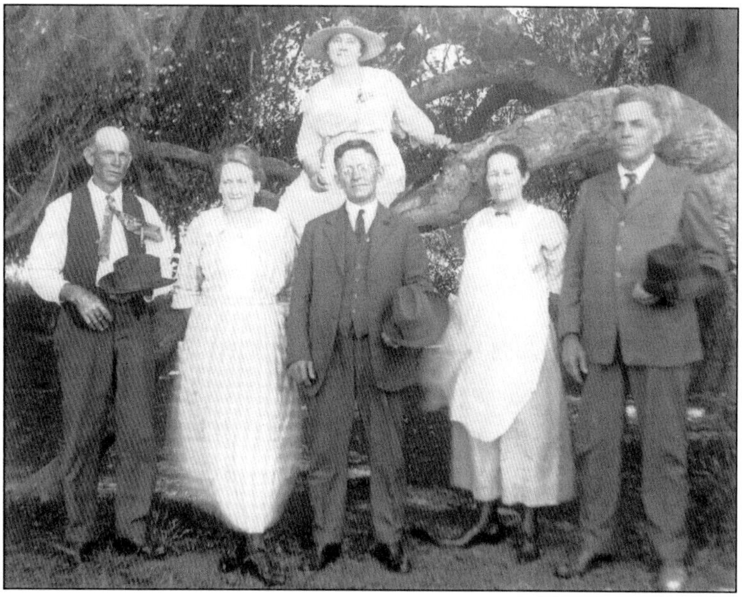

In place since the 1876 centennial, the Ione Homecoming started as a community picnic and has grown into a weekend-long festival. Members of the general committee of the first homecoming picnic have gathered here. Pictured from left to right are Fred Kirk, Susie Amick, George Yager, Hattie Heindel, and John W. Joses. Seated on the tree branch behind them is Cloudy Strong.

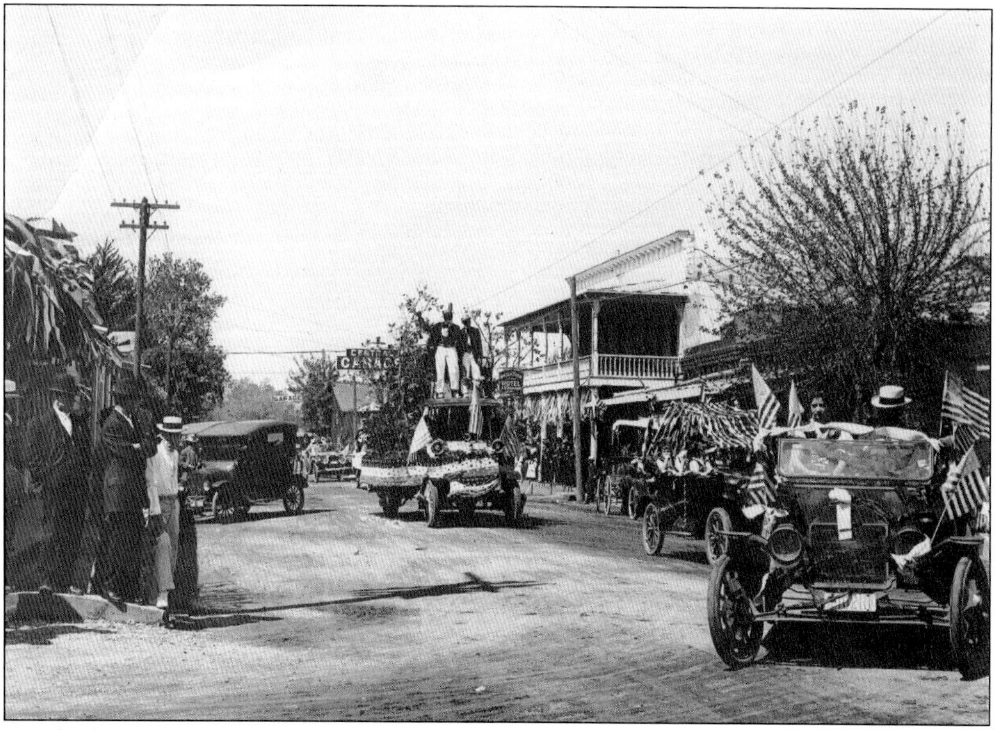

Parades have long been popular in Ione, with several occurring during the year to celebrate various holidays. In this 1920s photograph, cars carry revelers down Main Street during a Fourth of July celebration.

What would a fair or celebration be like without exhibits of domestic arts by the ladies of the community? These floral displays adorn a hall in Ione at the 1876 centennial celebration of the nation's independence. Toward the back are members of the picnic committee.

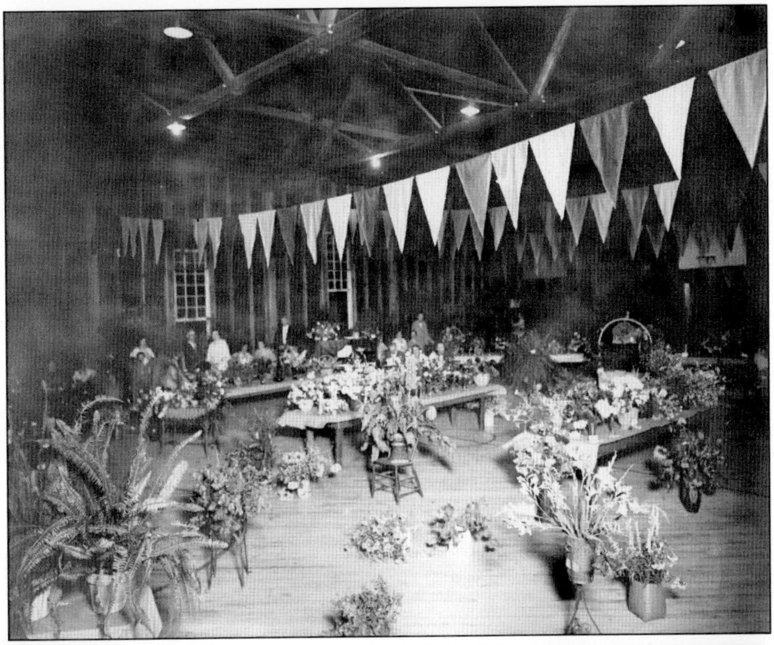

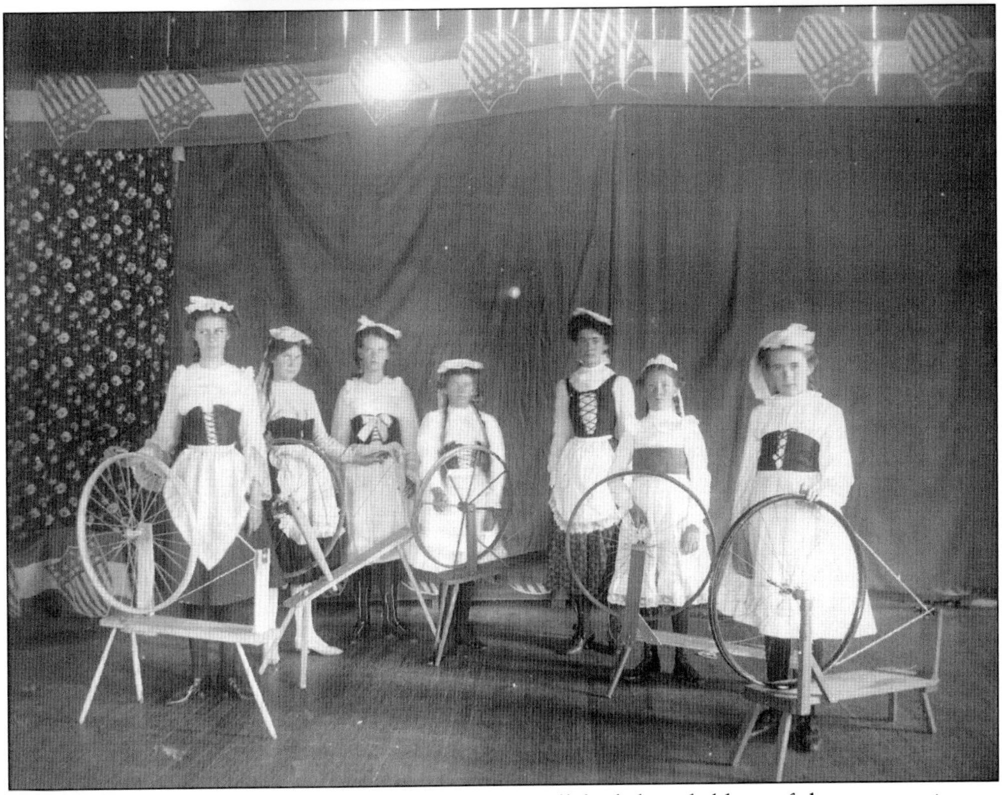

When visiting Ione during special occasions, one will find that children of the community are at the forefront of the celebration. Here girls don Colonial attire and pose with spinning wheels at a celebration of a patriot holiday in the late 1800s. Note the shields with stars and stripes decorating the stage above the girls' heads.

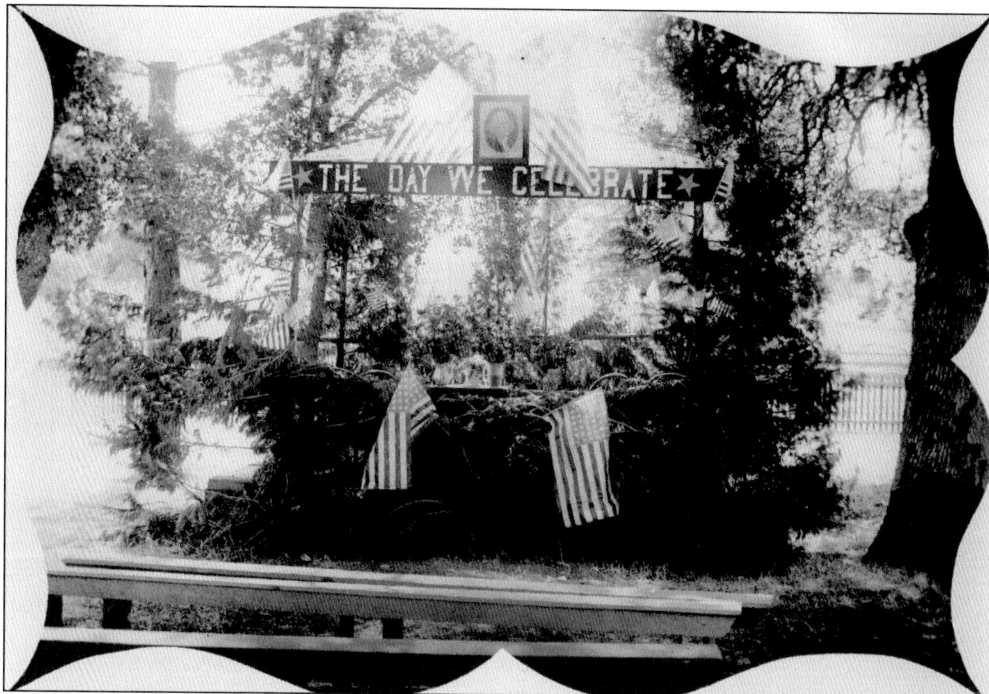

Birthdays of the founding fathers were cause for celebration during the good old days. In this 1860s photograph, the stage is set in Ione for guests of honor and speech making at a birthday party for George Washington. With the hectic pace of life these days, small-town festivities such as these seem to be more the rarity than the norm.

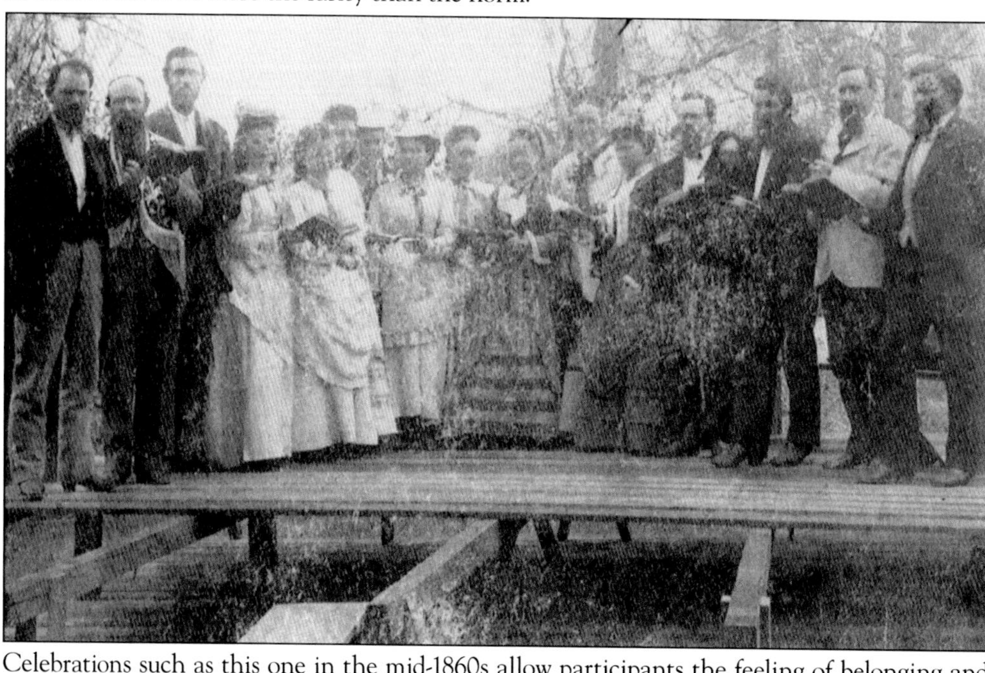

Celebrations such as this one in the mid-1860s allow participants the feeling of belonging and reinforce the solidarity of the community as a whole. This group may have come together to rejoice over the building of a new church, as it appears that they may be holding hymnals.

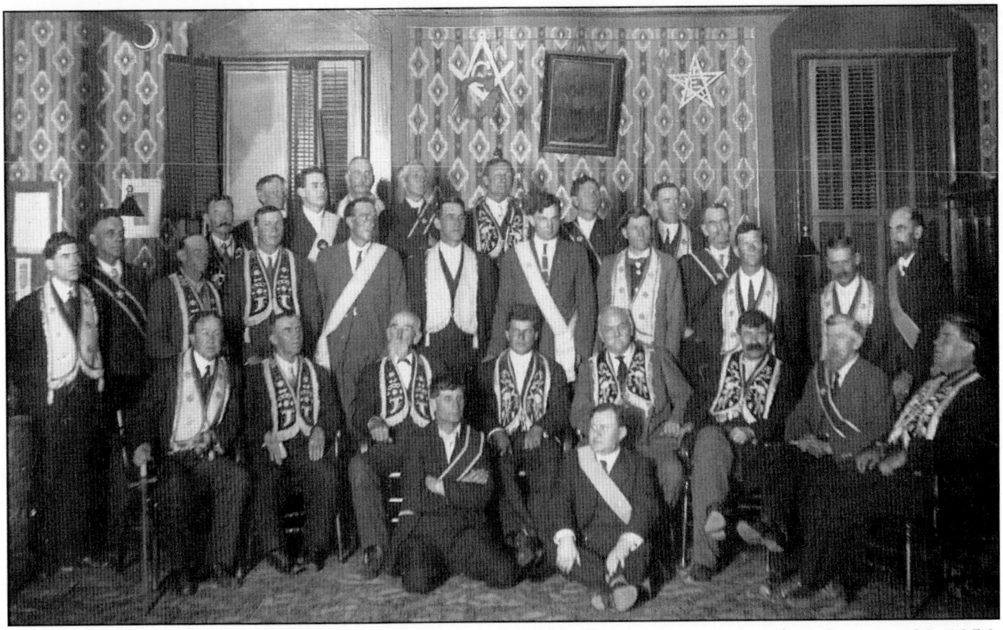

Ione Lodge No. 51 of the International Order of Odd Fellows was instituted on January 29, 1856, by John Doble, a charter member of Volcano Lodge No. 25. Doble is also known for his diaries, which are a rich source of Amador history. In 1868, working jointly with the Ione Masonic Lodge, the Odd Fellows erected a hall on Main Street. In 1976, dwindling membership forced the Ione Lodge to consolidate with Jackson Lodge No. 36.

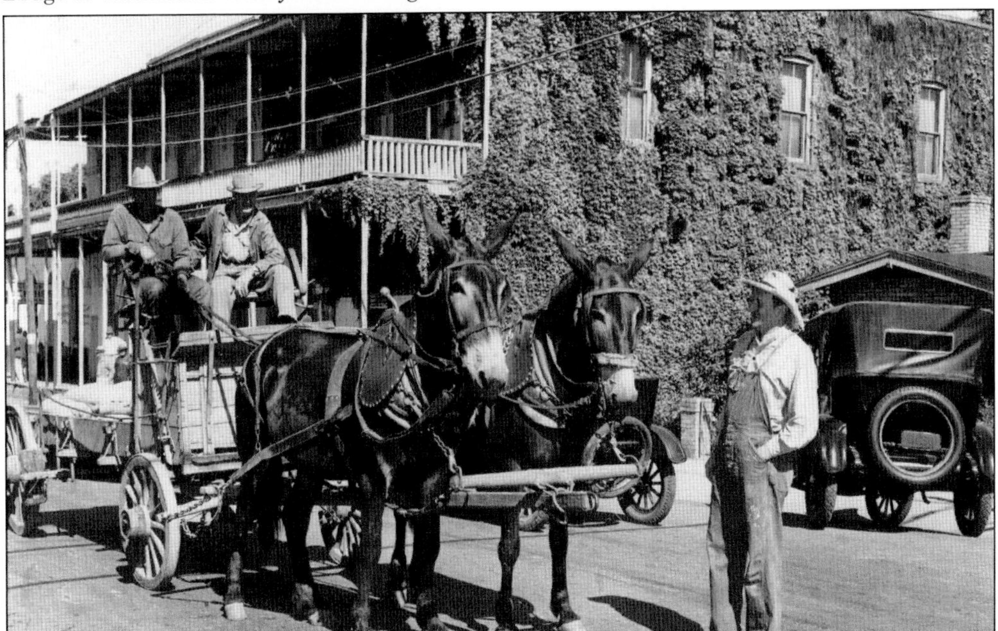

Hollywood has come to Amador County on many occasions, and the picturesque, old-town setting of Ione is a favorite of directors. Harold Colburn (right), who worked as an extra in the 1956 film *Come Next Spring*, looks over the mules used in the movie. For a time, Colburn owned the drugstore in Ione.

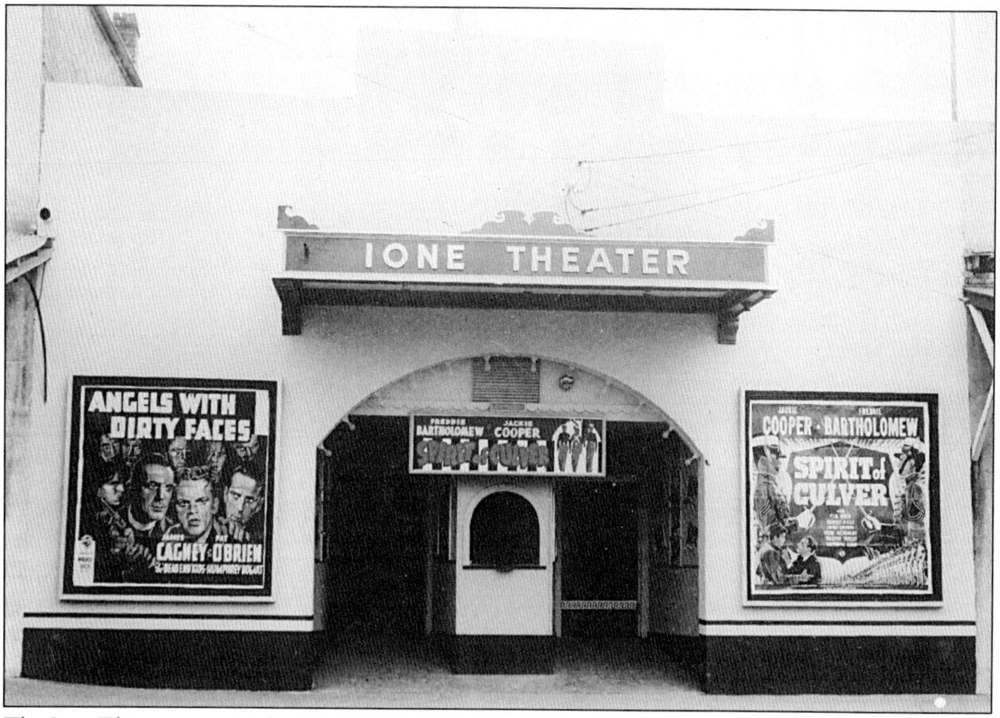

The Ione Theatre, pictured in 1938, was once a popular spot for young and old alike. Unfortunately, it has now gone the way of many other small-town movie houses and is no longer in operation. Ionians must travel to Jackson, Sacramento, or Stockton to enjoy the latest blockbusters.

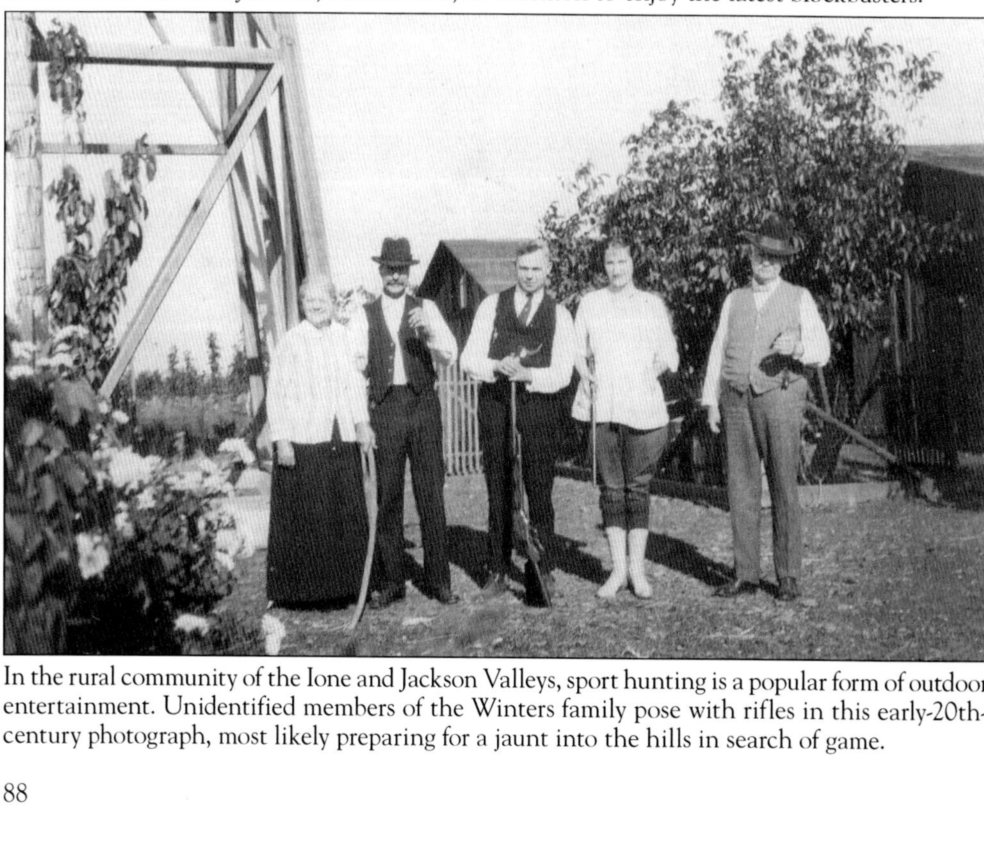

In the rural community of the Ione and Jackson Valleys, sport hunting is a popular form of outdoor entertainment. Unidentified members of the Winters family pose with rifles in this early-20th-century photograph, most likely preparing for a jaunt into the hills in search of game.

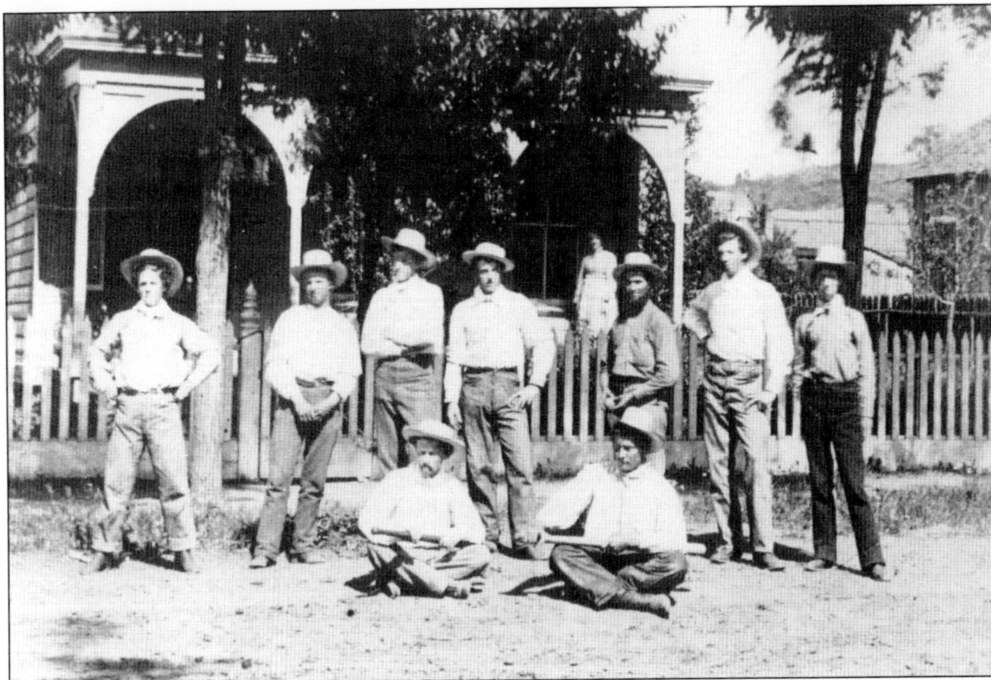

Nearly all Gold Rush communities had a baseball team—and often more than one. Ione Baseball Club players pose with a confident air, especially the slugger on the left, in this c. 1875 photograph.

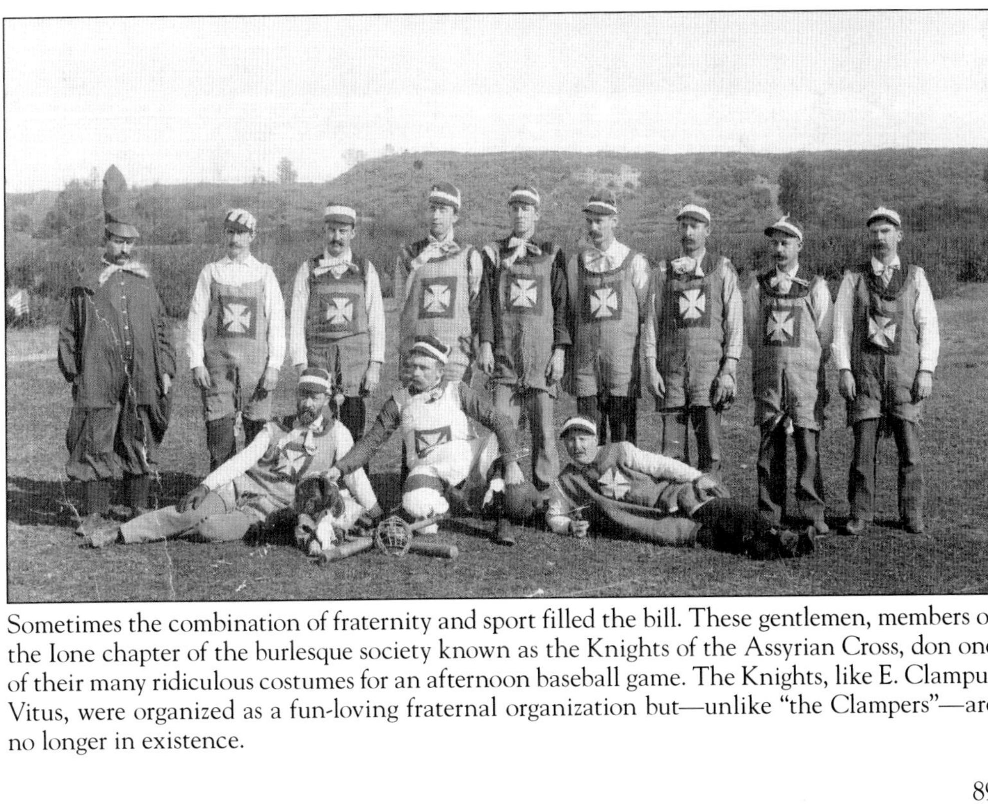

Sometimes the combination of fraternity and sport filled the bill. These gentlemen, members of the Ione chapter of the burlesque society known as the Knights of the Assyrian Cross, don one of their many ridiculous costumes for an afternoon baseball game. The Knights, like E. Clampus Vitus, were organized as a fun-loving fraternal organization but—unlike "the Clampers"—are no longer in existence.

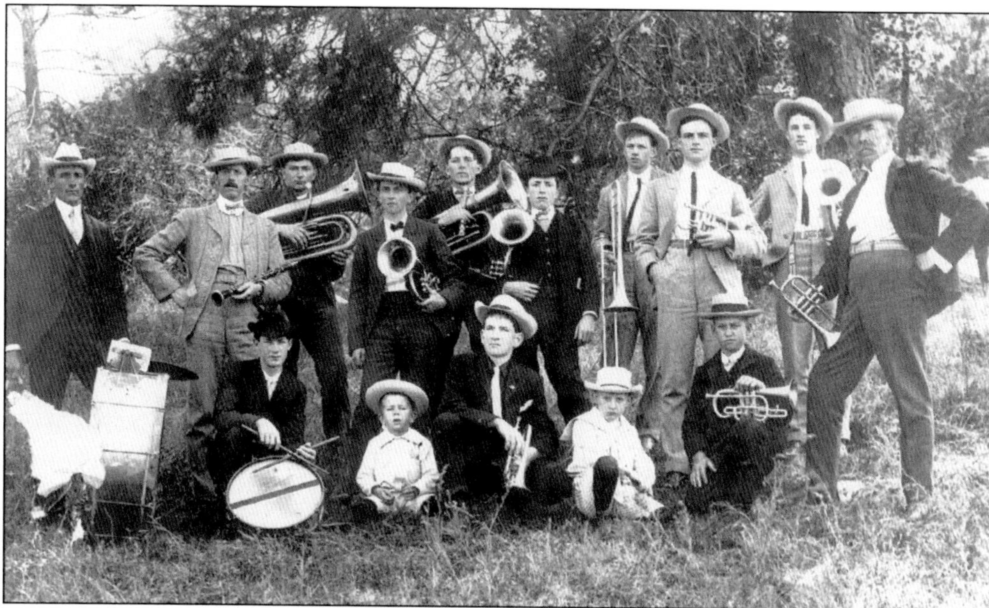

The Ione Boys Band performed at many local special events. Members pictured here are, from left to right: (first row) Albert Grover, ? Palmer, E. "Doc" Adams, ? Fairchild, and Herbert Fairchild; (second row) Paul Winters, unidentified, Arthur Winters, Ed Hawkins, Harry Burris, Carl Isaacs, Albert Sutherland, Edwin Waddell, Harold Waddell, and leader Mr. Palmer. This photograph was taken *c.* 1900.

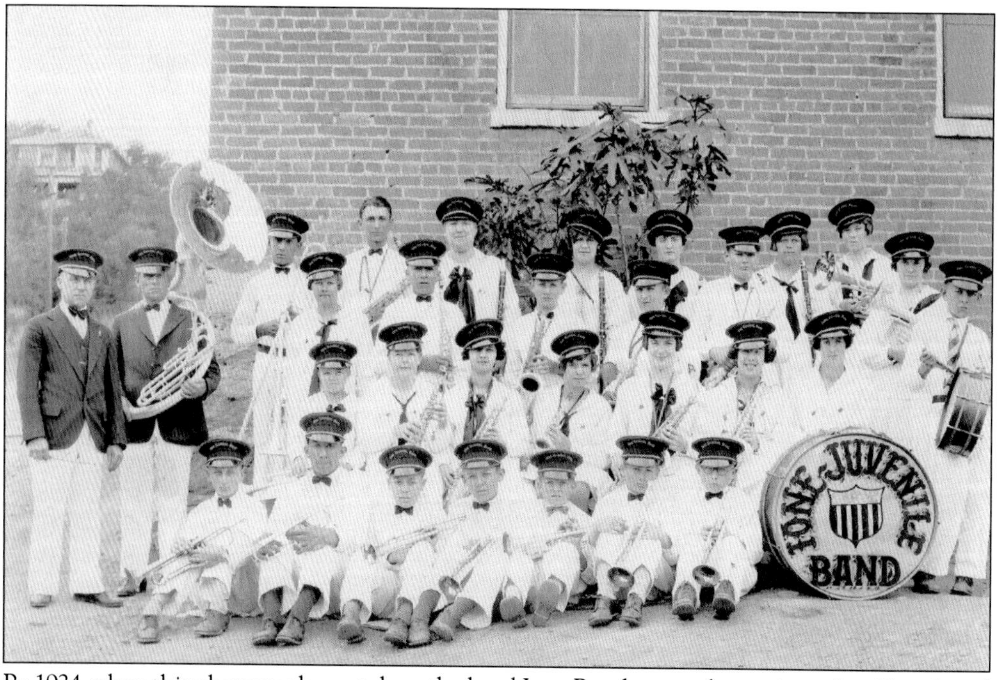

By 1924, when this photograph was taken, the local Ione Band was no longer just a boys' band, and the name had been changed to the Ione Juvenile Band. Although the author has identifications for all band members, the space allotted here is not enough to list them all. This photograph was taken outside the old Ione Elementary School.

Eight

The Jackson Valley and Beyond

Beneath the shadow of the Buena Vista Buttes stretches a fertile landscape known as the Jackson Valley. First inhabited by the native Miwok people, it became home to Gold Rush immigrants and was included in the controversial Arroyo Seco Land Grant. The first non-native settler to the valley, known as "Old Man Hitchcock," arrived sometime in the 1840s. In 1848, he sold his land to a man named Diggs, who set up a trading post and went into the beef business. Diggs sold out a year later to New Yorkers Charles Stone, Warren Nimms, and Fletcher Baker. By 1860, most of the land had been taken up in the valley, and settlement extended south to Boston Store and on down to the Mokelumne River. In addition to traditional ranching and farming, the valley has become home to several large vineyards and winery operations.

The search for gold in this area was concentrated to the south along the banks of the Mokelumne River. Mining camps like Camp Opra, Camp Union, and Lancha Plana, which sprang up between the valley and the river, are now but a memory. Within the Jackson Valley, minerals such as clay, coal, and sand were profitable commodities.

Today the Jackson Valley is also well known for its recreational offerings. It can be said that the heart of the valley is at Buena Vista, the four-corner settlement situated at the intersection of the two main roads passing through the valley. The Buena Vista tavern, a favorite meeting place for locals, has stood on this spot for over 100 years and is now accompanied by a restaurant and small store. Within several miles from Buena Vista are three lakes offering first-class outdoor recreation to both locals and visitors. A drive through this beautiful landscape will surely lure the visitor back again and again to enjoy both the scenery and the friendliness of the inhabitants.

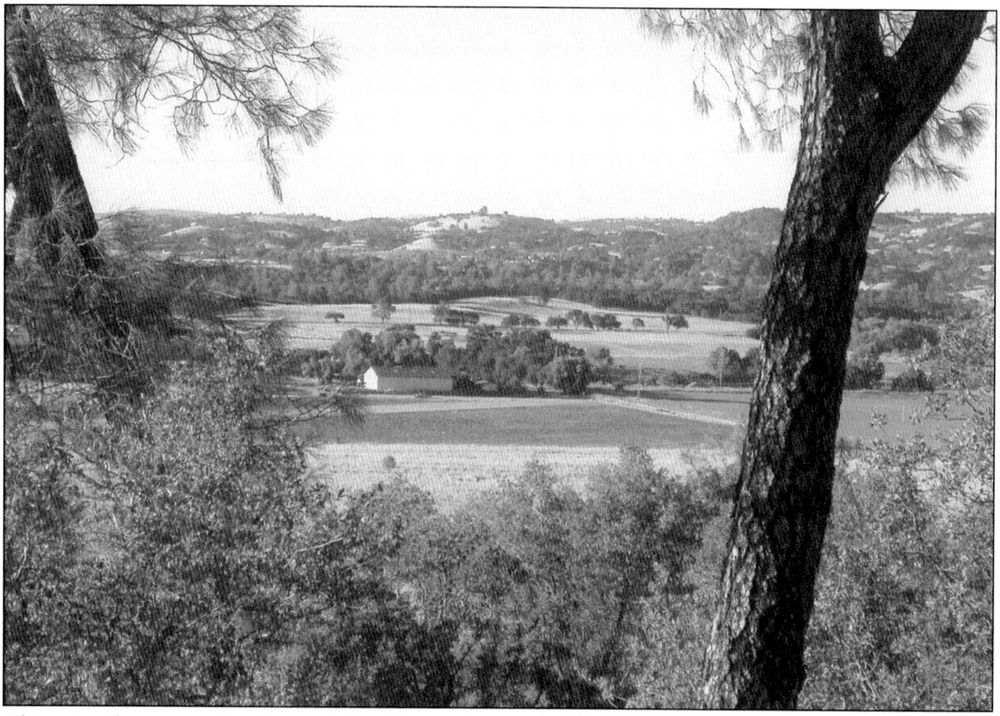

This view from atop the Buena Vista Buttes shows the Jackson Valley landscape and its bucolic atmosphere. With the exception of modern roads and homes, it remains much the same as it did a century ago. The barn at the center is located at the Waters ranch. Members of the Waters family have lived in the valley for more than 100 years. (Author's collection.)

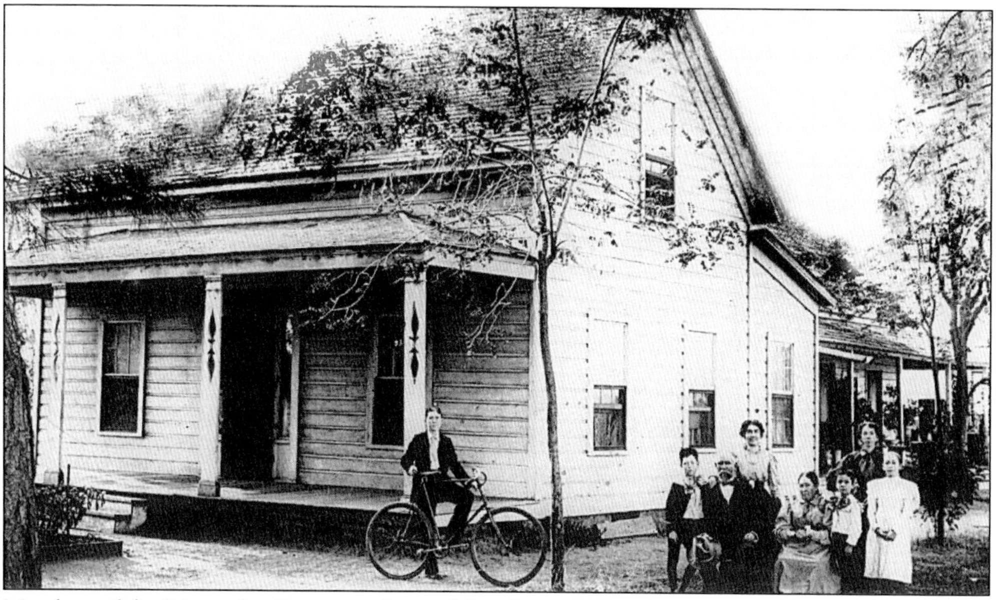

Members of the Ringer family pose in front of their home at Buena Vista. Jonathan Ringer traveled to the Jackson Valley in 1857. Shown from left to right are Albert Jonathan Ringer, Harrison George Ringer, Jonathan Ringer, Mary Amanda Ringer, Emily Elizabeth Ringer, Frank Maurice Ringer, Aida Elizabeth Ringer, and Alma Valentine Ringer Hart.

The Du Frene family has been livestock ranchers in the Jackson Valley for more than 100 years. W. D. Du Frene, the first to settle here, suffered through the land controversy over the Arroyo Seco Grant land. His son John Quincy Du Frene, known as a prosperous farmer, raised a family of four daughters and four sons. All of his sons became successful cattlemen. Eugene Du Frene, a descendant of this fine family, lives in the valley and carries on the tradition of raising livestock to this date.

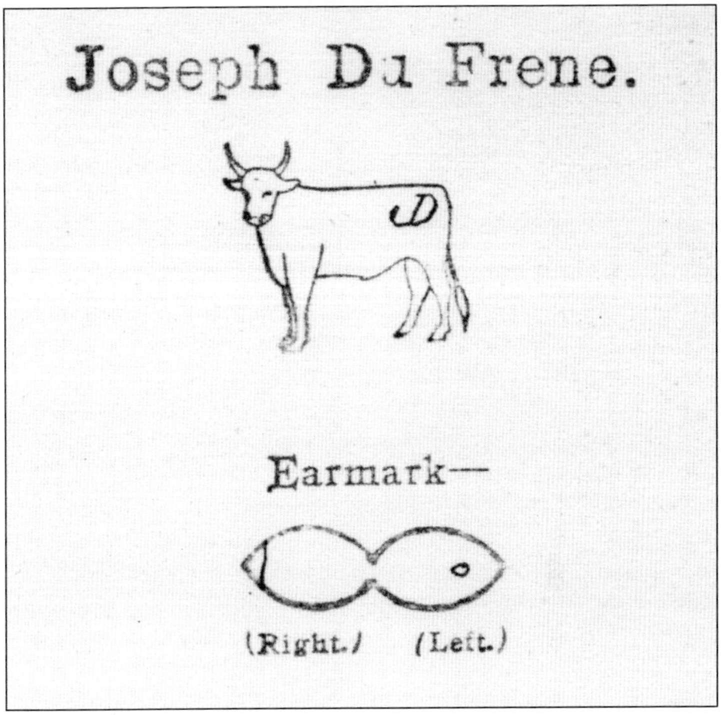

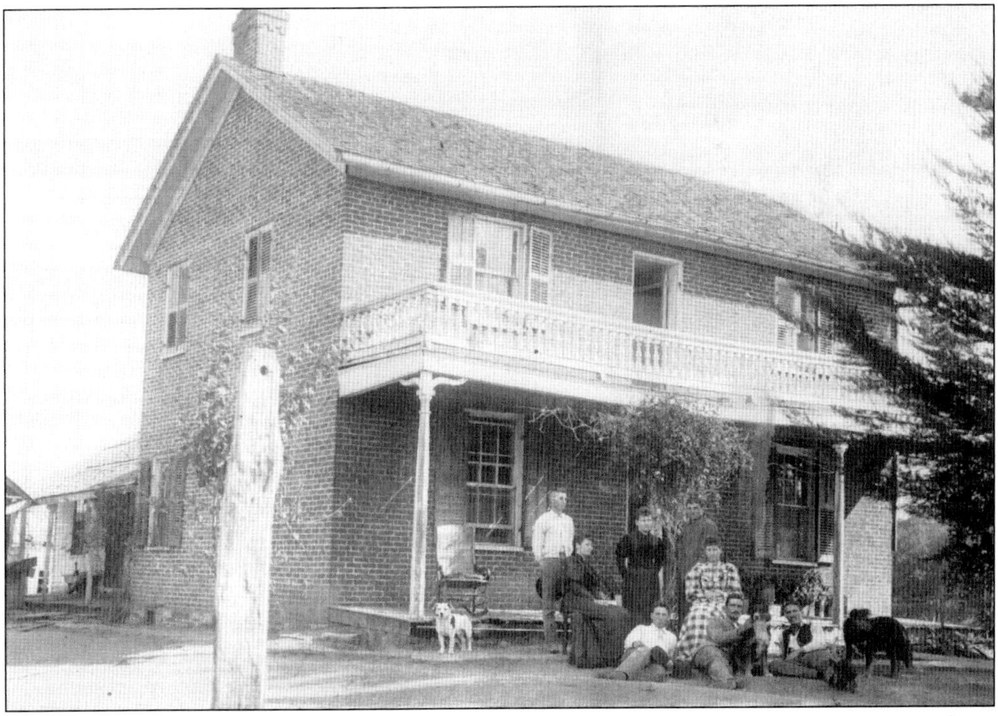

The Thompsons were another family who settled in the Jackson Valley in the early days. About 1860, William Carroll Thompson built this brick home, which still stands today near Buena Vista. Pictured here from left to right are George, Flora, Mary, William, Jane Thompson, James Rickey, and Homer and Cornelius Thompson.

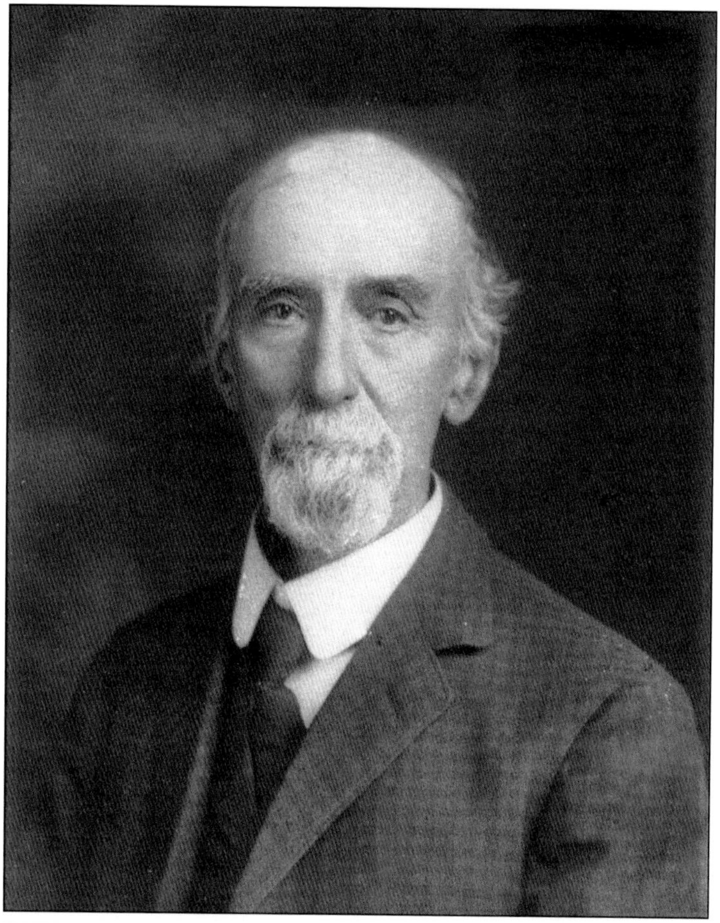

Many Argonauts immigrated to California in search of gold, but others came for land. Native Ohioan Christopher Columbus "C. C." Prouty arrived in California as a 12-year-old boy with his parents and siblings. The family traveled west in 1852, but close to the destination, C. C. lost his father to illness near Devil's Gate in eastern California. Following the family tradition of farming, he settled on a tract of land at the west end of the Jackson Valley along the banks of Jackson Creek. Two of his brothers, John and Simon, also took up land and farmed nearby. C. C. married Australia Bennett and fathered 14 children. Below, workers harvest hay on the C. C. Prouty ranch.

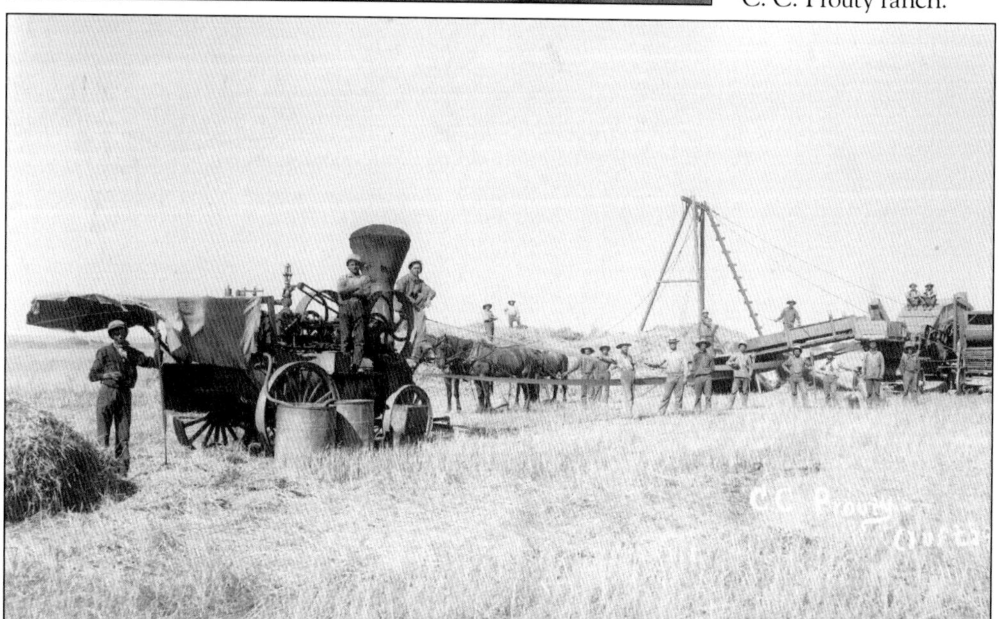

For over 150 years, Buena Vista has been the location of a store in the Jackson Valley. John Fitzsimmons, who came to the valley from Poverty Bar, purchased the store from William C. Richey in 1860 and operated it for more than 10 years. He also served as postmaster at Buena Vista and owned a large tract of ranch land in the valley, on which his descendants mined a great deal of coal.

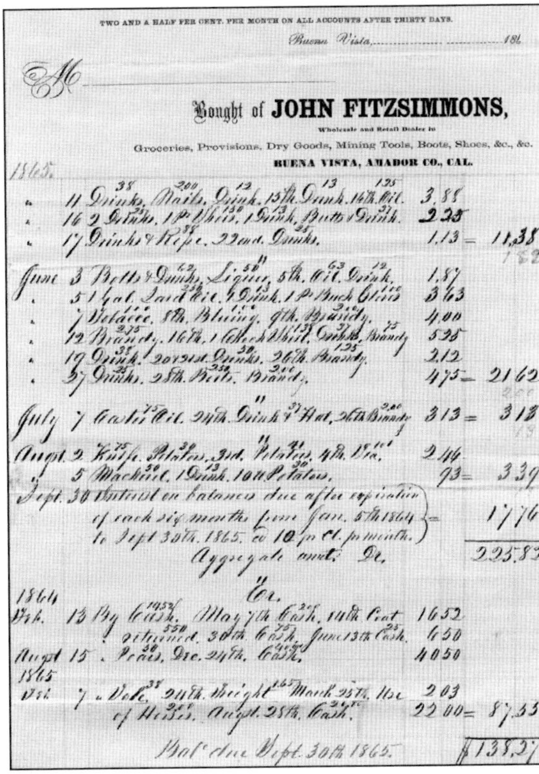

TWO AND A HALF PER CENT. PER MONTH ON ALL ACCOUNTS AFTER THIRTY DAYS.

Buena Vista,..................18

M

Bought of JOHN FITZSIMMONS,

Wholesale and Retail Dealer in

Groceries, Provisions, Dry Goods, Mining Tools, Boots, Shoes, &c., &c.

BUENA VISTA, AMADOR CO., CAL.

Bal. due Sept. 30th 1865. $138.27

The Oaks gated community, located near Buena Vista, offers residents the sociability of neighborhood living in a beautiful rural setting. In this photograph, residents relax on a hot summer day in the water at the swimming pool recreation area. Enjoying a dip are Richard Rice and Deborah Cook and their granddaughters, Amber Cara Sita Spinetta (second from left) and Sierra Lee Sumey (right).

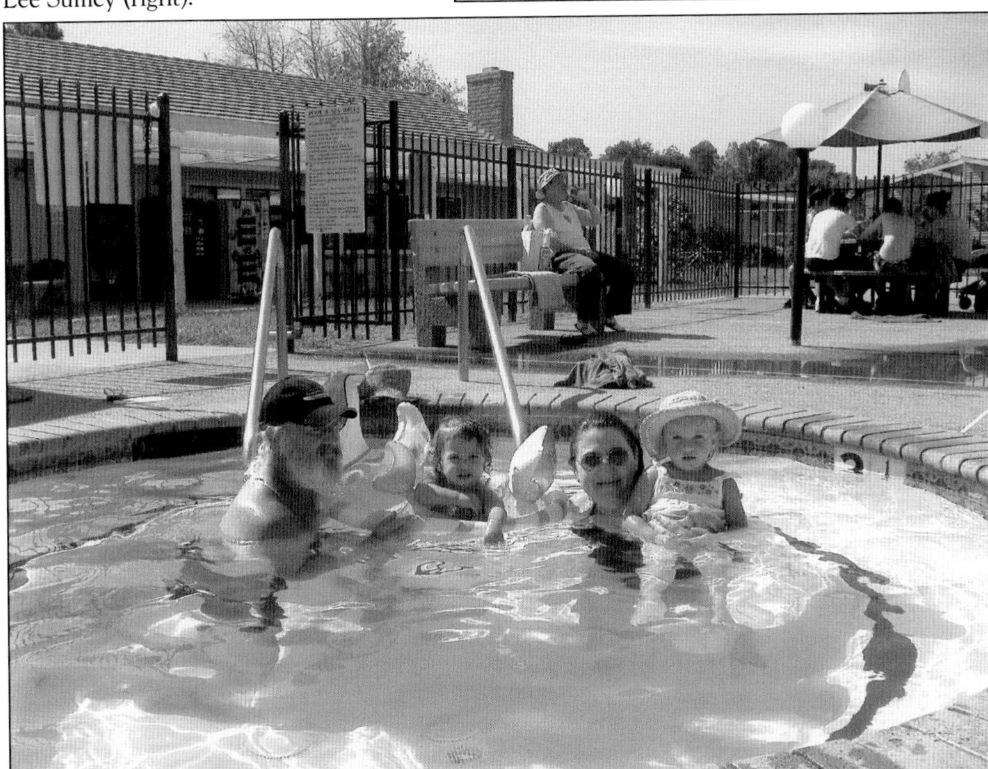

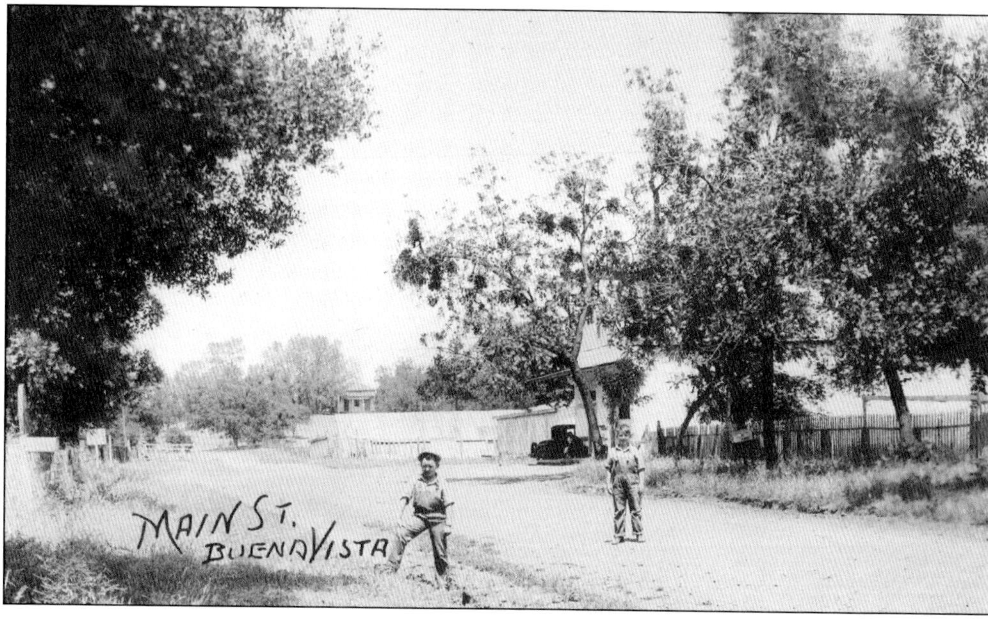

Shortly after World War I, the Buena Vista Store was purchased by Jacob Strohm. Buena Vista at that time was not much more than it is today. In the picture above, Strohm's sons Jacob and John pose along the "main street" of the settlement. The store can be seen at the right, surrounded by trees. The schoolhouse stands on the hill in the distance. In the picture below, two men pose in the doorway of the store, while Jacob's wife, Verona Grendall Strohm, stands in front of the building. Note that in both photographs the dance hall that stood to the right of the store is no longer there. Strohm razed that building after he purchased the lot. Today the old store is known as the Buena Vista Saloon and Restaurant.

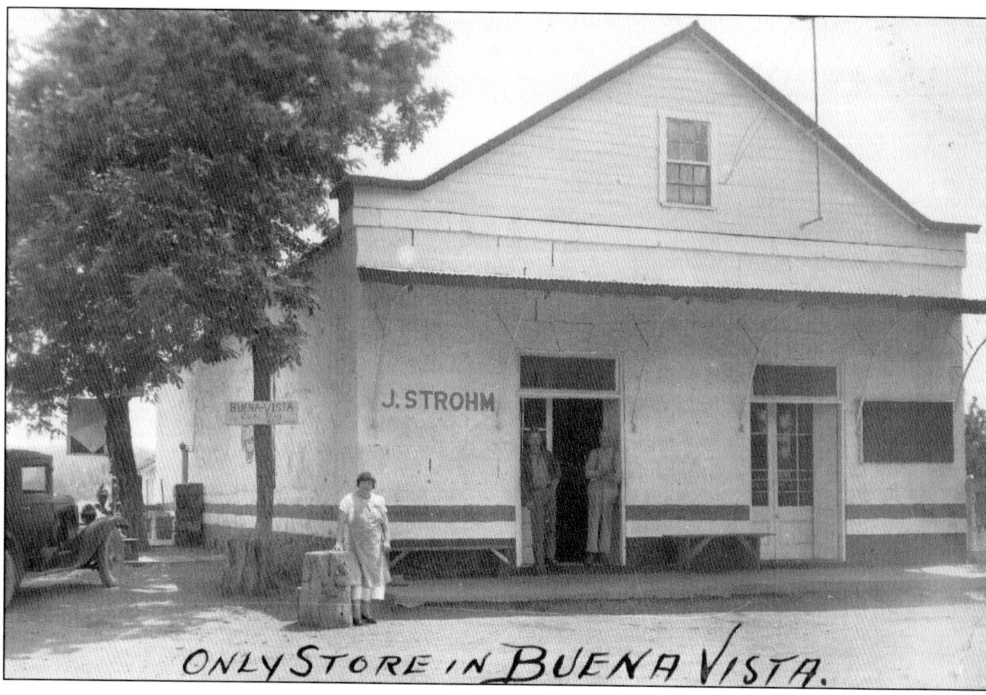

Every settlement needed a blacksmith shop, and this building housed just such a business for many years. A look inside the structure reveals that the framing supporting the building has been in place for more than 100 years. Those who owned the business and worked as the local smithy included a man named Tull, Richard Russell, partners McFadden and Horton, and the Norris brothers. (Author's collection.)

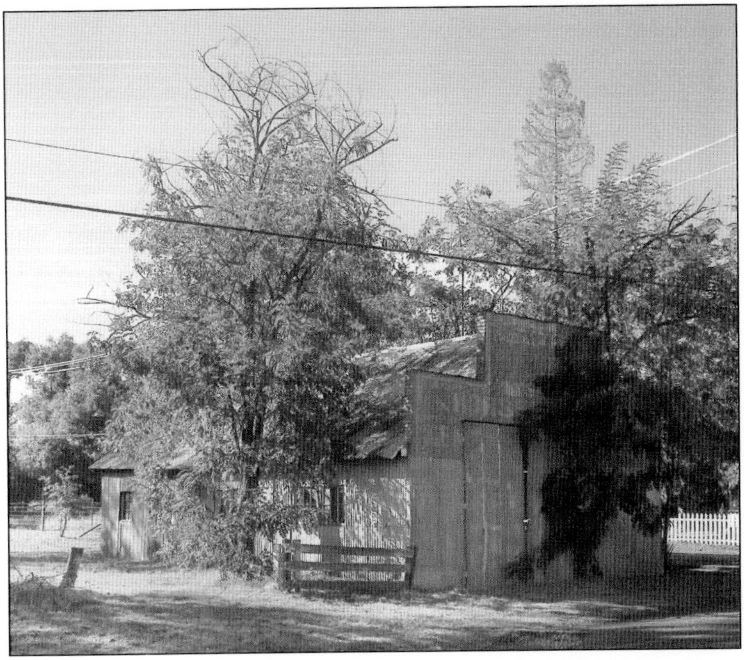

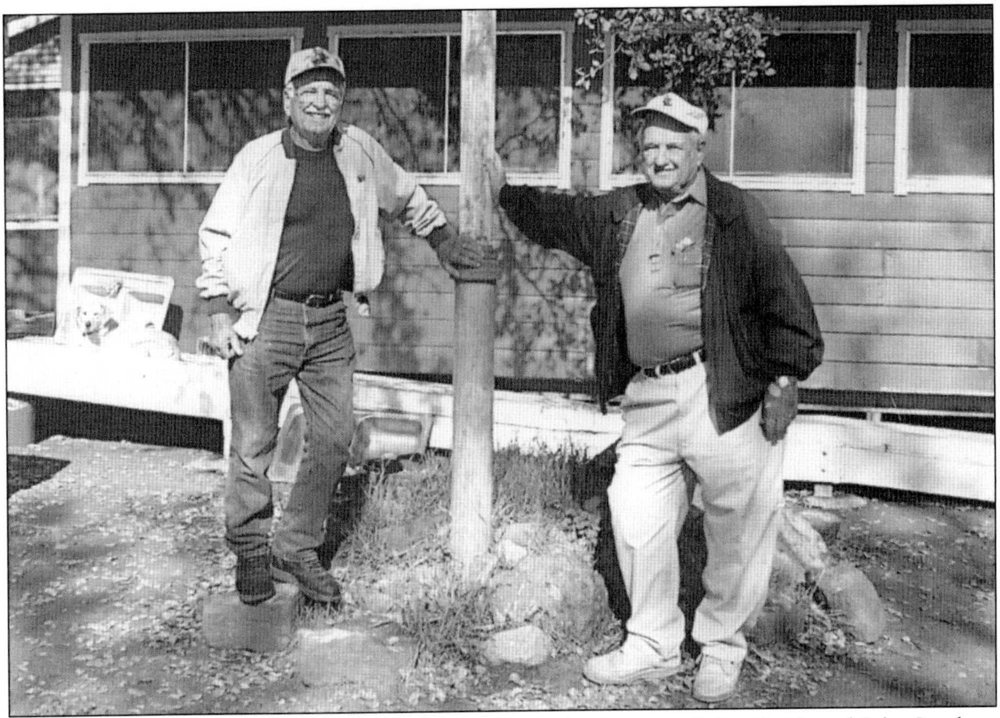

Many descendants of Jackson Valley settlers remain in the area. John (left) and Jake Strohm, the sons of Jacob and Verona Strohm, pose in front of the Buena Vista schoolhouse where they attended grammar school. For a time, their parents were owners of the Buena Vista Store. John still lives on his ranch in the Jackson Valley. Jake passed away in 2006.

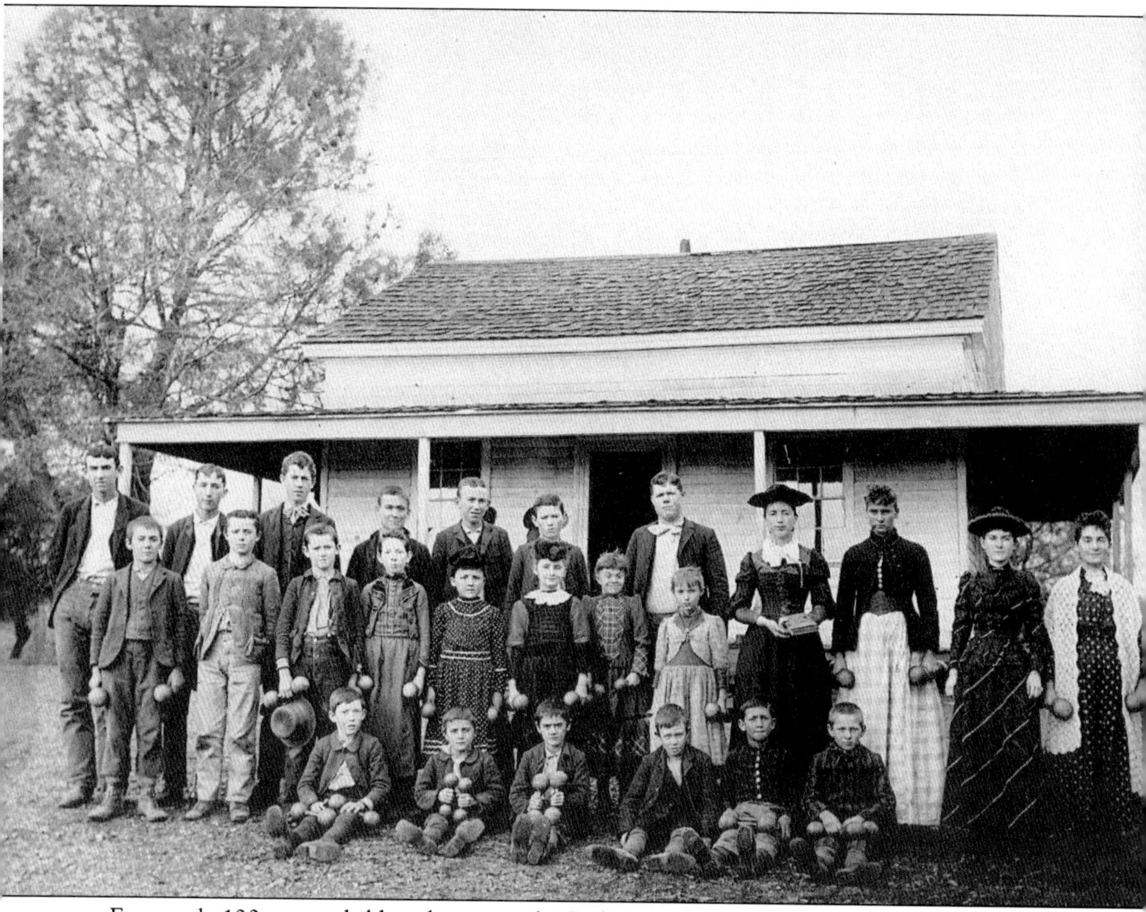

For nearly 100 years, children living in the Jackson Valley attended school in the same place. The original school was built in 1857, with Cyrus James teaching the first classes. Named the Jones School for a family that had a ranch near the Dry Creek Bridge, it later became known as the Jackson Valley School. Jesse D. Mason, in his *History of Amador County*, noted that the first schoolhouse was also used as a church. Seen from left to right are the following: (first row) Albert Ringer, Walter Milosovich, Toni Milosovich, Billy Kelly, Dan Hoover, and Johnny Walquist; (second row) unidentified, Lou Scully, Clarence Scully, Ada Ringer, unidentified, Lizzie Milosovich, Sarah Jane Fitzsimmons, and Ruby Norris; (third row) Jim Riley, Homer Thompson, John Scully, Edgar Tubbs, Ed Riley, Frank DuFrene, Bill Scully, teacher Maggie O'Brien, Dellia Hoover, Helen Ringer, and Mamie Ringer. One wonders why all the children are holding barbells.

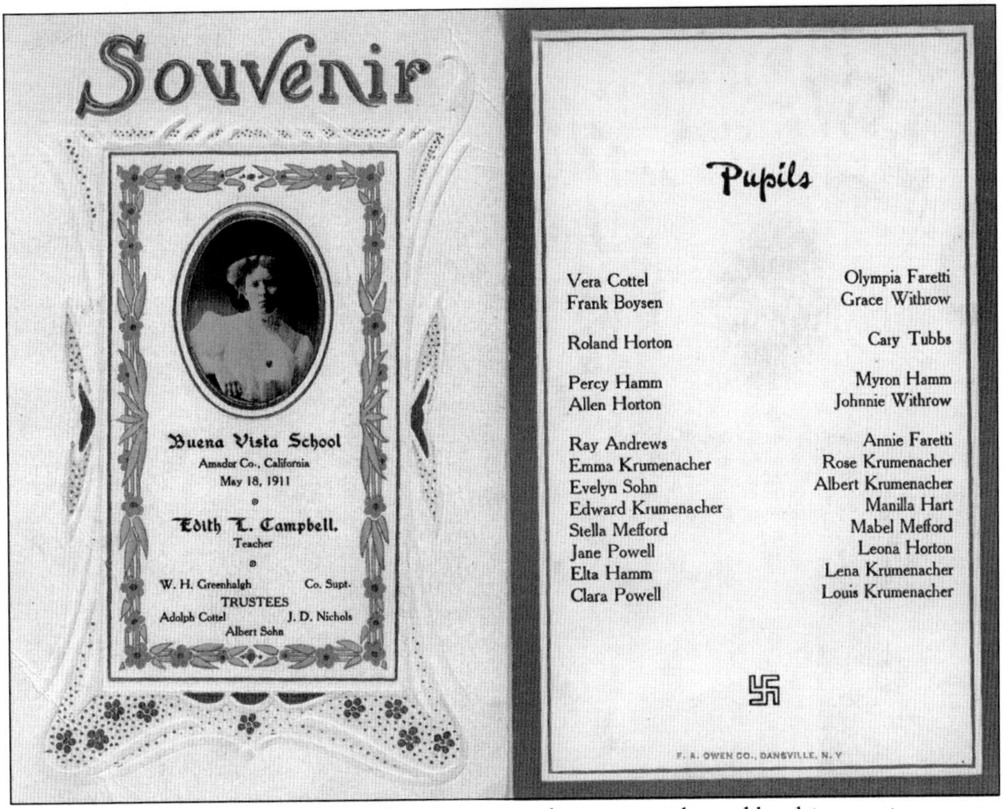

Souvenir

Buena Vista School
Amador Co., California
May 18, 1911

Edith L. Campbell.
Teacher

W. H. Greenhalgh Co. Supt.
TRUSTEES
Adolph Cottel J. D. Nichols
Albert Sohn

Pupils

Vera Cottel
Frank Boysen

Roland Horton

Percy Hamm
Allen Horton

Ray Andrews
Emma Krumenacher
Evelyn Sohn
Edward Krumenacher
Stella Mefford
Jane Powell
Elta Hamm
Clara Powell

Olympia Faretti
Grace Withrow

Cary Tubbs

Myron Hamm
Johnnie Withrow

Annie Faretti
Rose Krumenacher
Albert Krumenacher
Manilla Hart
Mabel Mefford
Leona Horton
Lena Krumenacher
Louis Krumenacher

F. A. OWEN CO., DANSVILLE, N. Y.

A souvenir graduation program has long been a tradition, as evidenced by this one given out to the 1911 graduating class of the Buena Vista Grammar School. The school was built in 1894 to replace the Jackson Valley School and was in use until the 1940s, when students in the valley were moved to the school in Ione.

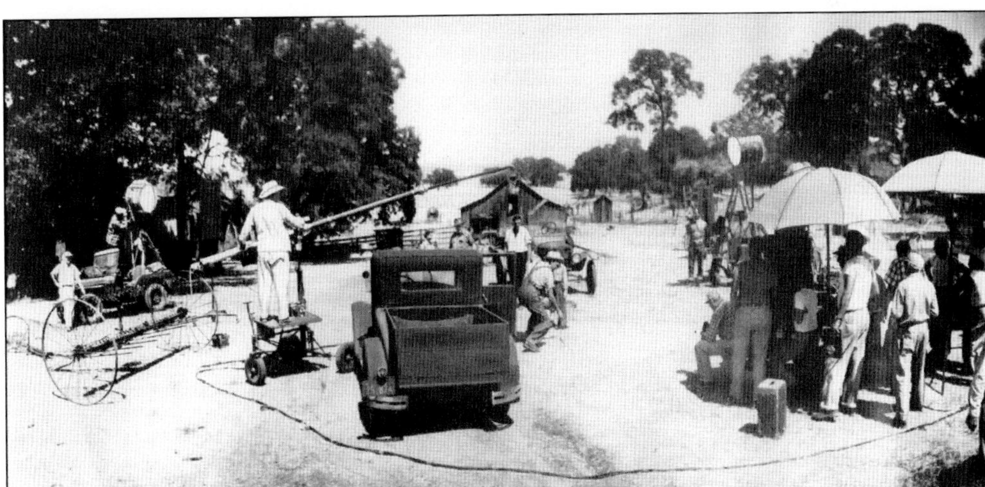

The pastoral scenery of the Jackson Valley is not only appealing to residents and visiting tourists but is a draw for Hollywood directors as well. This photograph was taken in 1956 during the filming of the movie *Come Next Spring*, which starred Walter Brennan, Anne Sheridan, Steve Cochran, and child actor Richard Eyer.

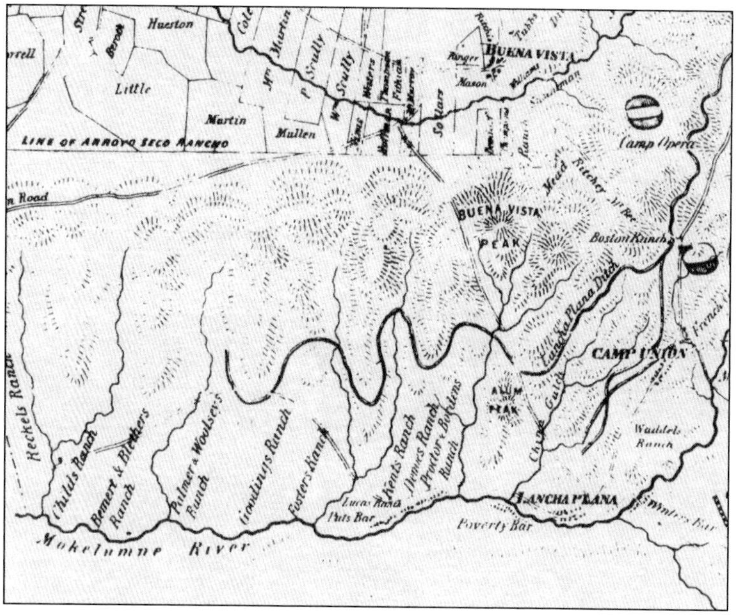

This section of the 1866 Amador County Map shows how well settled the area from Buena Vista south to the Mokelumne River had become within 15 years of the Gold Rush. Many of the ranches along the river were first named as bars, such as Goodyear's ranch, first known as Goodyear's Bar. After the placers had given up their gold, many of the miners turned their attention to ranching and farming.

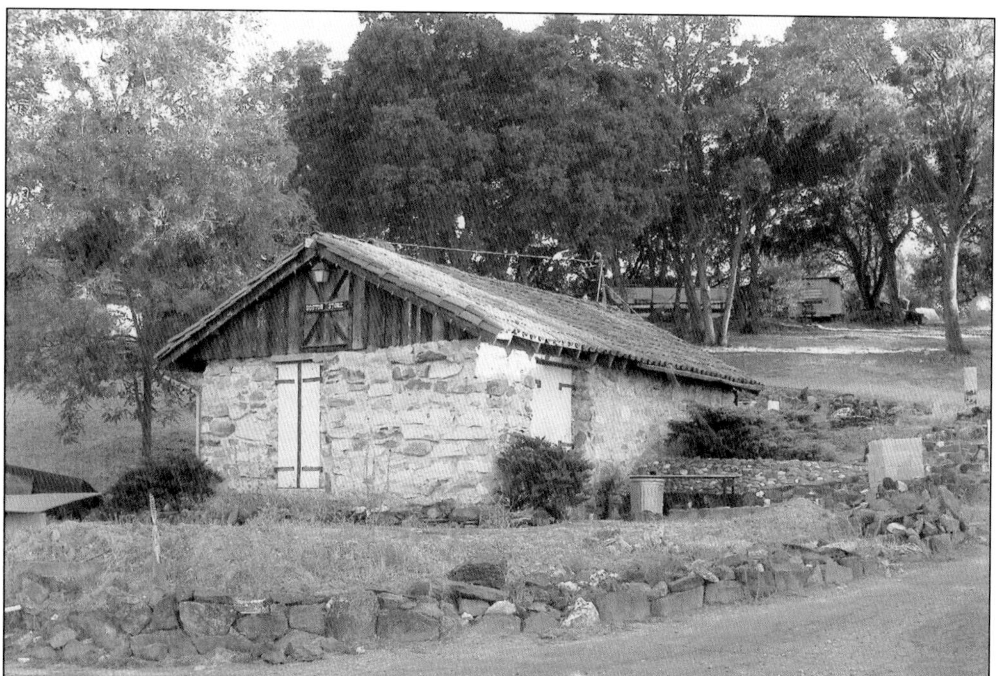

The Boston Store was a trading post located on the road from Buena Vista to the Mokelumne River. One of the first tracks to traverse the area, it was the main route from Sacramento to the southern goldfields. Like many other landmarks in the county, this building and the nearby stone well had fallen into decay and were restored to their present state in the 1960s. (Author's collection.)

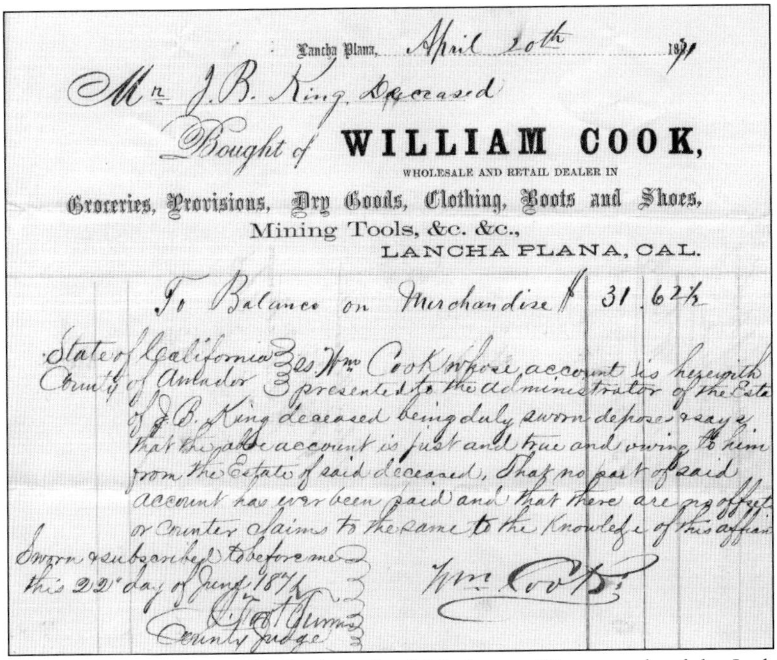

Lancha Plana, April 20th 1871

Mr. J.B. King, Deceased

Bought of **WILLIAM COOK,**

WHOLESALE AND RETAIL DEALER IN

Groceries, Provisions, Dry Goods, Clothing, Boots and Shoes,

Mining Tools, &c. &c.,

LANCHA PLANA, CAL.

To Balance on Merchandise $ 31 62½

State of California } ss. Wm Cook whose account is herewith
County of Amador } presented to the administrator of the Estate of J.B. King deceased being duly sworn deposes & says that the above account is just and true and owing to him from the Estate of said deceased, That no part of said account has ever been paid and that there are no offsets or counter claims to the same to the knowledge of this affiant

Sworn & subscribed to before me this 22d day of June 1871

[illegible] County Judge

Wm Cook

Lancha Plana, a mining camp established on the Mokelumne River south of the Jackson Valley, had such rich diggings that by 1850 it was a large settlement. Two years later, the first bridge was built across the river, and many merchants were doing a booming business. Then, in 1853, a devastating fire burned the entire town to the ground. Soon rebuilt, the settlement continued to thrive on mining profits. This photograph was taken around 1860, the time of the town's heyday. What was left of the town site was buried under the waters of Lake Camanche in 1964. The town site is California Historic Landmark No. 30. Also pictured is a bill head from the store of William Cook, who later dismantled his store and moved it stone by stone to Buena Vista.

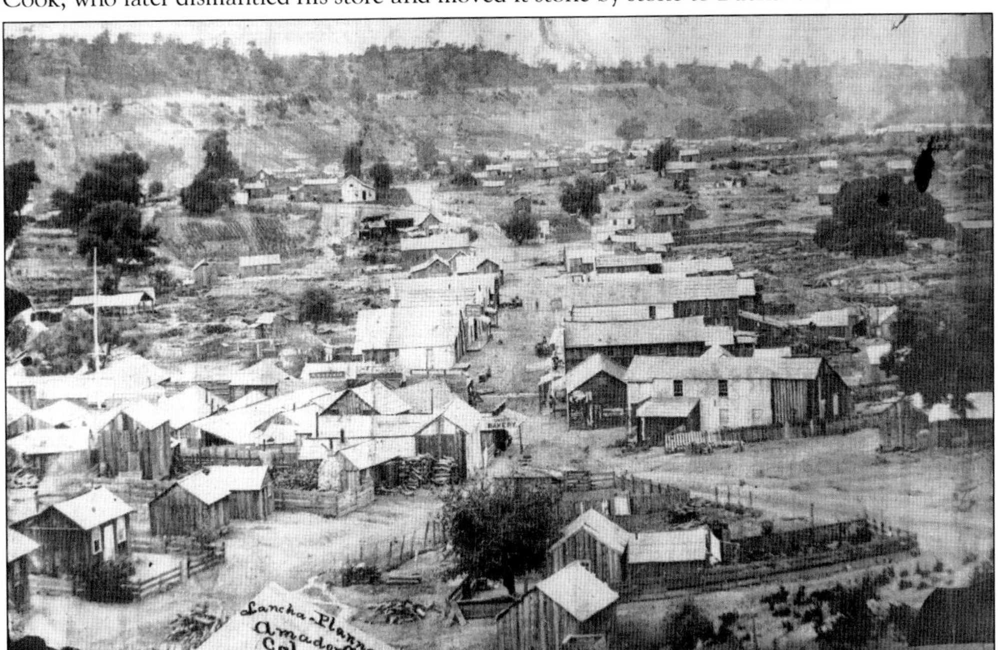

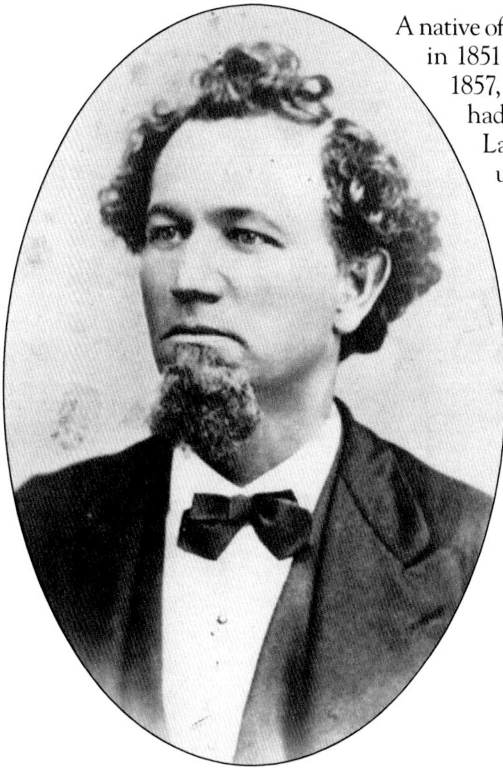

A native of Virginia, Dr. Charles Boarman came to California in 1851 at the age of 23 and settled in Sacramento. In 1857, he wed Mary Anna Morse Hills, with whom he had seven children. In 1859, the Boarmans moved to Lancha Plana, where Charles practiced medicine until his death in 1880. Boarman served as the Amador County physician for 17 years, and he was a founding member of the Society of California Pioneers.

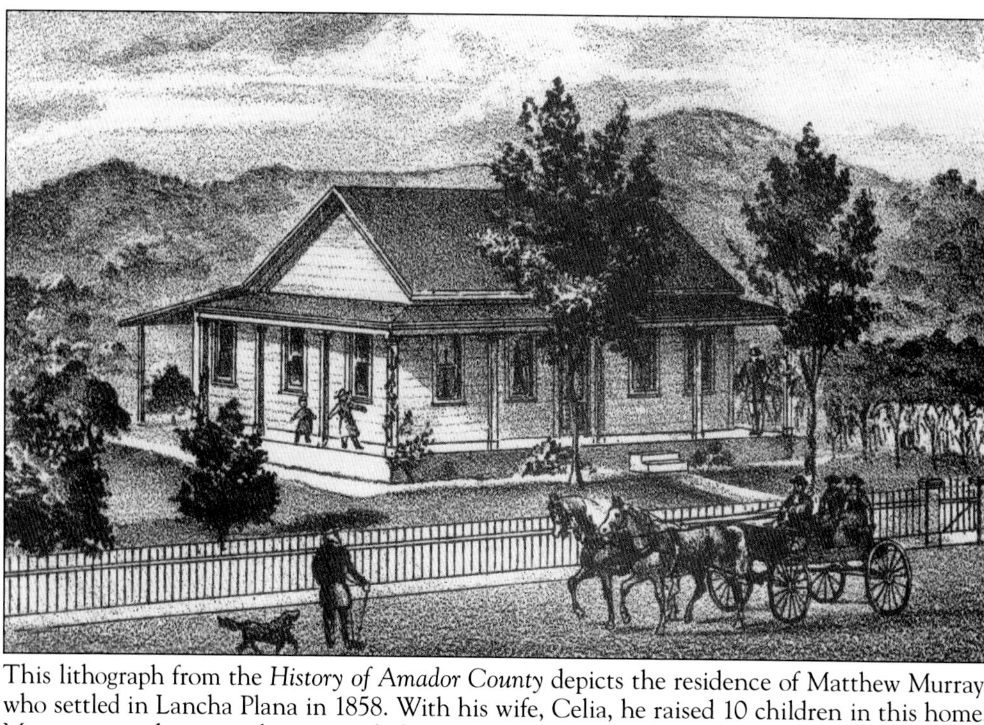

This lithograph from the *History of Amador County* depicts the residence of Matthew Murray, who settled in Lancha Plana in 1858. With his wife, Celia, he raised 10 children in this home. Murray pursued many endeavors, including running a mercantile business, owning and operating water ditches, and for a time serving as a county supervisor, sheriff, and judge.

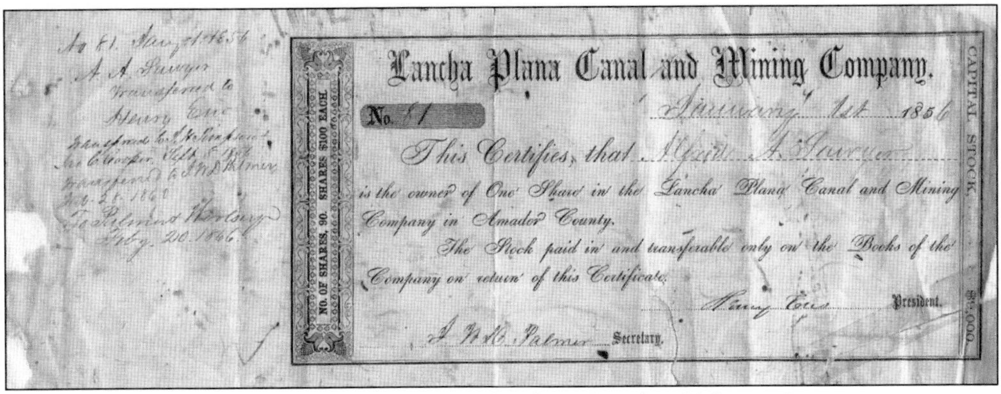

Lancha Plana Canal and Mining Company.

No.

This Certifies, that

is the owner of One Share in the Lancha Plana Canal and Mining Company in Amador County.

The Stock paid in and transferable only on the Books of the Company on return of this Certificate.

President.

Secretary.

NO. OF SHARES, 90. SHARES $100 EACH.

CAPITAL STOCK $9,000.

This rare 1856 stock certificate is from the Lancha Plana Canal and Mining Company, proprietors of the Lancha Plana ditch. The ditch took water from Jackson Creek and supplied it to Camp Opera, French Camp, and other mining camps as far as Putt's bar on the Mokelumne River. It traversed a total distance of about 30 miles and was built at a cost of about $30,000.

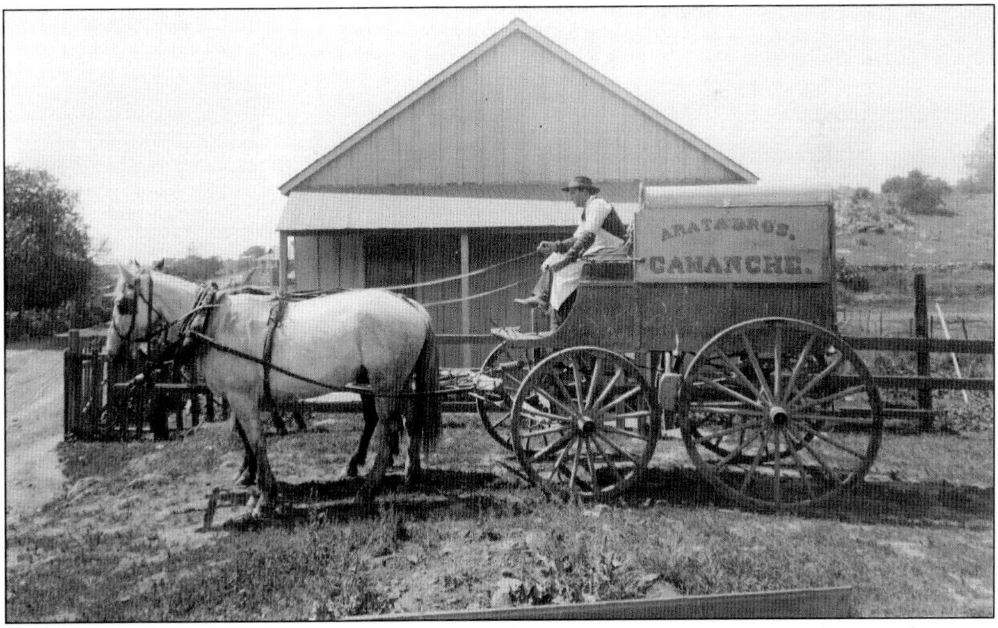

Another early mining town, now swallowed up by the waters of Lake Camanche, was the town of Camanche. This hamlet, like Lancha Plana, had a thriving business district and was home to many Italian families. Here Albert Arata, a Camanche merchant, makes a delivery in his wagon. The settlement was surrounded by ranches and farms, some of which farmed large crops of chrysanthemums grown for insecticidal use.

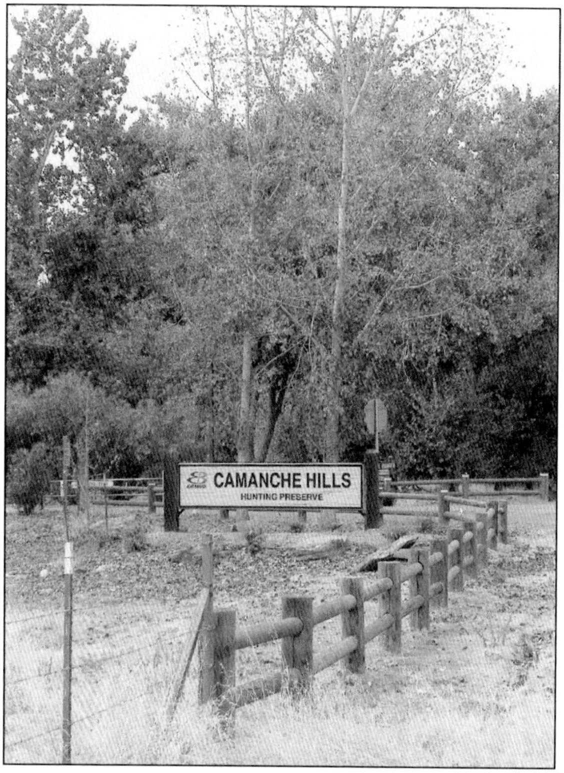

Land once occupied by towns, ranches, and farms now lies beneath the waters of Lake Camanche. This lake is one in a series of features composing a reclamation project managed by the East Bay Municipal Utility District (EBMUD) that delivers water from rivers and streams in Amador and Calaveras Counties to the San Francisco Bay Area. Completed in the 1960s, the Camanche project opened up new recreational opportunities in the area. Seen below is the marina at the Camanche North Shore Recreation Area. A look at the hillside on the left reveals how low the water level fell as a result of a dry 2006–2007 rainy season. The 1,500-acre Camanche Hills Hunting Preserve, also located on EBMUD property, is another popular recreation facility, offering hunters a variety of game birds as well as clay and skeet shooting. (Author's collection.)

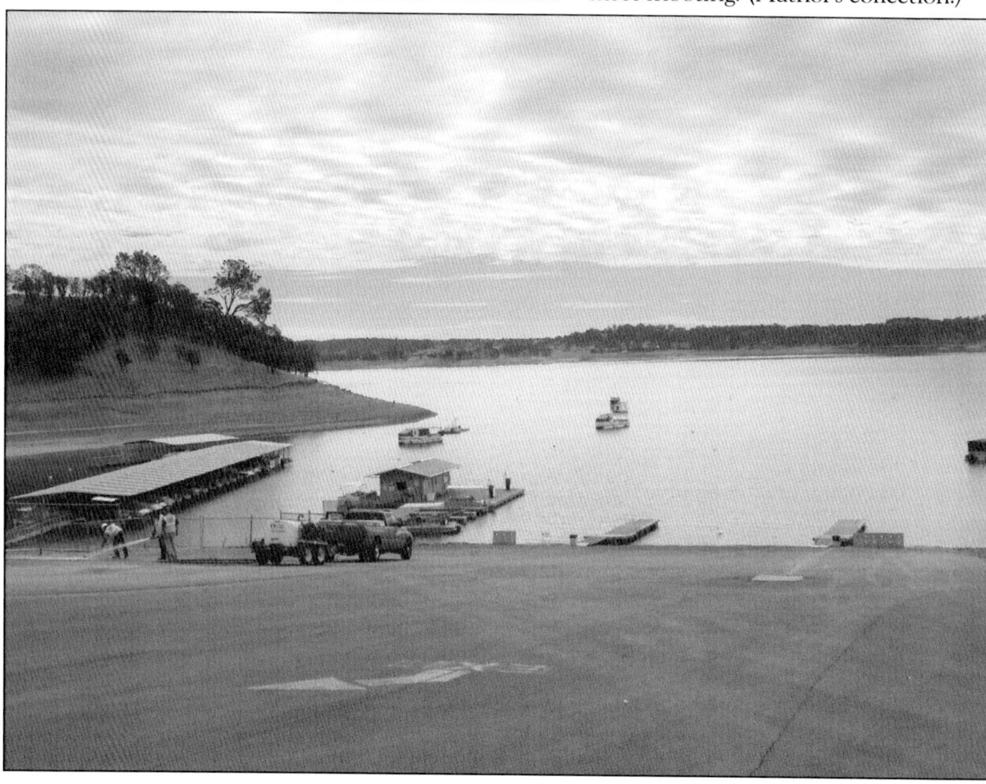

In 1956, landowners organized the Jackson Valley Irrigation District (JVID) to provide a reliable water source to meet the needs of farming. In 1965, Lake Amador was formed when JVID built a 1,000-foot-long earthen dam to contain the waters of Jackson Creek. The lake holds a total of 22,000 acre feet of water and has a maximum depth of 158 feet. The $2.3 million project was funded by a loan from the U.S. Bureau of Reclamation. Development of recreational facilities at the lake was funded under the Davis-Grunsky Act, administered by the California Department of Water Resources. A spillway was also built at the north end of Pardee Reservoir to serve as an alternative water source for JVID. The photograph at right is a view of the Buena Vista trout farm, taken from atop the Lake Amador dam. (Author's collection.)

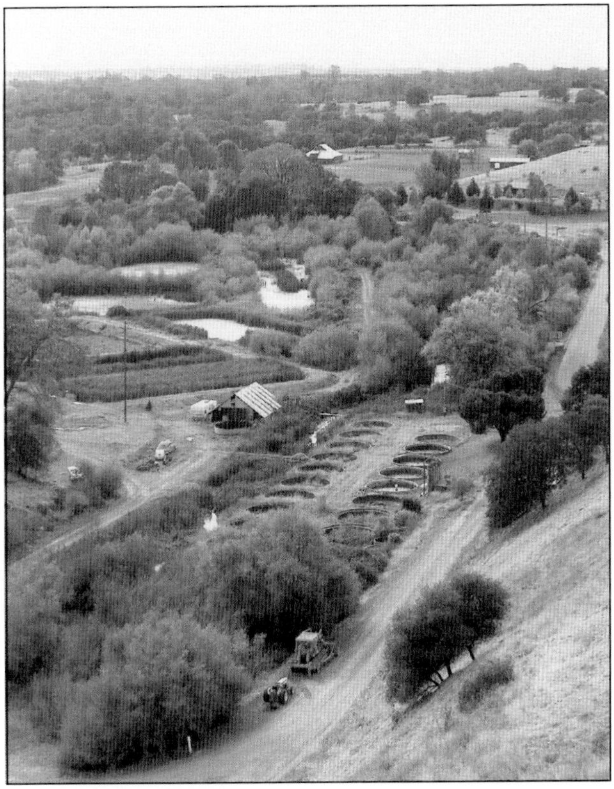

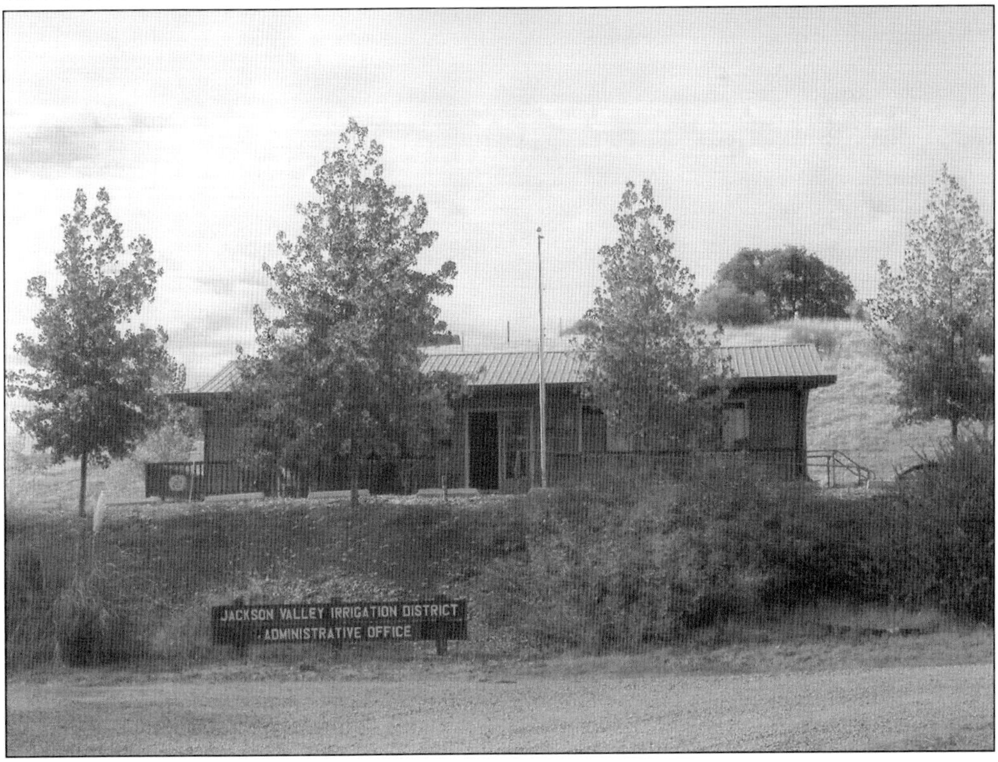

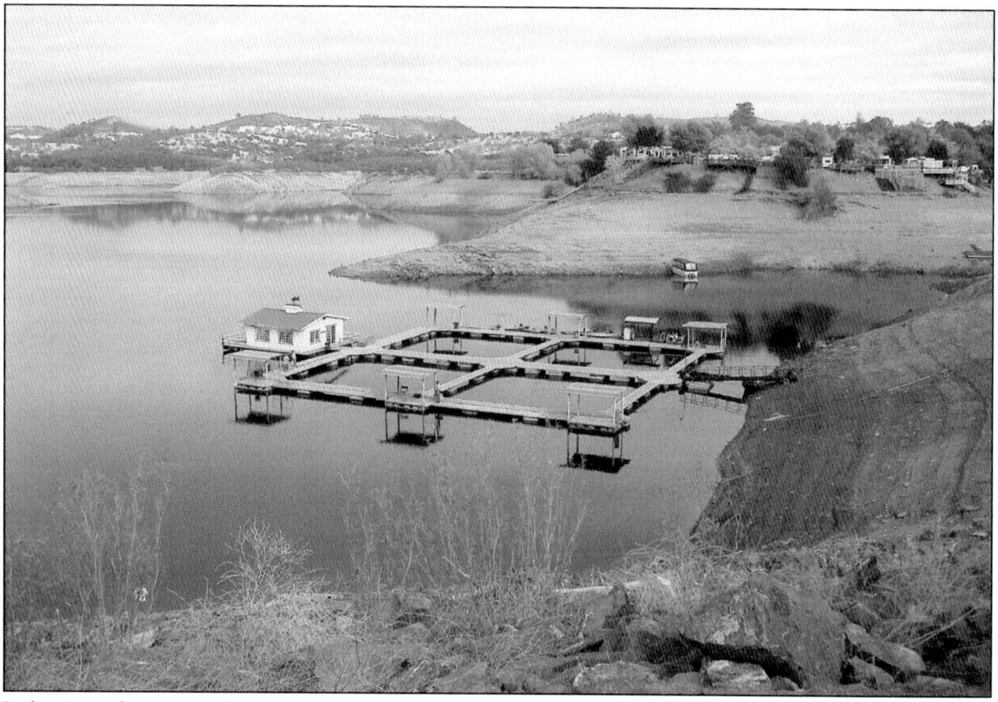

Lake Amador not only serves as a water source and recreational facility but is also home to a number of residents living in a lakeside mobile home park. This photograph provides a view of the residences on the hill across the lagoon. Note the extended distance between the homes and the dock and boathouse at the center, which was due to drought water levels. (Author's collection.)

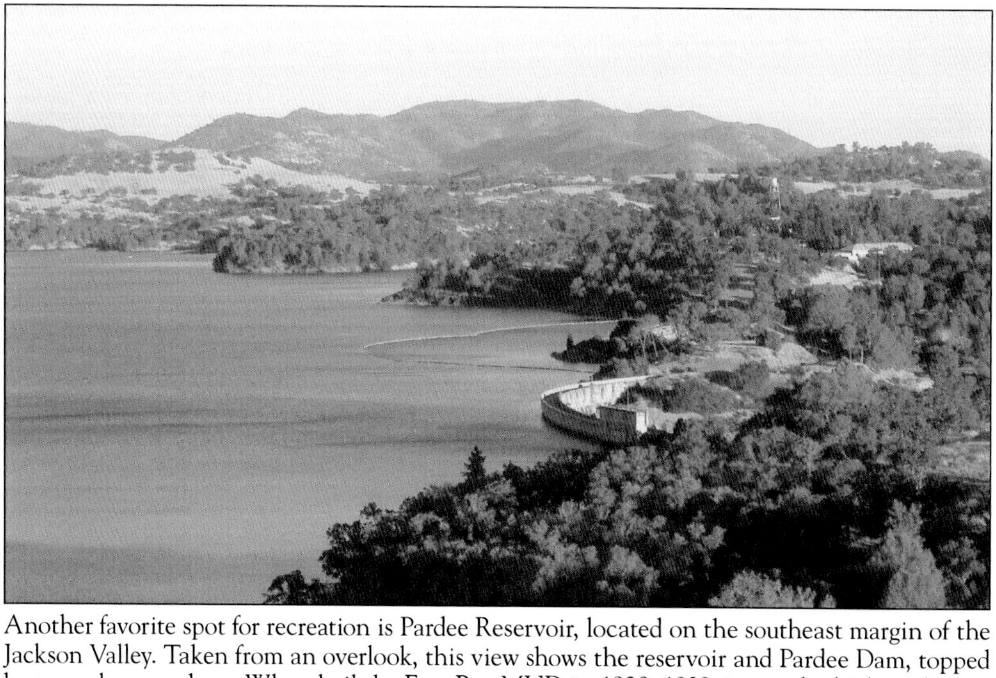

Another favorite spot for recreation is Pardee Reservoir, located on the southeast margin of the Jackson Valley. Taken from an overlook, this view shows the reservoir and Pardee Dam, topped by a one-lane roadway. When built by East Bay MUD in 1928–1929, it was the highest dam in the world. The reservoir was opened for public recreation in 1958. (Author's collection.)

Nine

Clay, Coal, and Sand

Amador County is known throughout the world as one of the richest sources of gold on the Mother Lode. What is not well known is that a profitable mining industry also took place in the western region of the county. In addition to the gold found in ancient rivers were beds of minerals that became the other golds of Amador: clay, coal, and quartz sand. Mining of these minerals began in the 1850s, when the first clay pits were opened in the vicinity of Carbondale.

The deposit in which these minerals are found is known as the Ione–Buena Vista Formation. It extends from Carbondale on the north, southward across the Ione and Jackson Valleys, and crosses the Mokelumne River drainage into Calaveras County, covering a total distance of about 12 miles. Within Amador County, the deposit is approximately four and a half miles wide.

The Ione–Buena Vista Deposit was formed during the Eocene period in a shallow sea that lay at the foot of the ancestral Sierra Nevada. At the time that the deposits were laid down, much of California west of the Sierra Nevada was covered in water, and the climate was warm and moist. This climate caused a deep weathering of the landscape, which led to the deposit of clays over large areas. As the climate became drier, these clays settled into land-locked lagoons and deltas. The clay beds that formed near Ione are not continuous throughout the formation but are found in pockets where they settled into the lagoons described above.

The minerals extracted from these deposits have brought both work and wealth to the families of the Ione and Jackson Valleys. In the early days, most of the mines were small-scale family operations that experienced eras of boom and bust, but over the past 150 years, some have evolved into large ventures conducted by international companies. In addition to clay, coal, and sand, other minerals, such as asbestos, chromite, mineral paint, pumice, talc, and gravel, have been mined in the region. Products generated from these minerals range from building cement to fine porcelain.

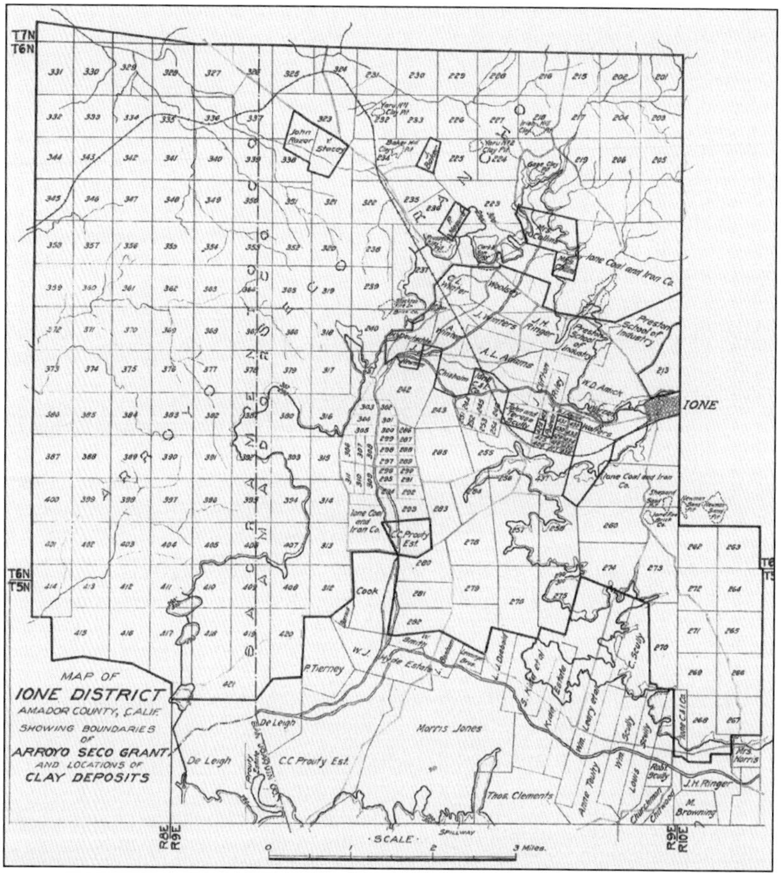

This 1928 map illustrates the distribution of clay deposits in the Ione and Jackson Valleys and the locations of some of the clay pits in operation at that time. Note that the Ione Coal and Iron Company has a number of clay pits. Also shown are the sites of several sand pits and many of the property owners in the region. (Courtesy California Division of Mines.)

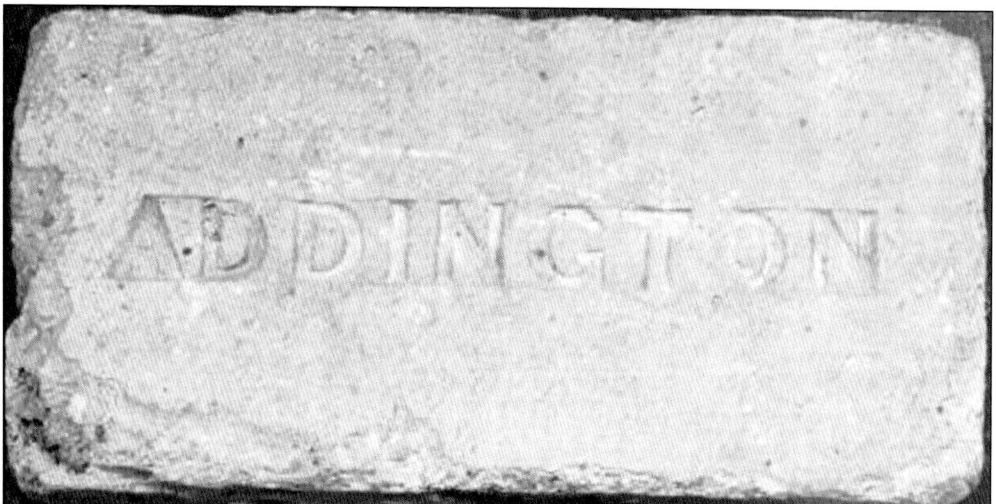

Absalom Addington was one of the first to mine clay near Carbondale. In 1859, he entered brick production in partnership with J. W. Orr and built several kilns on Pony Brown Road, west of Ione. The pottery firm became Addington and Son when Absalom's son Charlie joined him in the business. The Addingtons operated the business until 1884, when they sold out to J. B. Williams. (Author's collection.)

The Francis Reichling family poses in front of a shed at an early Ione Valley coal mine. The Reichlings were residents of Jackson, but with many business interests around the county they may have had an investment in the mine.

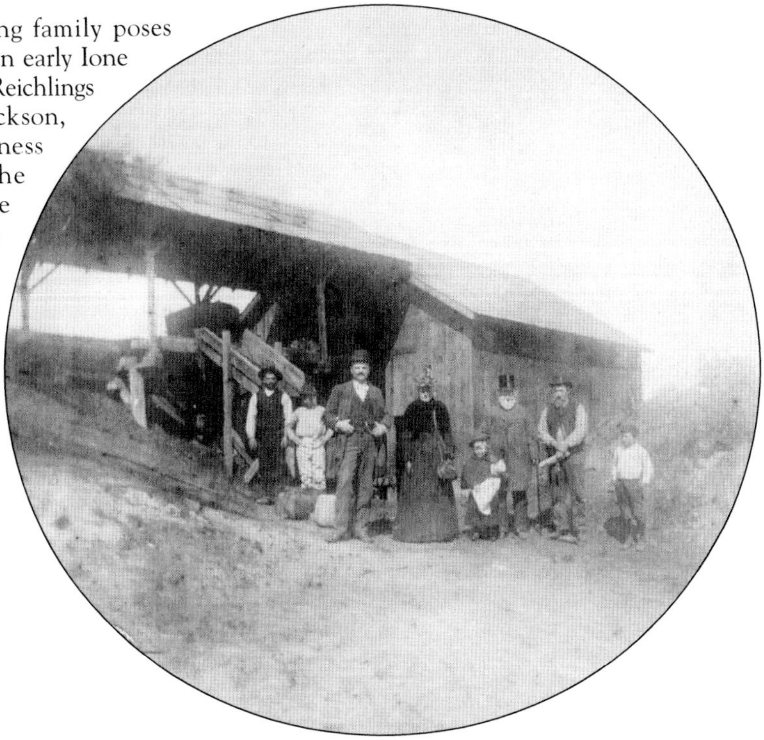

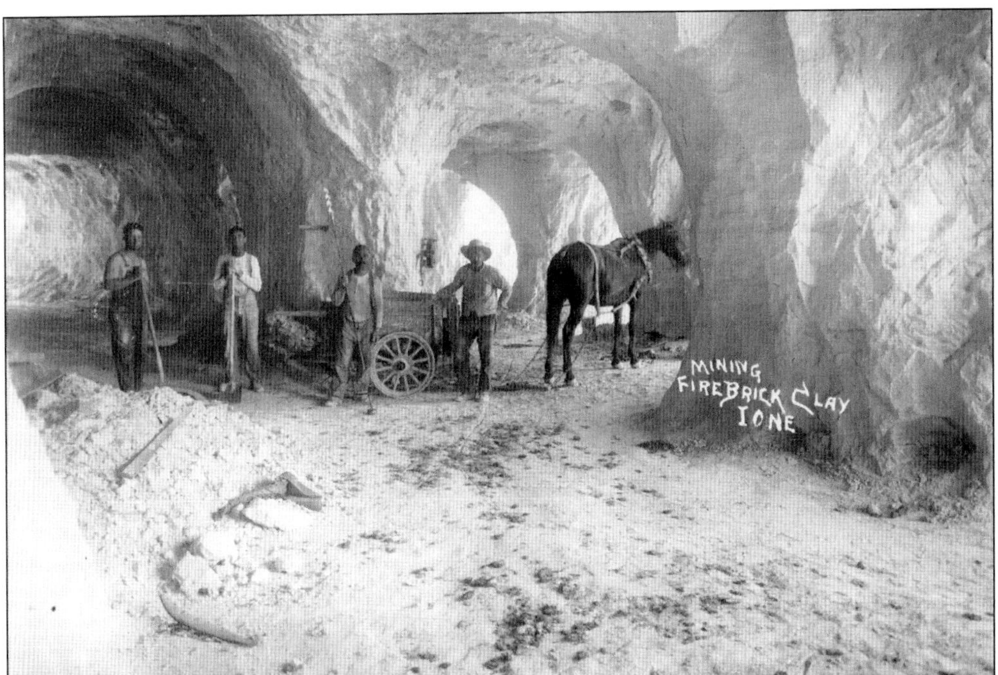

This early clay mine near Ione was worked using the room-and-pillar method. During this process, the deposit is accessed using explosives, and a tunnel entry is created into the hillside. The clay is mined by expanding the tunnel into areas that form rooms between which pillars are left intact to support the roof of the mine.

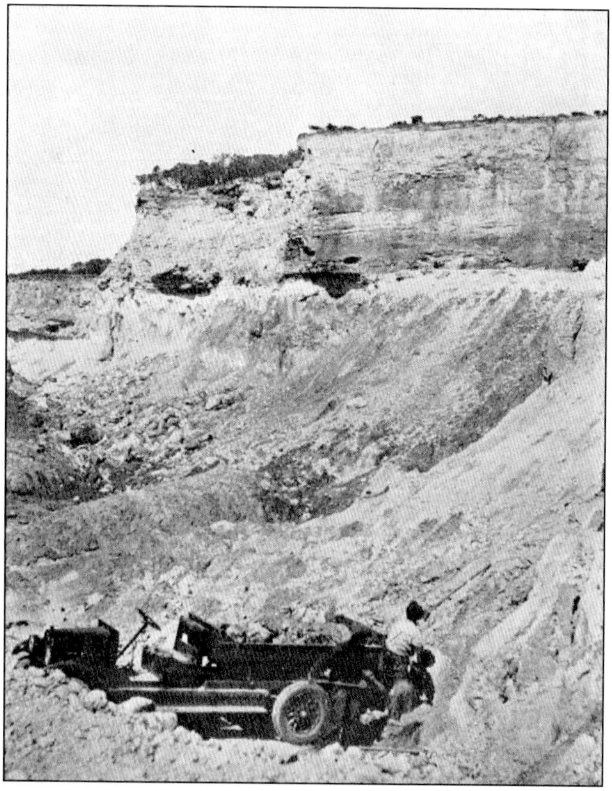

Open-pit mining was used extensively to extract clay and other minerals from the Ione–Buena Vista Formation. Typically, the overburden is stripped from the site, and then the minerals are removed and processed. As a rule, a vertical bank is worked with the height of the bank corresponding to the thickness of the deposit. In contrast to the pillar-and-room method, the result is a large open pit. The automobile pictured at left appears to be buried in rubble in the Newman clay pit. The dark spots in the clay bank are deposits of lignite coal, also mined from this site. Below is an 1880s view of the clay banks mined by the Ione Brick Works, for a time one of the largest brick producers in California.

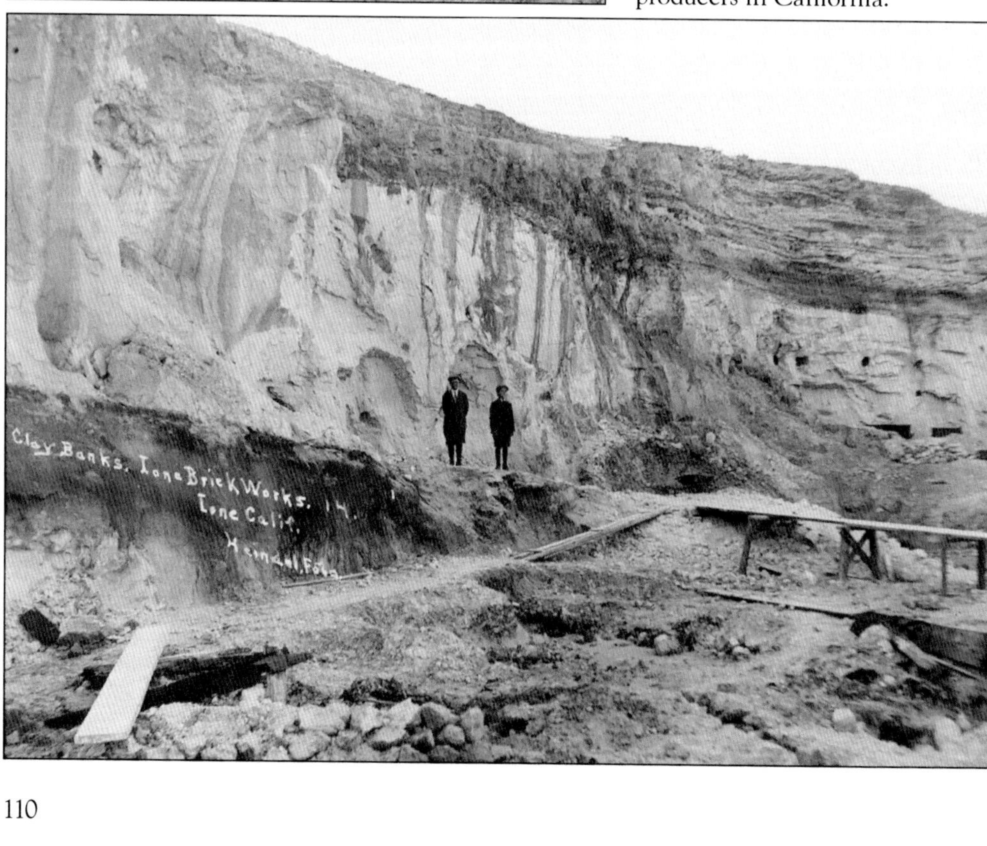

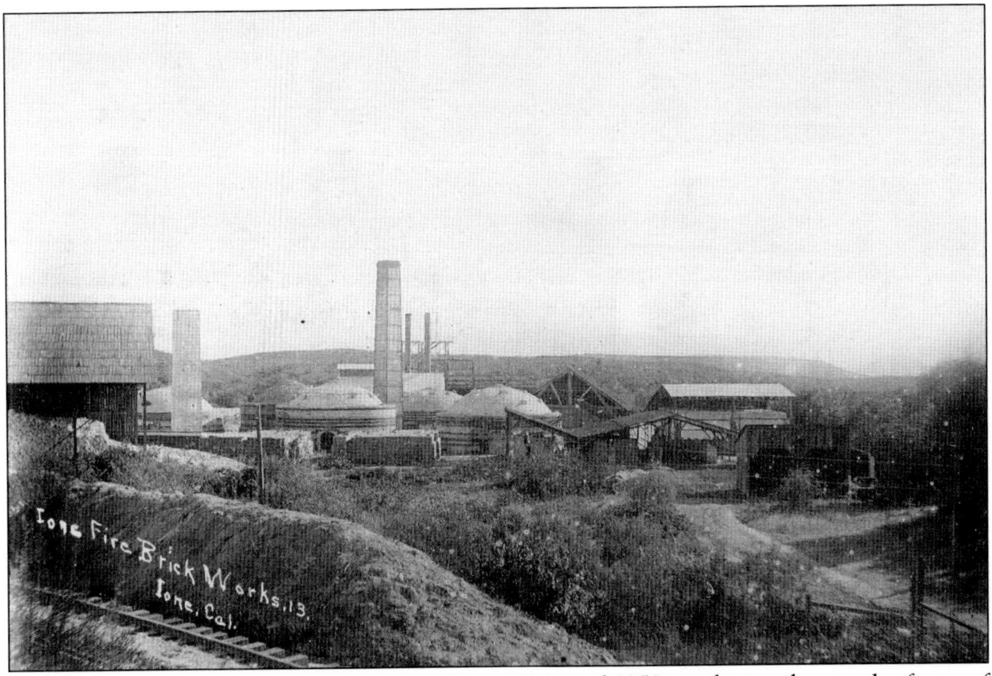

The Ione Fire Brick plant was in operation from 1906 until 1958, producing thousands of tons of bricks used for the lining of furnaces, kilns, and chimneys. In the 1920s, the plant was a subsidiary of the Stockton Fire Brick Company, and then was sold to Western Refractories in 1944. The plant is located about two miles southeast of Ione on a spur track of the Amador Central Railroad.

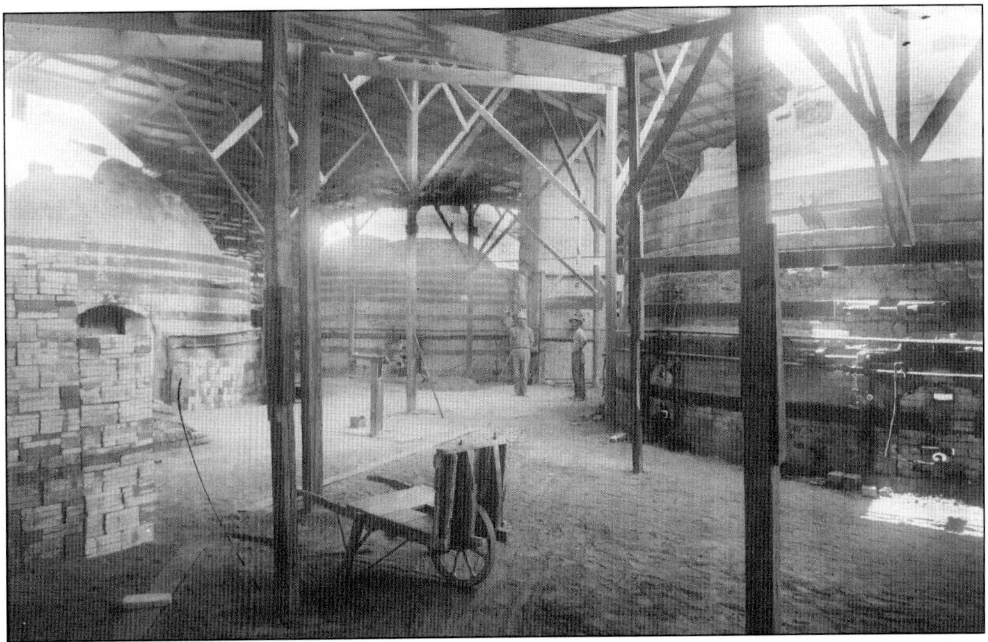

Sheds keep the weather off "green" bricks at the Ione Fire Brick plant. Bricks were most often dried in open yards in the sunshine. Three types of bricks were made at the Ione plant: stiff-mud, dry-press brick, and fire-clay brick. After drying, they were sent to one of six beehive-shaped, down-draft kilns to be fired. The entire process of firing took a total of 27 days.

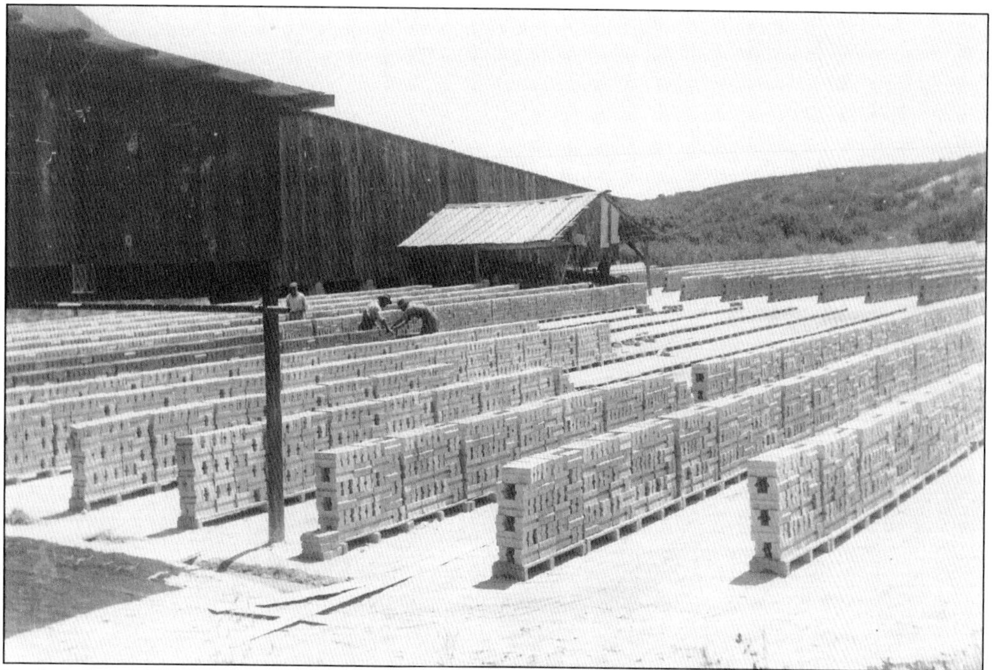

In this photograph, taken at the Ione Brick Company, bricks dry in the sun before being shipped off to construction sites. After 1876, most of these bricks were moved from the yards via train car, as seen on the previous page and in the following photograph.

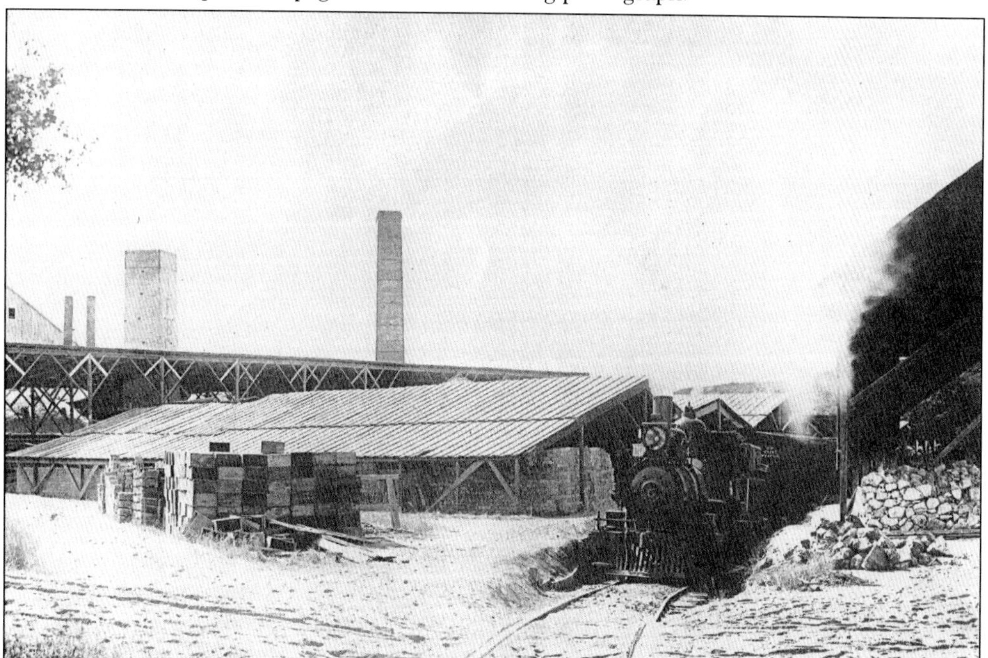

An engine prepares to pull a trainload of bricks from the Ione Brick Company works near Ione. Sidings were built off the main railroad line between Galt and Ione to various clay and coal mines in order to facilitate the shipment of these commodities in an expedited manner. The coal supply in the region was the main impetus for the Central Pacific to build a line into Ione.

Jacob Newman, merchant and investor, was involved in many business enterprises throughout Amador County in partnership with his brothers, including the clay industry. The Newman Clay Company mine, located a mile east of Ione, produced a red mottled clay and white sand. It was excavated as an open-pit mine. A picture of the mine is shown on page 110.

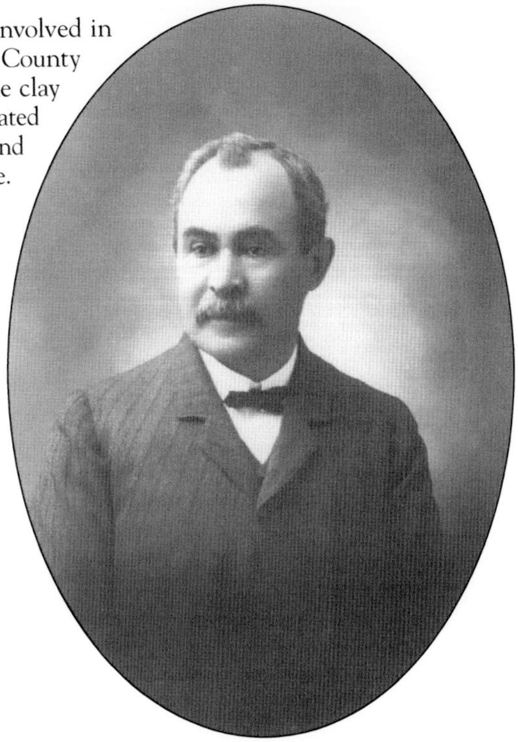

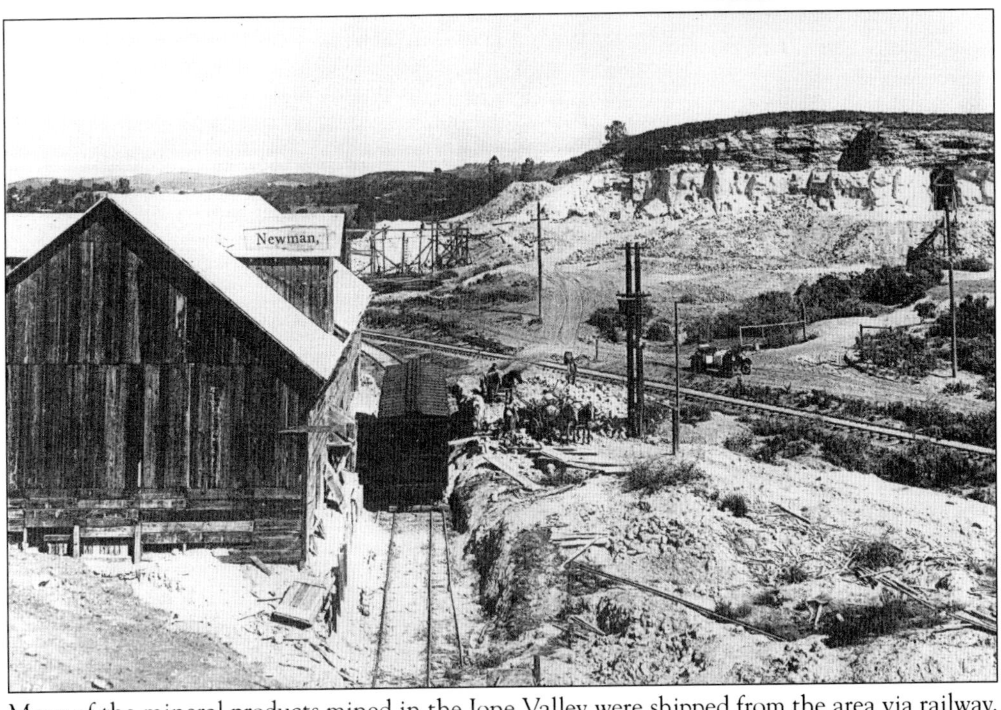

Many of the mineral products mined in the Ione Valley were shipped from the area via railway. Here a railcar sits on a siding next to a shed at the Newman Clay Company mine waiting to be loaded. Despite the arrival of rail transport and the automobile, the use of horse-drawn wagons had not yet been abandoned, as seen at the center of this image.

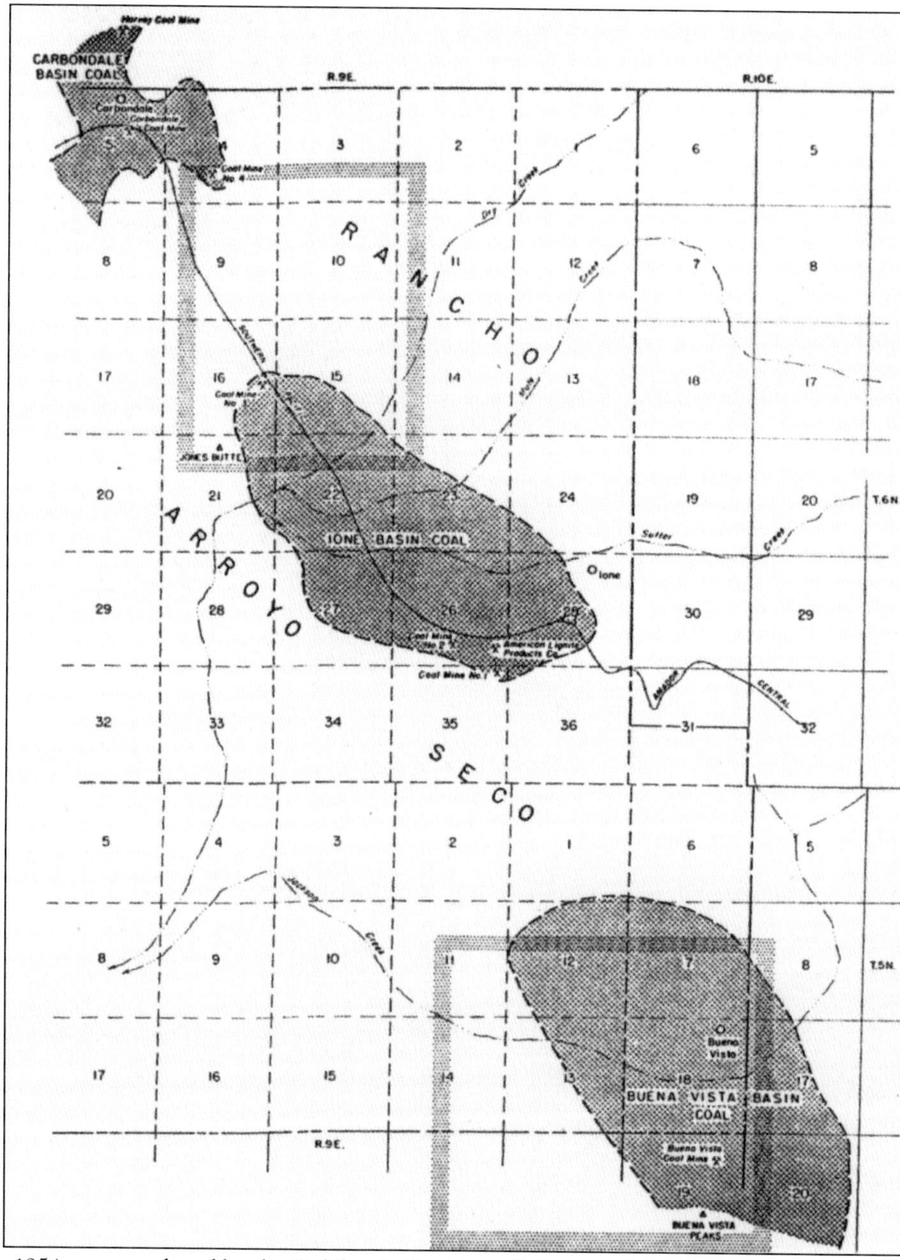

This 1954 map, produced by the California Division of Mines and Geology, shows the three coal basins found in the Ione–Buena Vista Formation. The mines noted on the map are just a few of those that were opened in the region. Coal mining first began here in the 1860s and continued intermittently until 1888. From about 1889 through 1902, activity increased and substantial amounts were taken from the Ione beds. After 1902 and until about 1947, production became sporadic due to competition with petroleum products. By 1915, only two mines were operating—the Harvey Mine and Coal Mine No. 4—both located near Carbondale. In 1927, a mining report noted that only three (these and the Buena Vista) were at work. Soon thereafter, coal mining stopped until 1947, when the Buena Vista Mine was reopened. By 1954, when this map was produced, the Buena Vista Mine was the only one still operating in Amador County. (Author's collection.)

The coal found in the Ione area is a low-grade type known as brown lignite. It occurs as flat beds within the clay deposits, is sometimes found in the shape of saucers or lenses, and has a somewhat waxy appearance. In this image of the Ione Brick Works clay pit, a deposit of lignite can be seen as the thick dark line several feet below the natural ground surface.

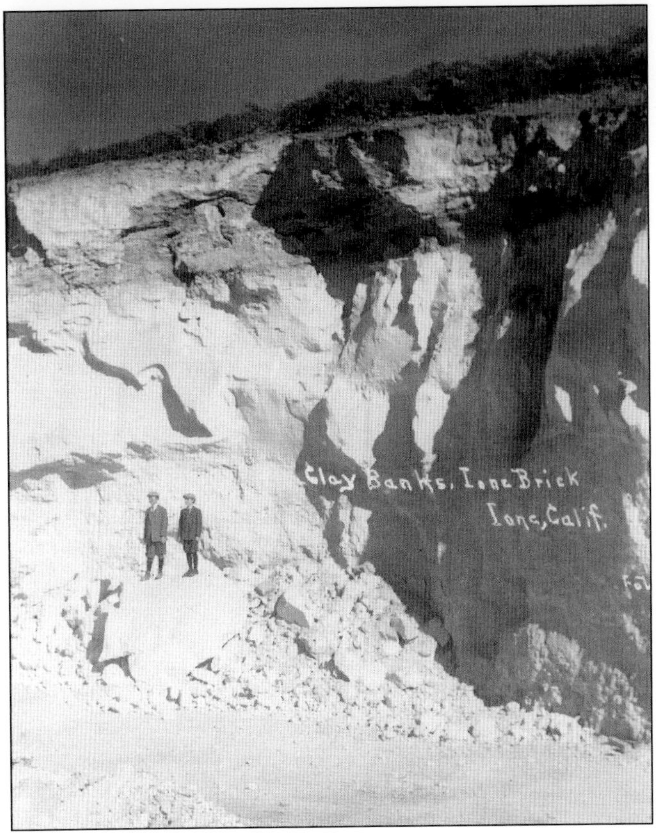

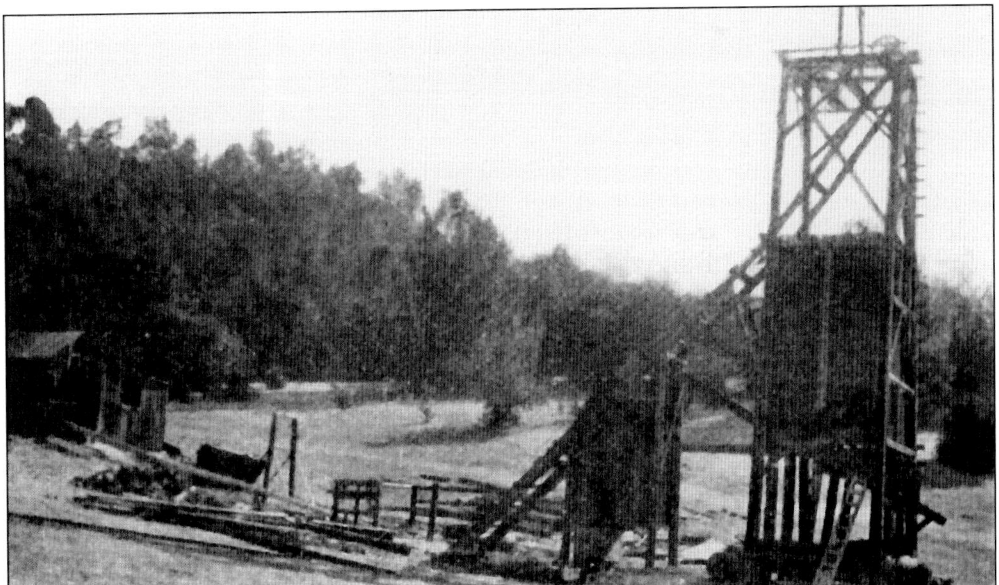

The Buena Vista Coal Mine, located at the foot of the Buena Vista Buttes in the Jackson Valley, was first opened by the Fitzsimmons family in the early 1900s. At that time, the coal was sold locally, and the Preston School of Industry was one of the biggest customers. Here the coal bed is 11 feet thick and topped with over 50 feet of clay and sand.

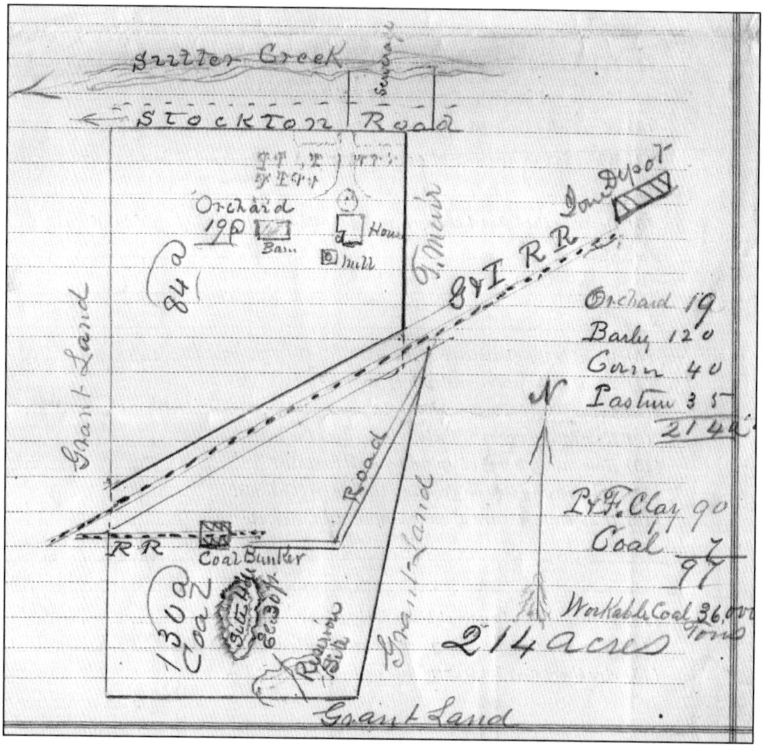

Coal, even low-grade lignite, was a valuable commodity to 19th-century industry. This 1889 map, prepared for a proposal to sell property to the State of California for the building of Preston School, details the availability of coal on the land and its convenient proximity to the railroad. During the late 1800s, the Central Pacific Railroad used coal from the area to power its locomotives in California.

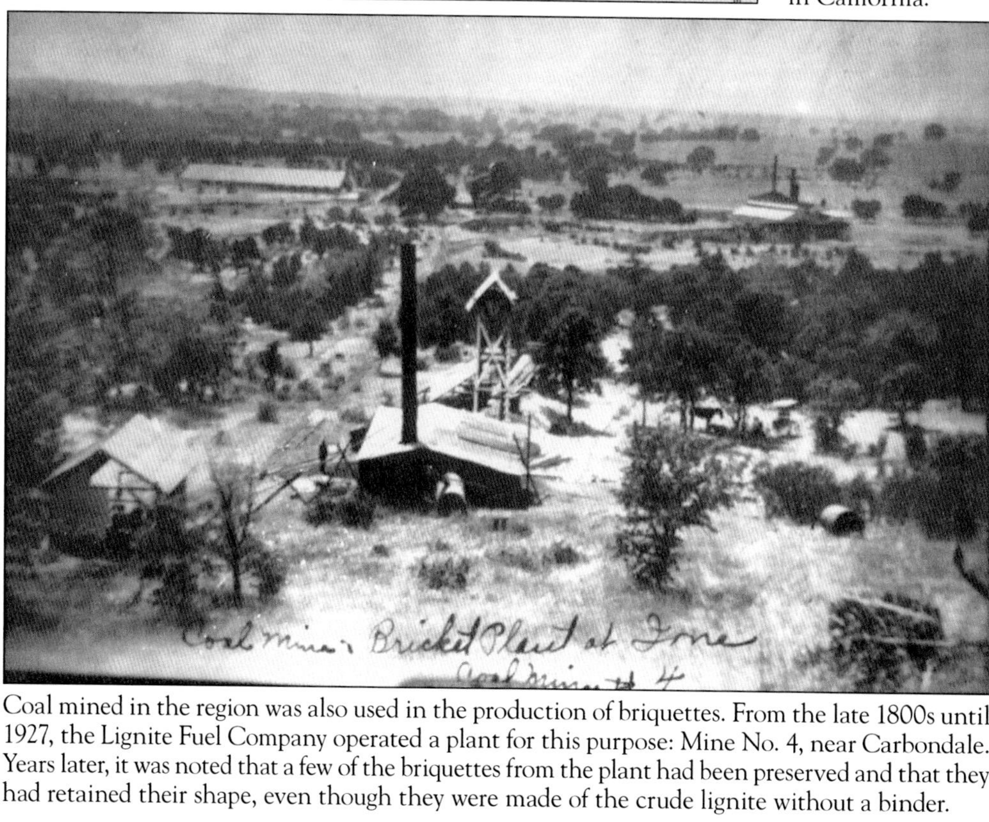

Coal mined in the region was also used in the production of briquettes. From the late 1800s until 1927, the Lignite Fuel Company operated a plant for this purpose: Mine No. 4, near Carbondale. Years later, it was noted that a few of the briquettes from the plant had been preserved and that they had retained their shape, even though they were made of the crude lignite without a binder.

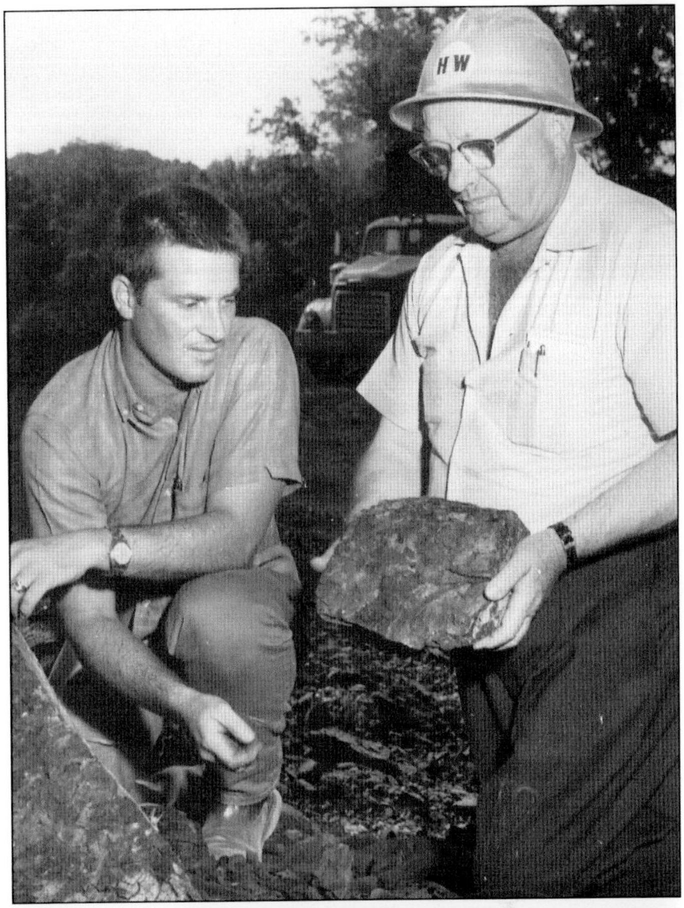

Frank Berry (right) and his son, of the Buena Vista lignite plant, look at a large chunk of coal taken from the mine. The Buena Vista Coal Mine (below) was one of the more productive in the region. It was opened in the early 1900s and worked sporadically for the next three decades. In the 1940s, it was found that the lignite at the site contained a high percentage of montan wax, suitable for industrial use. This wax, similar to carnauba wax but less expensive to produce, had a variety of uses, such as the production of carbon paper, phonograph records, polishes, and rubber. This discovery at Buena Vista provided a much-needed source for the American market. Prior to World War II, the United States relied on importing montan from Germany to meet manufacturing needs.

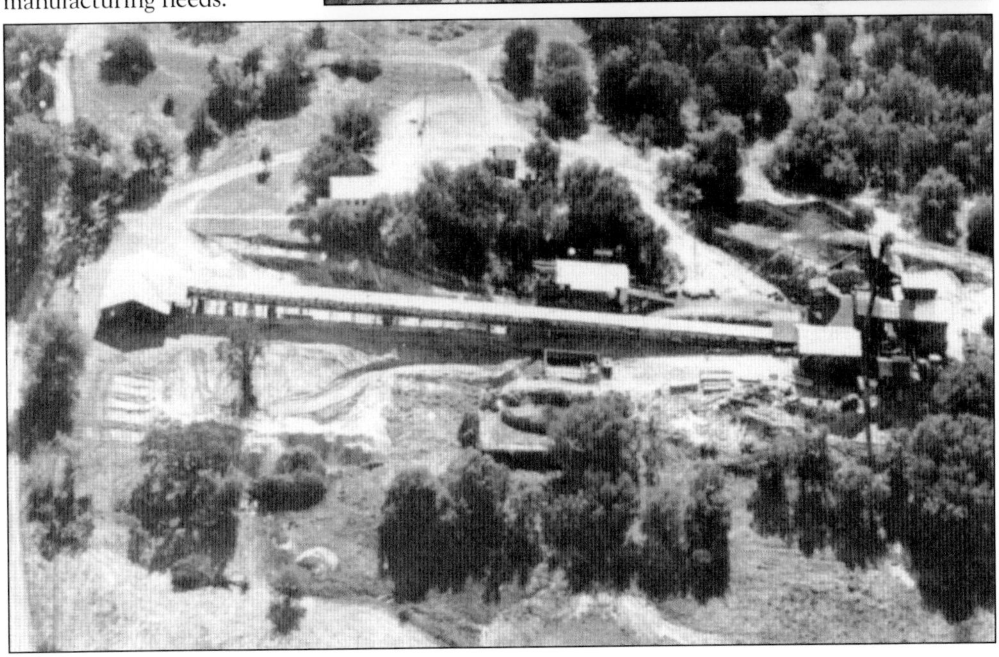

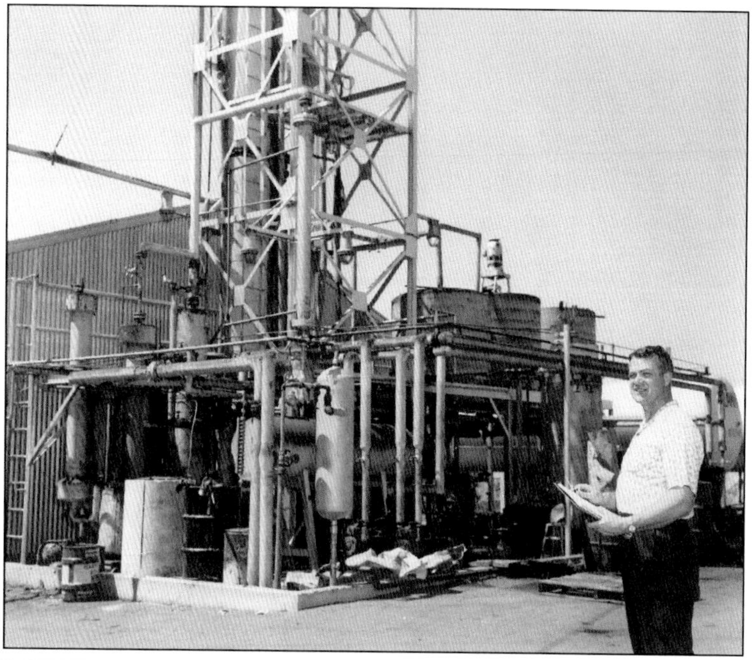

Joseph De Angelis, president of the American Lignite Products Company, stands next to the Buena Vista lignite plant. In 1947, the company constructed a plant to extract wax from the coal. In 1948, the plant burned and another was built; it was also destroyed by fire. A third plant, pictured here, was constructed in 1950. Over the next few years, production of wax at the plant averaged 50,000 pounds a month.

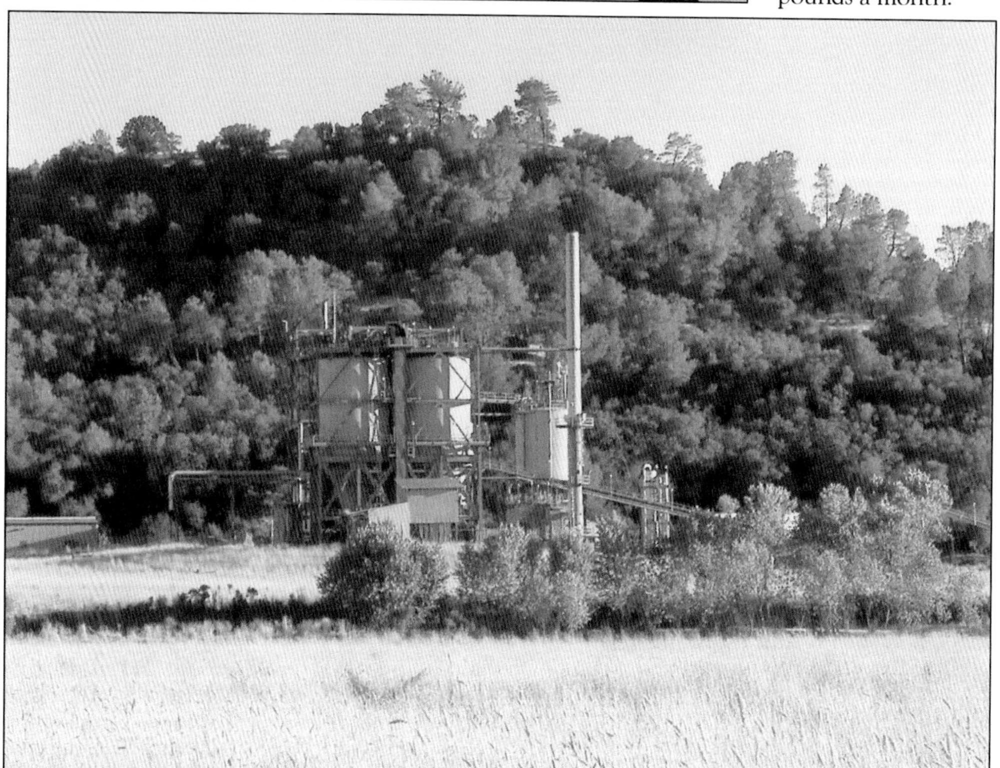

This cogeneration plant, constructed at the site of the Buena Vista Coal Mine in the 1980s, used lignite residue left from the production of montan wax to generate energy. Steam, and some electricity generated at the plant, was sold back to the wax plant and to Pacific Gas and Electric. The facility was last operated in 1999 by the Jackson Valley Energy Partners. (Author's collection.)

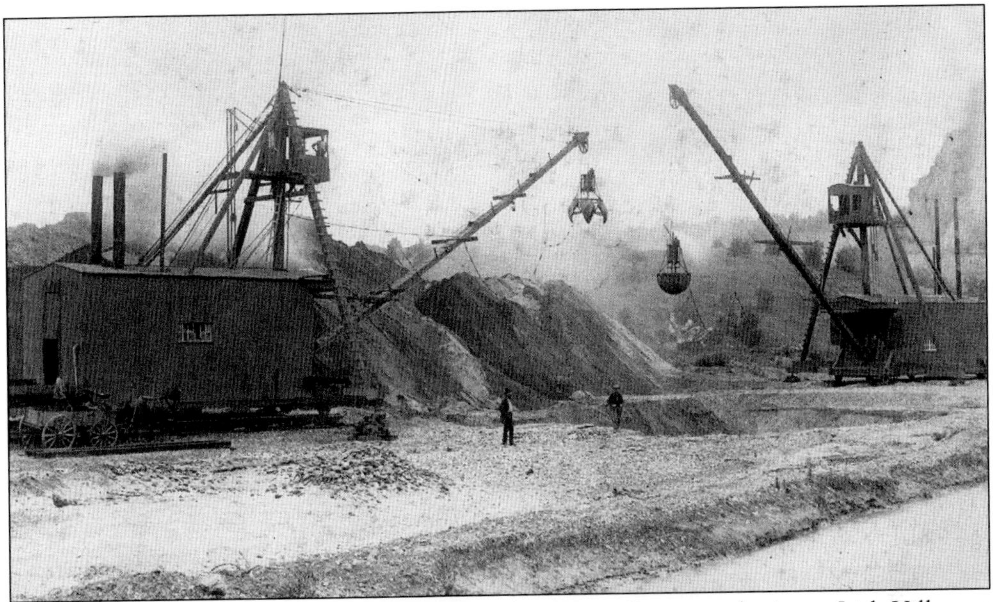

In this 1889 photograph, steam shovels work at the Arroyo Seco gravel mine at Irish Hill, west of Ione. The site was also known as the Lambing Mine, so named for Isaac Lambing, the first prospector at this location. This mine, among others near Irish Hill and to the west, produced megatons of gravel along with a fair amount of gold. Gravel mining continues today as a lucrative industry in the Ione Valley.

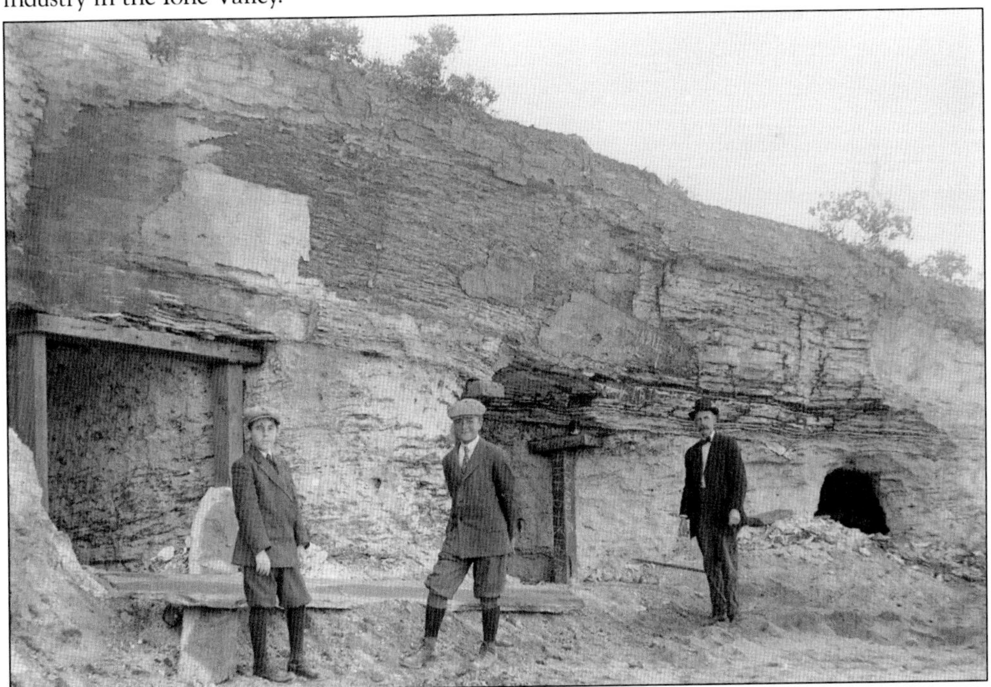

A group poses in front of a sand deposit mine in the Ione Valley. The sand is capped by a thick layer of slate, which can be seen as the horizontal layers above the shaft openings. Quartz sand deposits of the Ione–Buena Vista Formation were found suitable for the manufacture of glass, for use as flint in the production of porcelain, and in the composition of Portland cement.

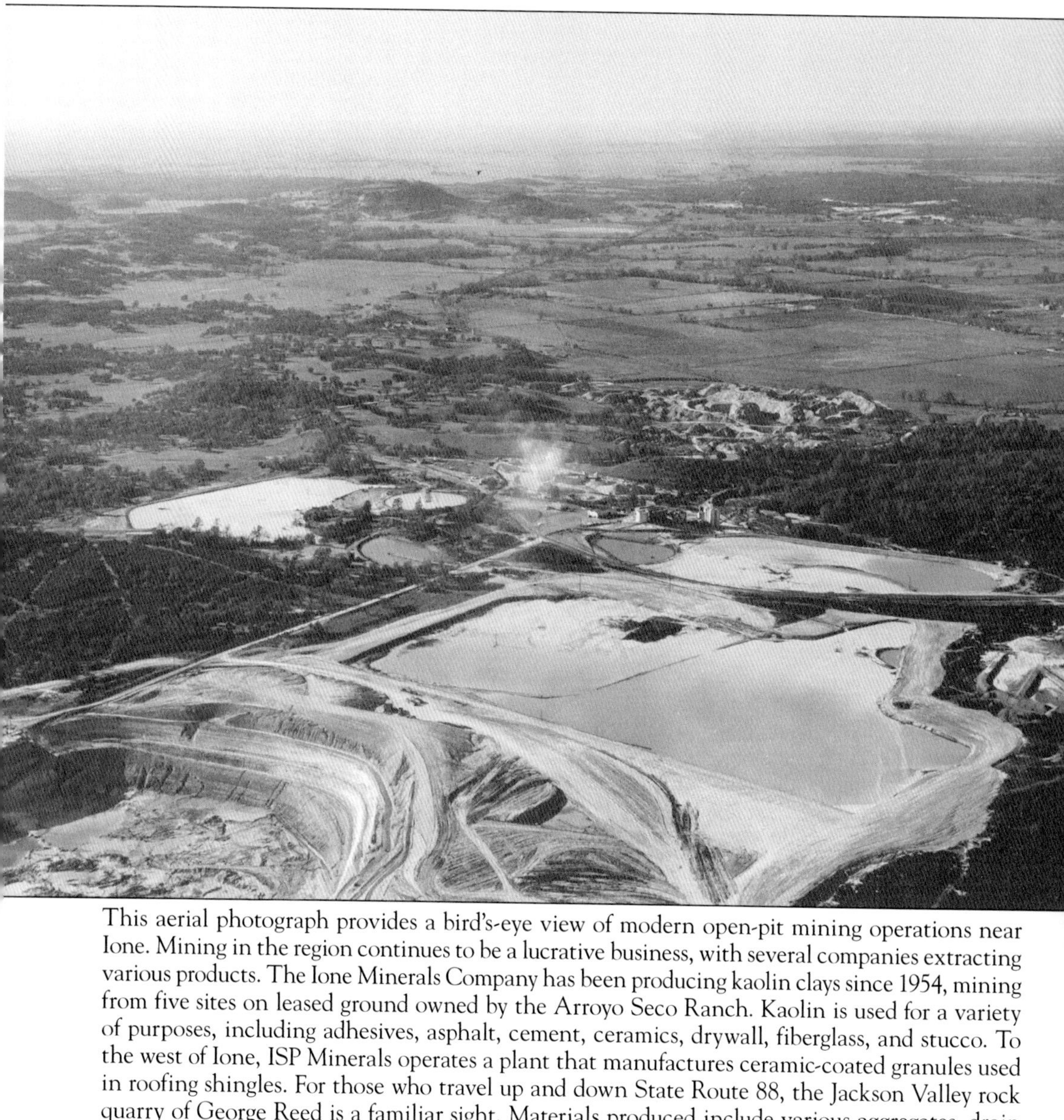

This aerial photograph provides a bird's-eye view of modern open-pit mining operations near Ione. Mining in the region continues to be a lucrative business, with several companies extracting various products. The Ione Minerals Company has been producing kaolin clays since 1954, mining from five sites on leased ground owned by the Arroyo Seco Ranch. Kaolin is used for a variety of purposes, including adhesives, asphalt, cement, ceramics, drywall, fiberglass, and stucco. To the west of Ione, ISP Minerals operates a plant that manufactures ceramic-coated granules used in roofing shingles. For those who travel up and down State Route 88, the Jackson Valley rock quarry of George Reed is a familiar sight. Materials produced include various aggregates, drain rock, base rock, derrick stone, and riprap. These companies, among others, continue the long tradition of mining in the Ione and Jackson Valleys; however, several factors, including the depletion of mineral sources, environmental concerns over pollution, threats to rare plant and animal species, noise, and traffic, may one day bring this historic industry to a halt.

Ten

A Modern Hamlet

Over the past 150 years, from when the first settlers arrived in the western valleys of Amador County into the 21st century, Ione has experienced many changes and yet managed to retain a small-town atmosphere. While residents consider it modern, visitors find that it still retains its quaintness with a friendly attitude. Many of the buildings that line Main Street have changed but little, and the landmark towers of Preston and the Methodist church still mark the skyline of this small hamlet.

Small towns throughout California have experienced changes in the nature of industry and employment over the last century, and Ione is no exception. Clay and coal mining have given way to careers in the department of corrections; grain for livestock is no longer ground at the local mill but purchased at the feed store; and many residents commute to cities in the Sacramento Valley to work. Despite these changes, the population has continued to increase.

In 1953, Ione became an incorporated city, elected a city council, and formed a police department. An increase in population over the past 50 years has expanded the footprint of the city to include new developments, while the small avenues that surround Main Street still house families in historic residences. In 1850, when the Ione Valley was a part of Calaveras County, the population was scattered far and wide and consisted mostly of the native people of the region. In 2000, when the last federal census was taken, the population of the town of Ione, at just over 7,000, was just about the same as the entire population of both the Ione and Jackson Valleys in 1850.

The many people that live in and around Ione are proud of their heritage and those who set the foundations of settlement here. Numerous monuments and markers can be found throughout the town, commemorating events and persons important to the history of the region, and local parks and celebrations continue to provide entertainment to the people.

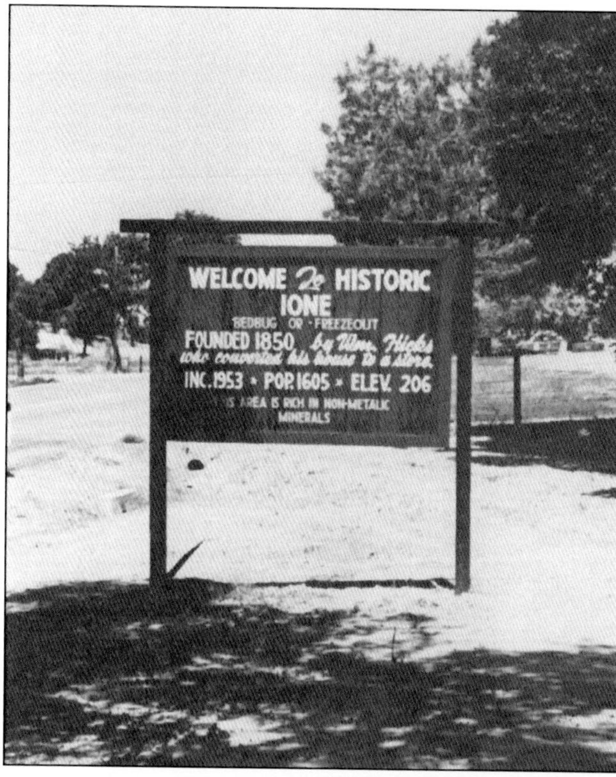

This sign, which once stood at the edge of town, greeted visitors for a number of years, proclaiming Ionians' pride in their history. Note the population at that time was 1,605, whereas in 2000 it was counted at 7,129 and continues to grow.

A visit to Ione provides one with a sense that the town is proud of its citizens and their contributions to society, and that the residents in turn are proud of the history of their home. Numerous plaques have been placed throughout this small city commemorating various events and people. This large memorial, dedicated in 1942, lists the men and women from Ione and the surrounding area who served in World War II.

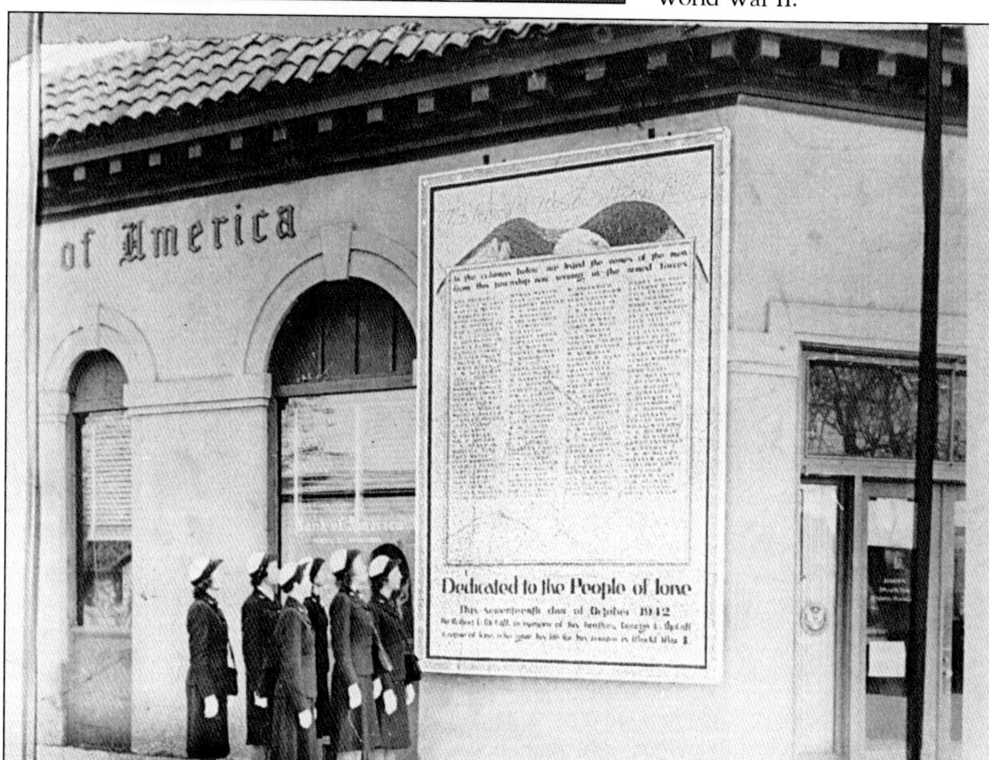

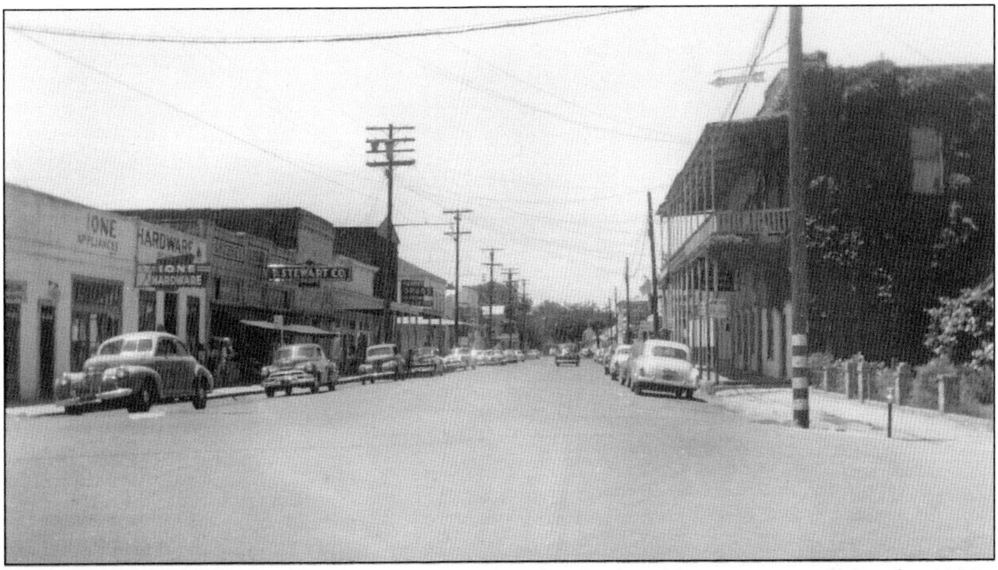

Throughout the 20th century, Ione continued to be the local business center. By the 1930s, when this photograph was taken, the once-dirt Main Street had been paved, and where wagons and stages once tracked, automobiles now parked in front of stores. Despite these changes, 19th-century stores like the Stewart Company still provided goods to the public.

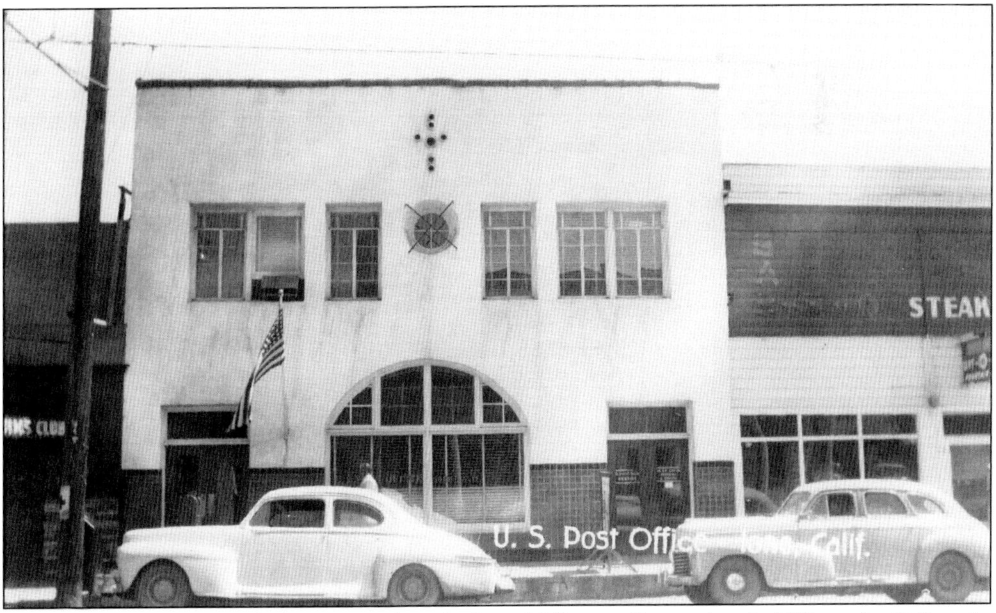

A U.S. Post Office branch first opened in the Ione Valley on September 3, 1852, at the Q Ranch. On February 16, 1857, it was moved into Ione City, where it has remained since. For a time, residents of the Jackson Valley had their own post office, variously known at Buena Vista and Ritchey, but today their mail is routed through this branch in Ione.

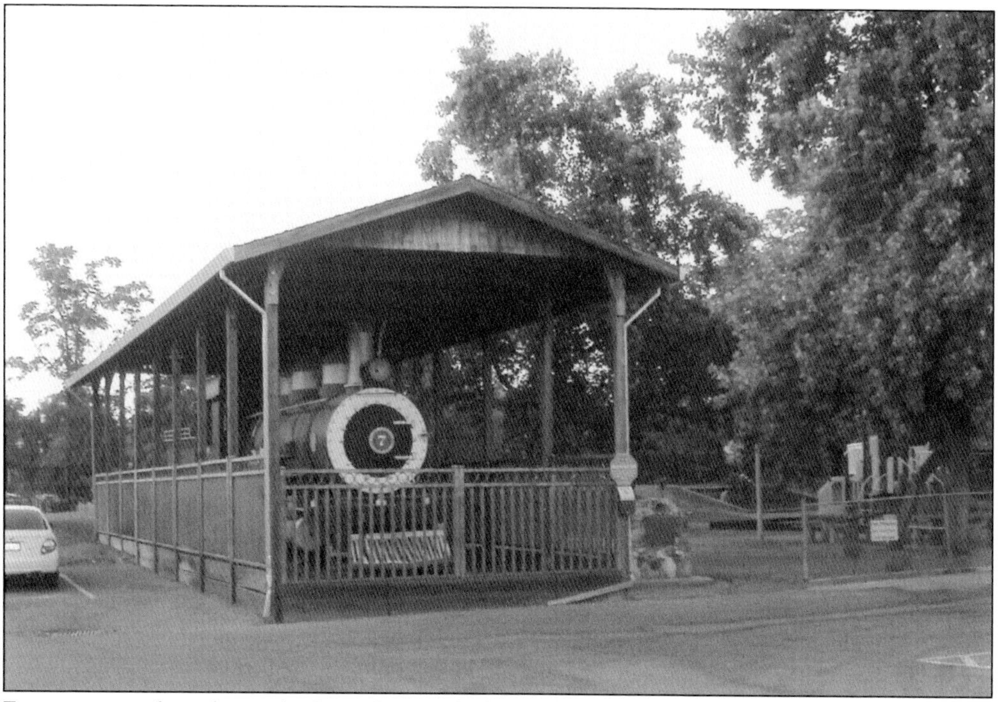

For visitors and residents, the Ione City Park, located one block off Main Street next to Sutter Creek, is a nice place to relax. Pictured here is old No. 7, "Iron Ivan," one of the locomotives used on the Ione and Eastern Railroad running between Ione and Martell. (Author's collection.)

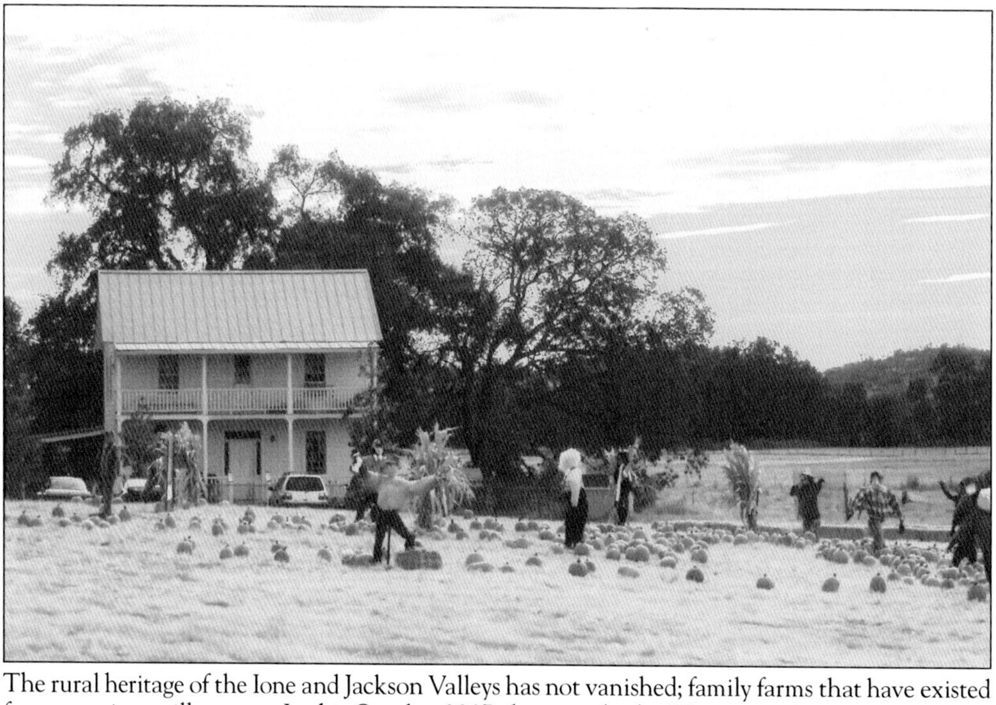

The rural heritage of the Ione and Jackson Valleys has not vanished; family farms that have existed for generations still operate. In this October 2007 photograph, the Winterport farm, once operated by the pioneer Winters brothers, offers a scenic pumpkin patch. (Author's collection.)

The rural setting of the Ione and Jackson Valleys, along with the hot, dry summers that occur here, make the region a prime target for wildfire. At the California Department of Forestry Academy, now known as the Cal Fire Academy, firefighters from far and wide are trained to fight wildfires. The academy is located just outside of Ione, between Preston and Mule Creek Prison. (Author's collection.)

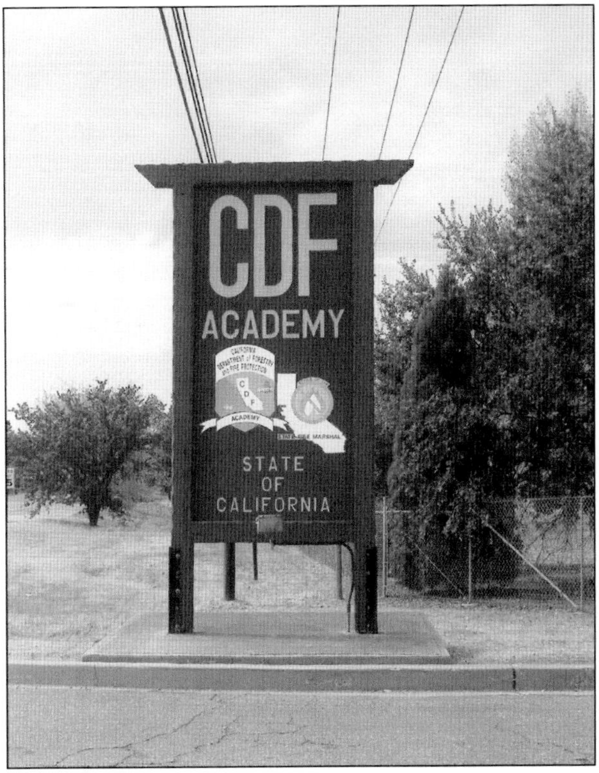

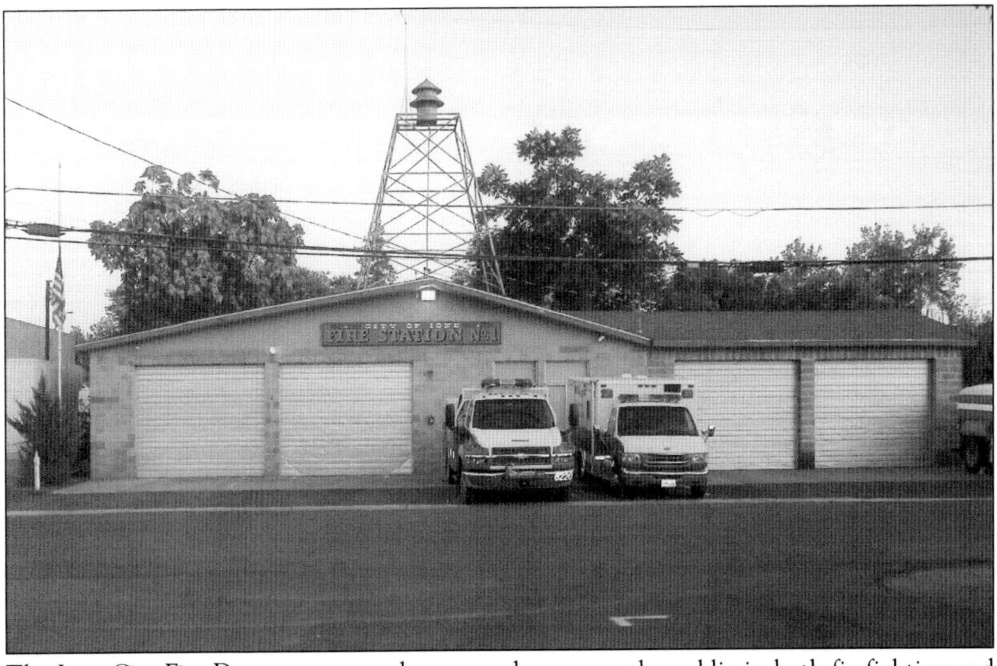

The Ione City Fire Department stands ever ready to serve the public in both firefighting and lifesaving roles. Local men and women have served the community in this capacity for more than 100 years, beginning when the first firefighters came at a moment's notice on a volunteer basis, battling flames with bucket lines. (Author's collection.)

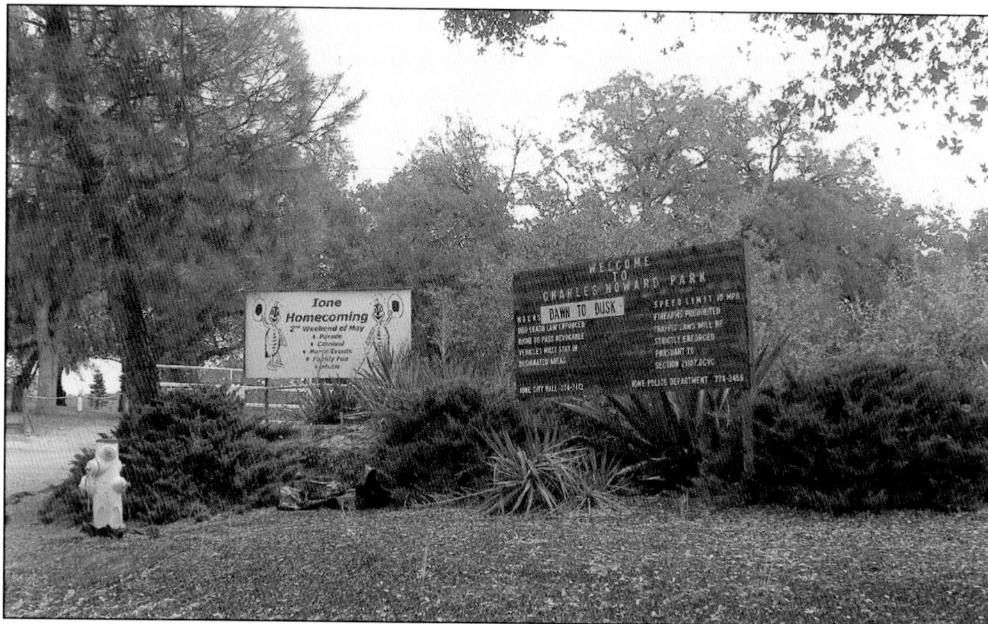

At the south edge of town is Charles Howard Park, named for the owner of famed racehorse Seabiscuit who once also owned the Rancho Arroyo Seco. Howard donated the tract of land on which the park is situated. In addition to picnic areas, the park includes Evalyn Bishop Hall, where many indoor events are held; soccer and softball fields; a skate park; an arena and stables; and playgrounds. (Author's collection.)

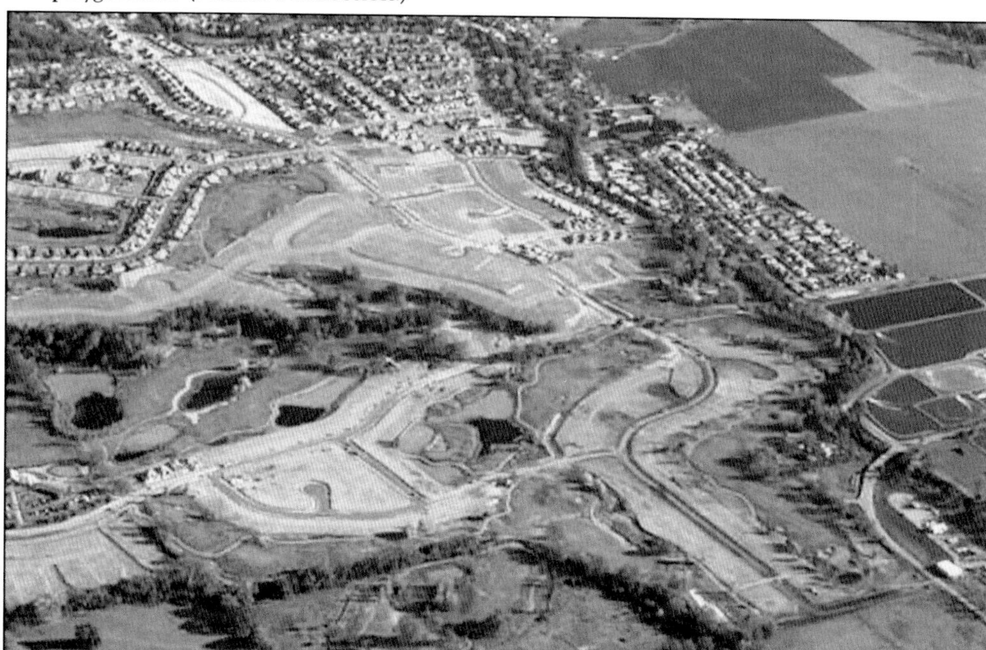

As the population of Ione has increased over the last several decades, new housing has been built to accommodate the need. This aerial view shows the Castle Oaks development just west of Ione, which includes both housing and a golf course. Residents of this upscale neighborhood can enjoy the atmosphere of rural America while retaining the amenities of a planned community.

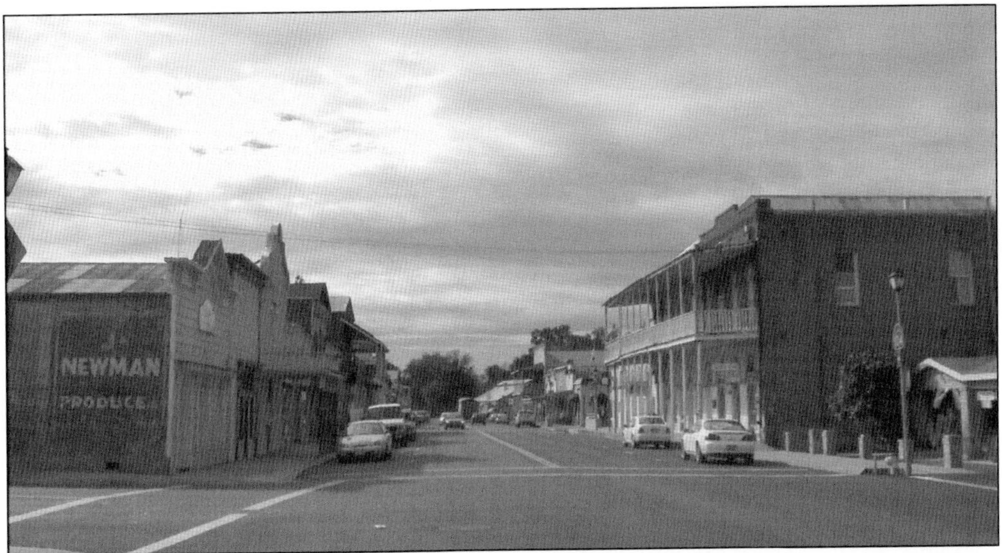

Despite the fast pace of 2007, Main Street retains its charm and quaintness. If it were not for the automobiles, street striping, and electric light poles, one might believe that this photograph was taken anytime over the past 100 years. Note the painted advertisement for Jacob Newman's store on the side of the building, standing the test of time for more than a century. (Author's collection.)

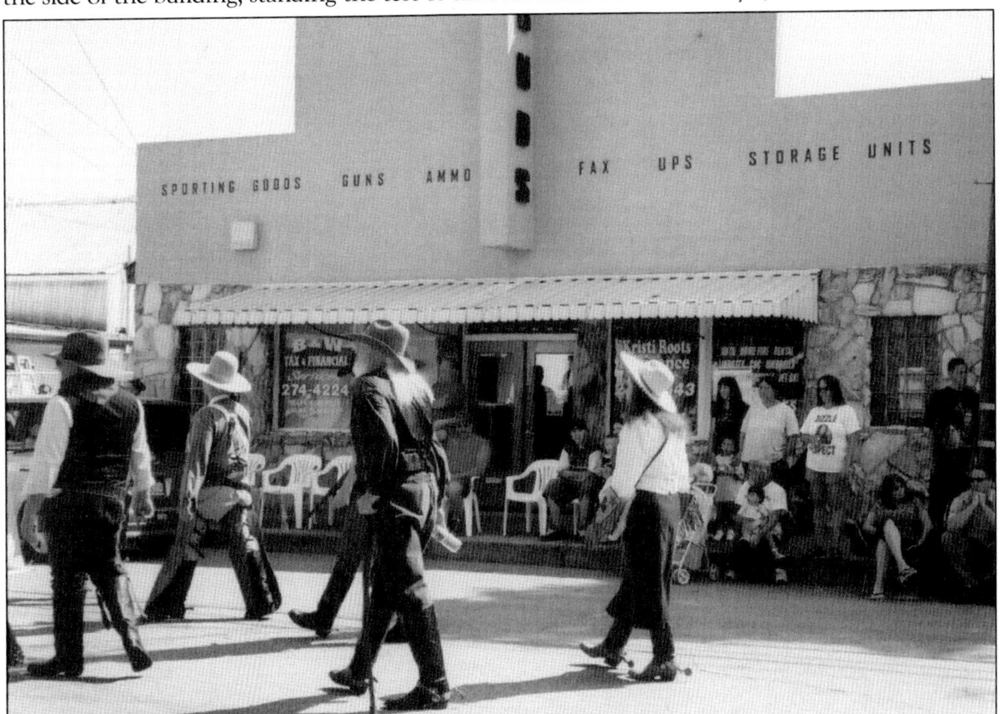

The Ione Homecoming celebration remains one of the most popular annual events, where residents line the streets to watch marching bands, floats, and other parade entries trek down Main Street. Here Sierra Six Guns and Sidekicks remind the spectators of their Western history. Members of the Old West reenactment group are, from left to right, Jay Lowman, Doug Dykes, Richard Rice, and author Deborah Cook. (Author's collection.)

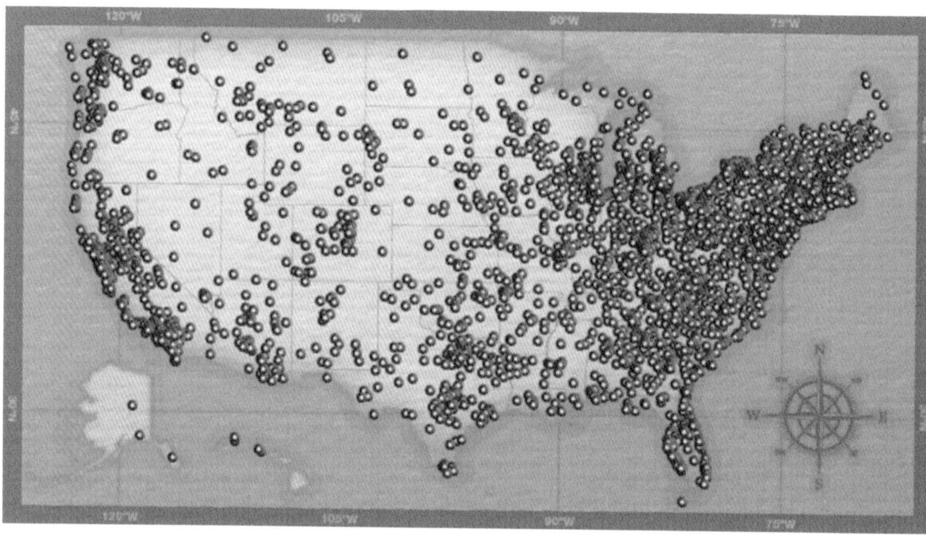